DISCOVERING KNOWLEDGE IN DATA

DISCOVERING KNOWLEDGE IN DATA

An Introduction to Data Mining

DANIEL T. LAROSE
Director of Data Mining
Central Connecticut State University

SHEFFIELD HALLAM UNIVERSITY
LEARNING CENTRE
WITHDRAWN FROM STOCK

A JOHN WILEY & SONS, INC., PUBLICATION

Published by John Wiley & Sons, Inc., Hoboken, New Jersey.
Published simultaneously in Canada.

For general information on our other products and services please contact our Customer Care Department within the U.S. at 877-762-2974, outside the U.S. at 317-572-3993 or fax 317-572-4002.

Wiley also publishes its books in a variety of electronic formats. Some content that appears in print, however, may not be available in electronic format.

Library of Congress Cataloging-in-Publication Data:

Larose, Daniel T.
Discovering knowledge in data : an introduction to data mining / Daniel T. Larose
p. cm.
Includes bibliographical references and index.
ISBN 0-471-66657-2 (cloth)
1. Data mining. I. Title.
QA76.9.D343L38 2005
006.3′12—dc22 2004003680

Printed in the United States of America

10 9 8 7 6

Dedication

To my parents,
And their parents,
And so on...

For my children,
And their children,
And so on...

CONTENTS

PREFACE

WHAT IS DATA MINING?

Data mining is predicted to be "one of the most revolutionary developments of the next decade," according to the online technology magazine *ZDNET News* (February 8, 2001). In fact, the *MIT Technology Review* chose data mining as one of ten emerging technologies that will change the world. According to the Gartner Group, "Data mining is the process of discovering meaningful new correlations, patterns and trends by sifting through large amounts of data stored in repositories, using pattern recognition technologies as well as statistical and mathematical techniques."

Because data mining represents such an important field, Wiley-Interscience and Dr. Daniel T. Larose have teamed up to publish a series of volumes on data mining, consisting initially of three volumes. The first volume in the series, *Discovering Knowledge in Data: An Introduction to Data Mining*, introduces the reader to this rapidly growing field of data mining.

WHY IS THIS BOOK NEEDED?

Human beings are inundated with data in most fields. Unfortunately, these valuable data, which cost firms millions to collect and collate, are languishing in warehouses and repositories. *The problem is that not enough trained human analysts are available who are skilled at translating all of the data into knowledge*, and thence up the taxonomy tree into wisdom. This is why this book is needed; it provides readers with:

- Models and techniques to uncover hidden nuggets of information
- Insight into how data mining algorithms work
- The experience of actually performing data mining on large data sets

Data mining is becoming more widespread every day, because it empowers companies to uncover profitable patterns and trends from their existing databases. Companies and institutions have spent millions of dollars to collect megabytes and terabytes of data but are not taking advantage of the valuable and actionable information hidden deep within their data repositories. However, as the practice of data mining becomes more widespread, companies that do not apply these techniques are in danger of falling behind and losing market share, because their competitors are using data mining and are thereby gaining the competitive edge. In *Discovering Knowledge in Data*, the step-by-step hands-on solutions of real-world business problems using widely available data mining techniques applied to real-world data sets will appeal to managers, CIOs, CEOs, CFOs, and others who need to keep abreast of the latest methods for enhancing return on investment.

DANGER! DATA MINING IS EASY TO DO BADLY

The plethora of new off-the-shelf software platforms for performing data mining has kindled a new kind of danger. The ease with which these GUI-based applications can manipulate data, combined with the power of the formidable data mining algorithms embedded in the black-box software currently available, make their misuse proportionally more hazardous.

Just as with any new information technology, *data mining is easy to do badly*. A little knowledge is especially dangerous when it comes to applying powerful models based on large data sets. For example, analyses carried out on unpreprocessed data can lead to erroneous conclusions, or inappropriate analysis may be applied to data sets that call for a completely different approach, or models may be derived that are built upon wholly specious assumptions. If deployed, these errors in analysis can lead to very expensive failures.

"WHITE BOX" APPROACH: UNDERSTANDING THE UNDERLYING ALGORITHMIC AND MODEL STRUCTURES

The best way to avoid these costly errors, which stem from a blind black-box approach to data mining, is to apply instead a "white-box" methodology, which emphasizes an understanding of the algorithmic and statistical model structures underlying the software. *Discovering Knowledge in Data* applies this white-box approach by:

- Walking the reader through the various algorithms
- Providing examples of the operation of the algorithm on actual large data sets
- Testing the reader's level of understanding of the concepts and algorithms
- Providing an opportunity for the reader to do some real data mining on large data sets

Algorithm Walk-Throughs

Discovering Knowledge in Data walks the reader through the operations and nuances of the various algorithms, using small-sample data sets, so that the reader gets a true appreciation of what is really going on inside the algorithm. For example, in Chapter 8, we see the updated cluster centers being updated, moving toward the center of their respective clusters. Also, in Chapter 9 we see just which type of network weights will result in a particular network node "winning" a particular record.

Applications of the Algorithms to Large Data Sets

Discovering Knowledge in Data provides examples of the application of various algorithms on actual large data sets. For example, in Chapter 7 a classification problem is attacked using a neural network model on a real-world data set. The resulting neural network topology is examined along with the network connection weights, as reported by the software. These data sets are included at the book series Web site, so that readers may follow the analytical steps on their own, using data mining software of their choice.

Chapter Exercises: Checking to Make Sure That You Understand It

Discovering Knowledge in Data includes over 90 chapter exercises, which allow readers to assess their depth of understanding of the material, as well as to have a little fun playing with numbers and data. These include conceptual exercises, which help to clarify some of the more challenging concepts in data mining, and "tiny data set" exercises, which challenge the reader to apply the particular data mining algorithm to a small data set and, step by step, to arrive at a computationally sound solution. For example, in Chapter 6 readers are provided with a small data set and asked to construct by hand, using the methods shown in the chapter, a C4.5 decision tree model, as well as a classification and regression tree model, and to compare the benefits and drawbacks of each.

Hands-on Analysis: Learn Data Mining by Doing Data Mining

Chapters 2 to 4 and 6 to 11 provide the reader with hands-on analysis problems, representing an opportunity for the reader to apply his or her newly acquired data mining expertise to solving real problems using large data sets. Many people learn by doing. *Discovering Knowledge in Data* provides a framework by which the reader can learn data mining by doing data mining. The intention is to mirror the real-world data mining scenario. In the real world, dirty data sets need cleaning; raw data needs to be normalized; outliers need to be checked. So it is with *Discovering Knowledge in Data*, where over 70 hands-on analysis problems are provided. In this way, the reader can "ramp up" quickly and be "up and running" his or her own data mining analyses relatively shortly.

For example, in Chapter 10 readers are challenged to uncover high-confidence, high-support rules for predicting which customer will be leaving a company's service. In Chapter 11 readers are asked to produce lift charts and gains charts for a set of classification models using a large data set, so that the best model may be identified.

DATA MINING AS A PROCESS

One of the fallacies associated with data mining implementation is that data mining somehow represents an isolated set of tools, to be applied by some aloof analysis department, and is related only inconsequentially to the mainstream business or research endeavor. Organizations that attempt to implement data mining in this way will see their chances of success greatly reduced. This is because data mining should be view as a *process*.

Discovering Knowledge in Data presents data mining as a well-structured *standard process*, intimately connected with managers, decision makers, and those involved in deploying the results. Thus, this book is not only for analysts but also for managers, who need to be able to communicate in the language of data mining. The particular standard process used is the CRISP–DM framework: the Cross-Industry Standard Process for Data Mining. CRISP–DM demands that data mining be seen as an entire process, from communication of the business problem through data collection and management, data preprocessing, model building, model evaluation, and finally, model deployment. Therefore, this book is not only for analysts and managers but also for data management professionals, database analysts, and decision makers.

GRAPHICAL APPROACH, EMPHASIZING EXPLORATORY DATA ANALYSIS

Discovering Knowledge in Data emphasizes a graphical approach to data analysis. There are more than 80 screen shots of actual computer output throughout the book, and over 30 other figures. Exploratory data analysis (EDA) represents an interesting and exciting way to "feel your way" through large data sets. Using graphical and numerical summaries, the analyst gradually sheds light on the complex relationships hidden within the data. *Discovering Knowledge in Data* emphasizes an EDA approach to data mining, which goes hand in hand with the overall graphical approach.

HOW THE BOOK IS STRUCTURED

Discovering Knowledge in Data provides a comprehensive introduction to the field. Case studies are provided showing how data mining has been utilized successfully (and not so successfully). Common myths about data mining are debunked, and common pitfalls are flagged, so that new data miners do not have to learn these lessons themselves.

The first three chapters introduce and follow the CRISP–DM standard process, especially the data preparation phase and data understanding phase. The next seven chapters represent the heart of the book and are associated with the CRISP–DM modeling phase. Each chapter presents data mining methods and techniques for a specific data mining task.

- Chapters 5, 6, and 7 relate to the *classification* task, examining the *k*-nearest neighbor (Chapter 5), decision tree (Chapter 6), and neural network (Chapter 7) algorithms.
- Chapters 8 and 9 investigate the *clustering* task, with hierarchical and *k*-means clustering (Chapter 8) and Kohonen network (Chapter 9) algorithms.
- Chapter 10 handles the *association* task, examining association rules through the a priori and GRI algorithms.
- Finally, Chapter 11 covers model evaluation techniques, which belong to the CRISP–DM evaluation phase.

DISCOVERING KNOWLEDGE IN DATA AS A TEXTBOOK

Discovering Knowledge in Data naturally fits the role of textbook for an introductory course in data mining. Instructors may appreciate:

- The presentation of data mining as a *process*
- The "white-box" approach, emphasizing an understanding of the underlying algorithmic structures:
  - algorithm walk-throughs
  - application of the algorithms to large data sets
  - chapter exercises
  - hands-on analysis
- The graphical approach, emphasizing exploratory data analysis
- The logical presentation, flowing naturally from the CRISP–DM standard process and the set of data mining tasks

Discovering Knowledge in Data is appropriate for advanced undergraduate or graduate courses. Except for one section in Chapter 7, no calculus is required. An introductory statistics course would be nice but is not required. No computer programming or database expertise is required.

ACKNOWLEDGMENTS

Discovering Knowledge in Data would have remained unwritten without the assistance of Val Moliere, editor, Kirsten Rohsted, editorial program coordinator, and Rosalyn Farkas, production editor, at Wiley-Interscience and Barbara Zeiders, who copyedited the work. Thank you for your guidance and perserverance.

I wish also to thank Dr. Chun Jin and Dr. Daniel S. Miller, my colleagues in the Master of Science in Data Mining program at Central Connecticut State University; Dr. Timothy Craine, the chair of the Department of Mathematical Sciences; Dr. Dipak K. Dey, chair of the Department of Statistics at the University of Connecticut; and Dr. John Judge, chair of the Department of Mathematics at Westfield State College. Your support was (and is) invaluable.

Thanks to my children, Chantal, Tristan, and Ravel, for sharing the computer with me. Finally, I would like to thank my wonderful wife, Debra J. Larose, for her patience, understanding, and proofreading skills. But words cannot express....

Daniel T. Larose, Ph.D.
Director, Data Mining @CCSU
www.ccsu.edu/datamining

CHAPTER 1

INTRODUCTION TO DATA MINING

WHAT IS DATA MINING?

WHY DATA MINING?

NEED FOR HUMAN DIRECTION OF DATA MINING

CROSS-INDUSTRY STANDARD PROCESS: CRISP–DM

CASE STUDY 1: ANALYZING AUTOMOBILE WARRANTY CLAIMS: EXAMPLE OF THE CRISP–DM INDUSTRY STANDARD PROCESS IN ACTION

FALLACIES OF DATA MINING

WHAT TASKS CAN DATA MINING ACCOMPLISH?

CASE STUDY 2: PREDICTING ABNORMAL STOCK MARKET RETURNS USING NEURAL NETWORKS

CASE STUDY 3: MINING ASSOCIATION RULES FROM LEGAL DATABASES

CASE STUDY 4: PREDICTING CORPORATE BANKRUPTCIES USING DECISION TREES

CASE STUDY 5: PROFILING THE TOURISM MARKET USING *k*-MEANS CLUSTERING ANALYSIS

About 13 million customers per month contact the West Coast customer service call center of the Bank of America, as reported by *CIO Magazine*'s cover story on data mining in May 1998 [1]. In the past, each caller would have listened to the same marketing advertisement, whether or not it was relevant to the caller's interests. However, "rather than pitch the product of the week, we want to be as relevant as possible to each customer," states Chris Kelly, vice president and director of database marketing at Bank of America in San Francisco. Thus, Bank of America's customer service representatives have access to individual customer profiles, so that the customer can be informed of new products or services that may be of greatest

Discovering Knowledge in Data: An Introduction to Data Mining, By Daniel T. Larose
ISBN 0-471-66657-2

interest to him or her. Data mining helps to identify the type of marketing approach for a particular customer, based on the customer's individual profile.

Former President Bill Clinton, in his November 6, 2002 address to the Democratic Leadership Council [2], mentioned that not long after the events of September 11, 2001, FBI agents examined great amounts of consumer data and found that five of the terrorist perpetrators were in the database. One of the terrorists possessed 30 credit cards with a combined balance totaling $250,000 and had been in the country for less than two years. The terrorist ringleader, Mohammed Atta, had 12 different addresses, two real homes, and 10 safe houses. Clinton concluded that we should proactively search through this type of data and that "if somebody has been here a couple years or less and they have 12 homes, they're either really rich or up to no good. It shouldn't be that hard to figure out which."

Brain tumors represent the most deadly cancer among children, with nearly 3000 cases diagnosed per year in the United States, nearly half of which are fatal. Eric Bremer [3], director of brain tumor research at Children's Memorial Hospital in Chicago, has set the goal of building a gene expression database for pediatric brain tumors, in an effort to develop more effective treatment. As one of the first steps in tumor identification, Bremer uses the Clementine data mining software suite, published by SPSS, Inc., to classify the tumor into one of 12 or so salient types. As we shall learn in Chapter 5 classification, is one of the most important data mining tasks.

These stories are examples of *data mining*.

WHAT IS DATA MINING?

According to the Gartner Group [4], "Data mining is the process of discovering meaningful new correlations, patterns and trends by sifting through large amounts of data stored in repositories, using pattern recognition technologies as well as statistical and mathematical techniques." There are other definitions:

- "Data mining is the analysis of (often large) observational data sets to find unsuspected relationships and to summarize the data in novel ways that are both understandable and useful to the data owner" (Hand et al. [5]).
- "Data mining is an interdisciplinary field bringing togther techniques from machine learning, pattern recognition, statistics, databases, and visualization to address the issue of information extraction from large data bases" (Evangelos Simoudis in Cabena et al. [6]).

Data mining is predicted to be "one of the most revolutionary developments of the next decade," according to the online technology magazine *ZDNET News* [7]. In fact, the *MIT Technology Review* [8] chose data mining as one of 10 emerging technologies that will change the world. "Data mining expertise is the most sought after..." among information technology professionals, according to the 1999 *Information Week* National Salary Survey [9]. The survey reports: "Data mining skills are in high demand this year, as organizations increasingly put data repositories online. Effectively analyzing information from customers, partners, and suppliers has become important to more companies. 'Many companies have implemented a data warehouse strategy and are now starting to look at what they can do with all that data,' says Dudley Brown, managing partner of BridgeGate LLC, a recruiting firm in Irvine, Calif."

How widespread is data mining? Which industries are moving into this area? Actually, the use of data mining is pervasive, extending into some surprising areas. Consider the following employment advertisement [10]:

STATISTICS INTERN: SEPTEMBER–DECEMBER 2003

Work with Basketball Operations

Resposibilities include:

- Compiling and converting data into format for use in statistical models
- Developing statistical forecasting models using regression, logistic regression, **data mining**, etc.
- Using statistical packages such as Minitab, SPSS, XLMiner

Experience in developing statistical models a differentiator, but not required.

Candidates who have completed advanced statistics coursework with a strong knowledge of basketball and the love of the game should forward your résumé and cover letter to:

Boston Celtics
Director of Human Resources
151 Merrimac Street
Boston, MA 02114

Yes, the Boston Celtics are looking for a data miner. Perhaps the Celtics' data miner is needed to keep up with the New York Knicks, who are using IBM's Advanced Scout data mining software [11]. Advanced Scout, developed by a team led by Inderpal Bhandari, is designed to detect patterns in data. A big basketball fan, Bhandari approached the New York Knicks, who agreed to try it out. The software depends on the data kept by the National Basketball Association, in the form of "events" in every game, such as baskets, shots, passes, rebounds, double-teaming, and so on. As it turns out, the data mining uncovered a pattern that the coaching staff had evidently missed. When the Chicago Bulls double-teamed Knicks' center Patrick Ewing, the Knicks' shooting percentage was extremely low, even though double-teaming should open up an opportunity for a teammate to shoot. Based on this information, the coaching staff was able to develop strategies for dealing with the double-teaming situation. Later, 16 of the 29 NBA teams also turned to Advanced Scout to mine the play-by-play data.

WHY DATA MINING?

While waiting in line at a large supermarket, have you ever just closed your eyes and listened? What do you hear, apart from the kids pleading for candy bars? You might hear the beep, beep, beep of the supermarket scanners, reading the bar codes on the grocery items, ringing up on the register, and storing the data on servers located at the supermarket headquarters. Each beep indicates a new row in the database, a new "observation" in the information being collected about the shopping habits of your family and the other families who are checking out.

Clearly, a lot of data is being collected. However, what is being learned from all this data? What knowledge are we gaining from all this information? Probably, depending on the supermarket, not much. As early as 1984, in his book *Megatrends* [12], John Naisbitt observed that "we are drowning in information but starved for knowledge." The problem today is not that there is not enough data and information streaming in. We are, in fact, inundated with data in most fields. Rather, the problem is that there are not enough trained *human* analysts available who are skilled at translating all of this data into knowledge, and thence up the taxonomy tree into wisdom.

The ongoing remarkable growth in the field of data mining and knowledge discovery has been fueled by a fortunate confluence of a variety of factors:

- The explosive growth in data collection, as exemplified by the supermarket scanners above
- The storing of the data in data warehouses, so that the entire enterprise has access to a reliable current database
- The availability of increased access to data from Web navigation and intranets
- The competitive pressure to increase market share in a globalized economy
- The development of off-the-shelf commercial data mining software suites
- The tremendous growth in computing power and storage capacity

NEED FOR HUMAN DIRECTION OF DATA MINING

Many software vendors market their analytical software as being plug-and-play out-of-the-box applications that will provide solutions to otherwise intractable problems without the need for human supervision or interaction. Some early definitions of data mining followed this focus on automation. For example, Berry and Linoff, in their book *Data Mining Techniques for Marketing, Sales and Customer Support* [13], gave the following definition for data mining: "Data mining is the process of exploration and analysis, *by automatic or semi-automatic means*, of large quantities of data in order to discover meaningful patterns and rules" (emphasis added). Three years later, in their sequel, *Mastering Data Mining* [14], the authors revisit their definition of data mining and state: "If there is anything we regret, it is the phrase 'by automatic or semi-automatic means' . . . because we feel there has come to be too much focus on the automatic techniques and not enough on the exploration and analysis. This has misled many people into believing that data mining is a product that can be bought rather than a discipline that must be mastered."

Very well stated! Automation is no substitute for human input. As we shall learn shortly, humans need to be actively involved at every phase of the data mining process. Georges Grinstein of the University of Massachusetts at Lowell and AnVil, Inc., stated it like this [15]:

> Imagine a black box capable of answering any question it is asked. Any question. Will this eliminate our need for human participation as many suggest? Quite the opposite. The fundamental problem still comes down to a human interface issue. How do I phrase the question correctly? How do I set up the parameters to get a solution that is applicable in the particular case I am interested in? How do I get the results in reasonable time and in a form that I can understand? Note that all the questions connect the discovery process to me, for my human consumption.

Rather than asking where humans fit into data mining, we should instead inquire about how we may design data mining into the very human process of problem solving.

Further, the very power of the formidable data mining algorithms embedded in the black-box software currently available makes their misuse proportionally more dangerous. Just as with any new information technology, *data mining is easy to do badly*. Researchers may apply inappropriate analysis to data sets that call for a completely different approach, for example, or models may be derived that are built upon wholly specious assumptions. Therefore, an understanding of the statistical and mathematical model structures underlying the software is required.

CROSS-INDUSTRY STANDARD PROCESS: CRISP–DM

There is a temptation in some companies, due to departmental inertia and compartmentalization, to approach data mining haphazardly, to reinvent the wheel and duplicate effort. A cross-industry standard was clearly required that is industry-neutral, tool-neutral, and application-neutral. The Cross-Industry Standard Process for Data Mining (CRISP–DM) [16] was developed in 1996 by analysts representing DaimlerChrysler, SPSS, and NCR. CRISP provides a nonproprietary and freely available standard process for fitting data mining into the general problem-solving strategy of a business or research unit.

According to CRISP–DM, a given data mining project has a life cycle consisting of six phases, as illustrated in Figure 1.1. Note that the phase sequence is *adaptive*. That is, the next phase in the sequence often depends on the outcomes associated with the preceding phase. The most significant dependencies between phases are indicated by the arrows. For example, suppose that we are in the modeling phase. Depending on the behavior and characteristics of the model, we may have to return to the data preparation phase for further refinement before moving forward to the model evaluation phase.

The iterative nature of CRISP is symbolized by the outer circle in Figure 1.1. Often, the solution to a particular business or research problem leads to further questions of interest, which may then be attacked using the same general process as before.

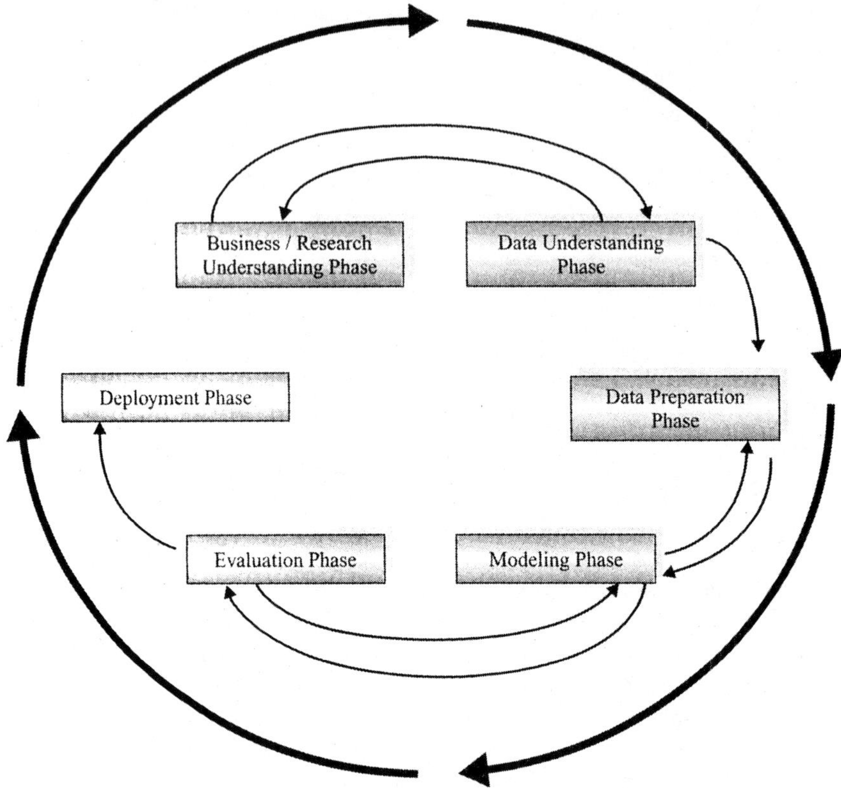

Figure 1.1 CRISP–DM is an iterative, adaptive process.

Lessons learned from past projects should always be brought to bear as input into new projects. Following is an outline of each phase. Although conceivably, issues encountered during the evaluation phase can send the analyst back to any of the previous phases for amelioration, for simplicity we show only the most common loop, back to the modeling phase.

CRISP–DM: The Six Phases

1. *Business understanding phase.* The first phase in the CRISP–DM standard process may also be termed the research understanding phase.
   a. Enunciate the project objectives and requirements clearly in terms of the business or research unit as a whole.
   b. Translate these goals and restrictions into the formulation of a data mining problem definition.
   c. Prepare a preliminary strategy for achieving these objectives.
2. *Data understanding phase*
   a. Collect the data.

   b. Use exploratory data analysis to familiarize yourself with the data and discover initial insights.
   c. Evaluate the quality of the data.
   d. If desired, select interesting subsets that may contain actionable patterns.

3. *Data preparation phase*
   a. Prepare from the initial raw data the final data set that is to be used for all subsequent phases. This phase is very labor intensive.
   b. Select the cases and variables you want to analyze and that are appropriate for your analysis.
   c. Perform transformations on certain variables, if needed.
   d. Clean the raw data so that it is ready for the modeling tools.

4. *Modeling phase*
   a. Select and apply appropriate modeling techniques.
   b. Calibrate model settings to optimize results.
   c. Remember that often, several different techniques may be used for the same data mining problem.
   d. If necessary, loop back to the data preparation phase to bring the form of the data into line with the specific requirements of a particular data mining technique.

5. *Evaluation phase*
   a. Evaluate the one or more models delivered in the modeling phase for quality and effectiveness before deploying them for use in the field.
   b. Determine whether the model in fact achieves the objectives set for it in the first phase.
   c. Establish whether some important facet of the business or research problem has not been accounted for sufficiently.
   d. Come to a decision regarding use of the data mining results.

6. *Deployment phase*
   a. Make use of the models created: Model creation does not signify the completion of a project.
   b. Example of a simple deployment: Generate a report.
   c. Example of a more complex deployment: Implement a parallel data mining process in another department.
   d. For businesses, the customer often carries out the deployment based on your model.

You can find out much more information about the CRISP–DM standard process at `www.crisp-dm.org`. Next, we turn to an example of a company applying CRISP–DM to a business problem.

CASE STUDY 1

ANALYZING AUTOMOBILE WARRANTY CLAIMS: EXAMPLE OF THE CRISP–DM INDUSTRY STANDARD PROCESS IN ACTION [17]

Quality assurance continues to be a priority for automobile manufacturers, including Daimler Chrysler. Jochen Hipp of the University of Tubingen, Germany, and Guido Lindner of DaimlerChrysler AG, Germany, investigated patterns in the warranty claims for DaimlerChrysler automobiles.

1. Business Understanding Phase

DaimlerChrysler's objectives are to reduce costs associated with warranty claims and improve customer satisfaction. Through conversations with plant engineers, who are the technical experts in vehicle manufacturing, the researchers are able to formulate specific business problems, such as the following:

- Are there interdependencies among warranty claims?
- Are past warranty claims associated with similar claims in the future?
- Is there an association between a certain type of claim and a particular garage?

The plan is to apply appropriate data mining techniques to try to uncover these and other possible associations.

2. Data Understanding Phase

The researchers make use of DaimlerChrysler's Quality Information System (QUIS), which contains information on over 7 million vehicles and is about 40 gigabytes in size. QUIS contains production details about how and where a particular vehicle was constructed, including an average of 30 or more sales codes for each vehicle. QUIS also includes warranty claim information, which the garage supplies, in the form of one of more than 5000 possible potential causes.

The researchers stressed the fact that the database was entirely unintelligible to domain nonexperts: "So experts from different departments had to be located and consulted; in brief a task that turned out to be rather costly." They emphasize that analysts should not underestimate the importance, difficulty, and potential cost of this early phase of the data mining process, and that shortcuts here may lead to expensive reiterations of the process downstream.

3. Data Preparation Phase

The researchers found that although relational, the QUIS database had limited SQL access. They needed to select the cases and variables of interest manually, and then manually derive new variables that could be used for the modeling phase. For example, the variable *number of days from selling date until first claim* had to be derived from the appropriate date attributes.

They then turned to proprietary data mining software, which had been used at DaimlerChrysler on earlier projects. Here they ran into a common roadblock—that the data format requirements varied from algorithm to algorithm. The result was further exhaustive preprocessing of the data, to transform the attributes into a form usable for model algorithms. The researchers mention that the data preparation phase took much longer than they had planned.

4. Modeling Phase

Since the overall business problem from phase 1 was to investigate dependence among the warranty claims, the researchers chose to apply the following techniques: (1) Bayesian networks and (2) association rules. Bayesian networks model uncertainty by explicitly representing the conditional dependencies among various components, thus providing a graphical visualization of the dependency relationships among the components. As such, Bayesian networks represent a natural choice for modeling dependence among warranty claims. The mining of association rules is covered in Chapter 10. Association rules are also a natural way to investigate dependence among warranty claims since the confidence measure represents a type of conditional probability, similar to Bayesian networks.

The details of the results are confidential, but we can get a general idea of the type of dependencies uncovered by the models. One insight the researchers uncovered was that a particular combination of construction specifications doubles the probability of encountering an automobile electrical cable problem. DaimlerChrysler engineers have begun to investigate how this combination of factors can result in an increase in cable problems.

The researchers investigated whether certain garages had more warranty claims of a certain type than did other garages. Their association rule results showed that, indeed, the confidence levels for the rule "If garage *X*, then cable problem," varied considerably from garage to garage. They state that further investigation is warranted to reveal the reasons for the disparity.

5. Evaluation Phase

The researchers were disappointed that the support for sequential-type association rules was relatively small, thus precluding generalization of the results, in their opinion. Overall, in fact, the researchers state: "In fact, we did not find any rule that our domain experts would judge as interesting, at least at first sight." According to this criterion, then, the models were found to be lacking in effectiveness and to fall short of the objectives set for them in the business understanding phase. To account for this, the researchers point to the "legacy" structure of the database, for which automobile parts were categorized by garages and factories for historic or technical reasons and not designed for data mining. They suggest adapting and redesigning the database to make it more amenable to knowledge discovery.

6. Deployment Phase

The researchers have identified the foregoing project as a pilot project, and as such, do not intend to deploy any large-scale models from this first iteration. After the pilot project, however, they have applied the lessons learned from this project, with the goal of integrating their methods with the existing information technology environment at DaimlerChrysler. To further support the original goal of lowering claims costs, they intend to develop an intranet offering mining capability of QUIS for all corporate employees.

What lessons can we draw from this case study? First, the general impression one draws is that uncovering hidden nuggets of knowledge in databases is a rocky road. In nearly every phase, the researchers ran into unexpected roadblocks and difficulties. This tells us that actually applying data mining for the first time in a company requires asking people to do something new and different, which is not always welcome. Therefore, if they expect results, corporate management must be 100% supportive of new data mining initiatives.

Another lesson to draw is that intense human participation and supervision is required at every stage of the data mining process. For example, the algorithms require specific data formats, which may require substantial preprocessing (see Chapter 2). Regardless of what some software vendor advertisements may claim, you can't just purchase some data mining software, install it, sit back, and watch it solve all your problems. Data mining is not magic. Without skilled human supervision, blind use of data mining software will only provide you with the wrong answer to the wrong question applied to the wrong type of data. The wrong analysis is worse than no analysis, since it leads to policy recommendations that will probably turn out to be expensive failures.

Finally, from this case study we can draw the lesson that there is no guarantee of positive results when mining data for actionable knowledge, any more than when one is mining for gold. Data mining is not a panacea for solving business problems. But used properly, by people who understand the models involved, the data requirements, and the overall project objectives, data mining can indeed provide actionable and highly profitable results.

FALLACIES OF DATA MINING

Speaking before the U.S. House of Representatives Subcommittee on Technology, Information Policy, Intergovernmental Relations, and Census, Jen Que Louie, president of Nautilus Systems, Inc., described four fallacies of data mining [18]. Two of these fallacies parallel the warnings we described above.

- ***Fallacy 1.*** There are data mining tools that we can turn loose on our data repositories and use to find answers to our problems.
  - *Reality.* There are no automatic data mining tools that will solve your problems mechanically "while you wait." Rather, data mining is a process, as we have seen above. CRISP–DM is one method for fitting the data mining process into the overall business or research plan of action.
- ***Fallacy 2.*** The data mining process is autonomous, requiring little or no human oversight.
  - *Reality.* As we saw above, the data mining process requires significant human interactivity at each stage. Even after the model is deployed, the introduction of new data often requires an updating of the model. Continuous quality monitoring and other evaluative measures must be assessed by human analysts.
- ***Fallacy 3.*** Data mining pays for itself quite quickly.
  - *Reality.* The return rates vary, depending on the startup costs, analysis personnel costs, data warehousing preparation costs, and so on.
- ***Fallacy 4.*** Data mining software packages are intuitive and easy to use.
  - *Reality.* Again, ease of use varies. However, data analysts must combine subject matter knowledge with an analytical mind and a familiarity with the overall business or research model.

To the list above, we add two additional common fallacies:

- ***Fallacy 5.*** Data mining will identify the causes of our business or research problems.
  - *Reality.* The knowledge discovery process will help you to uncover patterns of behavior. Again, it is up to humans to identify the causes.
- ***Fallacy 6.*** Data mining will clean up a messy database automatically.
  - *Reality.* Well, not automatically. As a preliminary phase in the data mining process, data preparation often deals with data that has not been examined or used in years. Therefore, organizations beginning a new data mining operation will often be confronted with the problem of data that has been lying around for years, is stale, and needs considerable updating.

The discussion above may have been termed *what data mining cannot or should not do*. Next we turn to a discussion of what data mining can do.

WHAT TASKS CAN DATA MINING ACCOMPLISH?

Next, we investigate the main tasks that data mining is usually called upon to accomplish. The following list shows the most common data mining tasks.

- Description
- Estimation
- Prediction
- Classification
- Clustering
- Association

Description

Sometimes, researchers and analysts are simply trying to find ways to *describe* patterns and trends lying within data. For example, a pollster may uncover evidence that those who have been laid off are less likely to support the present incumbent in the presidential election. Descriptions of patterns and trends often suggest possible explanations for such patterns and trends. For example, those who are laid off are now less well off financially than before the incumbent was elected, and so would tend to prefer an alternative.

Data mining models should be as *transparent* as possible. That is, the results of the data mining model should describe clear patterns that are amenable to intuitive interpretation and explanation. Some data mining methods are more suited than others to transparent interpretation. For example, decision trees provide an intuitive and human-friendly explanation of their results. On the other hand, neural networks are comparatively opaque to nonspecialists, due to the nonlinearity and complexity of the model.

High-quality description can often be accomplished by *exploratory data analysis*, a graphical method of exploring data in search of patterns and trends. We look at exploratory data analysis in Chapter 3.

Estimation

Estimation is similar to classification except that the target variable is numerical rather than categorical. Models are built using "complete" records, which provide the value of the target variable as well as the predictors. Then, for new observations, estimates of the value of the target variable are made, based on the values of the predictors. For example, we might be interested in estimating the systolic blood pressure reading of a hospital patient, based on the patient's age, gender, body-mass index, and blood sodium levels. The relationship between systolic blood pressure and the predictor variables in the training set would provide us with an estimation model. We can then apply that model to new cases.

Examples of estimation tasks in business and research include:

- Estimating the amount of money a randomly chosen family of four will spend for back-to-school shopping this fall.
- Estimating the percentage decrease in rotary-movement sustained by a National Football League running back with a knee injury.
- Estimating the number of points per game that Patrick Ewing will score when double-teamed in the playoffs.
- Estimating the grade-point average (GPA) of a graduate student, based on that student's undergraduate GPA.

Consider Figure 1.2, where we have a scatter plot of the graduate grade-point averages (GPAs) against the undergraduate GPAs for 1000 students. Simple linear regression allows us to find the line that best approximates the relationship between these two variables, according to the least-squares criterion. The regression line, indicated in blue in Figure 1.2, may then be used to estimate the graduate GPA of a student given that student's undergraduate GPA. Here, the equation of the regression line (as produced by the statistical package *Minitab*, which also produced the graph) is $\hat{y} = 1.24 + 0.67x$. This tells us that the estimated graduate GPA $\hat{y}$ equals 1.24 plus

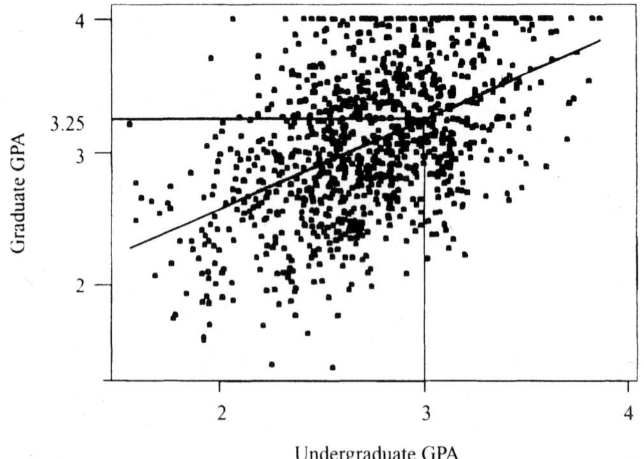

Figure 1.2 Regression estimates lie on the regression line.

0.67 times the student's undergraduate GPA. For example, if your undergrad GPA is 3.0, your estimated graduate GPA is $\hat{y} = 1.24 + 0.67(3) = 3.25$. Note that this point $(x = 3.0,\ \hat{y} = 3.25)$ lies precisely on the regression line, as do all linear regression predictions.

The field of statistical analysis supplies several venerable and widely used estimation methods. These include point estimation and confidence interval estimations, simple linear regression and correlation, and multiple regression. We examine these methods in Chapter 4. Neural networks (Chapter 7) may also be used for estimation.

Prediction

Prediction is similar to classification and estimation, except that for prediction, the results lie in the future. Examples of prediction tasks in business and research include:

- Predicting the price of a stock three months into the future (Figure 1.3)
- Predicting the percentage increase in traffic deaths next year if the speed limit is increased
- Predicting the winner of this fall's baseball World Series, based on a comparison of team statistics
- Predicting whether a particular molecule in drug discovery will lead to a profitable new drug for a pharmaceutical company

Any of the methods and techniques used for classification and estimation may also be used, under appropriate circumstances, for prediction. These include the traditional statistical methods of point estimation and confidence interval estimations, simple linear regression and correlation, and multiple regression, investigated in Chapter 4, as well as data mining and knowledge discovery methods such as neural network (Chapter 7), decision tree (Chapter 6), and k-nearest neighbor (Chapter 5) methods. An application of prediction using neural networks is examined later in the chapter in Case Study 2.

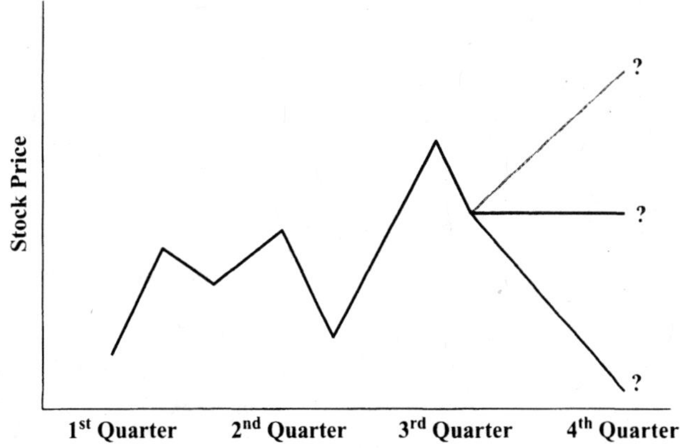

Figure 1.3 Predicting the price of a stock three months in the future.

Classification

In classification, there is a target categorical variable, such as *income bracket*, which, for example, could be partitioned into three classes or categories: high income, middle income, and low income. The data mining model examines a large set of records, each record containing information on the target variable as well as a set of input or predictor variables. For example, consider the excerpt from a data set shown in Table 1.1. Suppose that the researcher would like to be able to *classify* the income brackets of persons not currently in the database, based on other characteristics associated with that person, such as age, gender, and occupation. This task is a classification task, very nicely suited to data mining methods and techniques. The algorithm would proceed roughly as follows. First, examine the data set containing both the predictor variables and the (already classified) target variable, *income bracket*. In this way, the algorithm (software) "learns about" which combinations of variables are associated with which income brackets. For example, older females may be associated with the high-income bracket. This data set is called the *training set*. Then the algorithm would look at new records, for which no information about income bracket is available. Based on the classifications in the training set, the algorithm would assign classifications to the new records. For example, a 63-year-old female professor might be classified in the high-income bracket.

Examples of classification tasks in business and research include:

- Determining whether a particular credit card transaction is fraudulent
- Placing a new student into a particular track with regard to special needs
- Assessing whether a mortgage application is a good or bad credit risk
- Diagnosing whether a particular disease is present
- Determining whether a will was written by the actual deceased, or fraudulently by someone else
- Identifying whether or not certain financial or personal behavior indicates a possible terrorist threat

For example, in the medical field, suppose that we are interested in classifying the type of drug a patient should be prescribed, based on certain patient characteristics, such as the age of the patient and the patient's sodium/potassium ratio. Figure 1.4 is a scatter plot of patients' sodium/potassium ratio against patients' ages for a sample of 200 patients. The particular drug prescribed is symbolized by the shade of the points. Light gray points indicate drug Y; medium gray points indicate drug A or X;

TABLE 1.1 Excerpt from Data Set for Classifying Income

Subject	Age	Gender	Occupation	Income Bracket
001	47	F	Software engineer	High
002	28	M	Marketing consultant	Middle
003	35	M	Unemployed	Low
⋮				

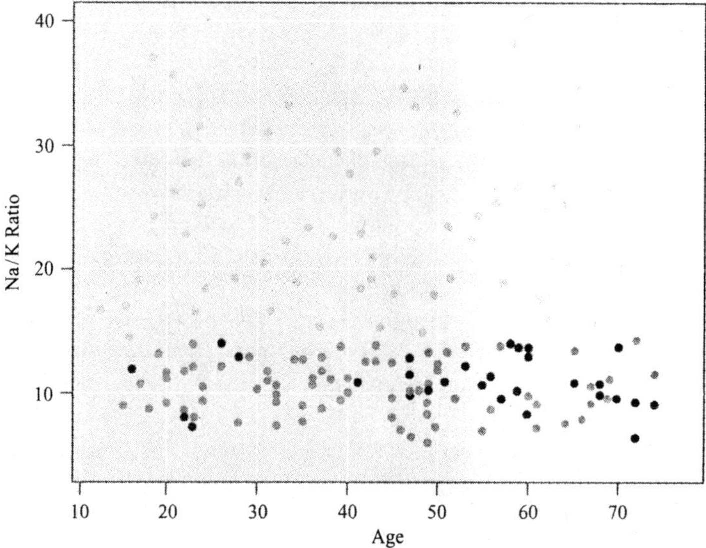

Figure 1.4 Which drug should be prescribed for which type of patient?

dark gray points indicate drug B or C. This plot was generated using the Clementine data mining software suite, published by SPSS.

In this scatter plot, Na/K (sodium/potassium ratio) is plotted on the Y (vertical) axis and age is plotted on the X (horizontal) axis. Suppose that we base our prescription recommendation on this data set.

1. Which drug should be prescribed for a young patient with a high sodium/potassium ratio?
   - Young patients are on the left in the graph, and high sodium/potassium ratios are in the upper half, which indicates that previous young patients with high sodium/potassium ratios were prescribed drug Y (light gray points). The recommended prediction classification for such patients is drug Y.
2. Which drug should be prescribed for older patients with low sodium/potassium ratios?
   - Patients in the lower right of the graph have been taking different prescriptions, indicated by either dark gray (drugs B and C) or medium gray (drugs A and X). Without more specific information, a definitive classification cannot be made here. For example, perhaps these drugs have varying interactions with beta-blockers, estrogens, or other medications, or are contraindicated for conditions such as asthma or heart disease.

Graphs and plots are helpful for understanding two- and three-dimensional relationships in data. But sometimes classifications need to be based on many different predictors, requiring a many-dimensional plot. Therefore, we need to turn to more sophisticated models to perform our classification tasks. Common data mining methods used for classification are k-nearest neighbor (Chapter 5), decision tree (Chapter 6), and neural network (Chapter 7). An application of classification using decision trees is examined in Case Study 4.

Clustering

Clustering refers to the grouping of records, observations, or cases into classes of similar objects. A *cluster* is a collection of records that are similar to one another, and dissimilar to records in other clusters. Clustering differs from classification in that there is no target variable for clustering. The clustering task does not try to classify, estimate, or predict the value of a target variable. Instead, clustering algorithms seek to segment the entire data set into relatively homogeneous subgroups or clusters, where the similarity of the records within the cluster is maximized and the similarity to records outside the cluster is minimized.

Claritas, Inc. [19] is in the clustering business. Among the services they provide is a demographic profile of each of the geographic areas in the country, as defined by zip code. One of the clustering mechanisms they use is the PRIZM segmentation system, which describes every U.S. zip code area in terms of distinct lifestyle types (Table 1.2). Just go to the company's Web site [19], enter a particular zip code, and you are shown the most common PRIZM clusters for that zip code.

What do these clusters mean? For illustration, let's look up the clusters for zip code 90210, Beverly Hills, California. The resulting clusters for zip code 90210 are:

- *Cluster 01:* Blue Blood Estates
- *Cluster 10:* Bohemian Mix
- *Cluster 02:* Winner's Circle
- *Cluster 07:* Money and Brains
- *Cluster 08:* Young Literati

TABLE 1.2 The 62 Clusters Used by the PRIZM Segmentation System

01 Blue Blood Estates	02 Winner's Circle	03 Executive Suites	04 Pools & Patios
05 Kids & Cul-de-Sacs	06 Urban Gold Coast	07 Money & Brains	08 Young Literati
09 American Dreams	10 Bohemian Mix	11 Second City Elite	12 Upward Bound
13 Gray Power	14 Country Squires	15 God's Country	16 Big Fish, Small Pond
17 Greenbelt Families	18 Young Influentials	19 New Empty Nests	20 Boomers & Babies
21 Suburban Sprawl	22 Blue-Chip Blues	23 Upstarts & Seniors	24 New Beginnings
25 Mobility Blues	26 Gray Collars	27 Urban Achievers	28 Big City Blend
29 Old Yankee Rows	30 Mid-City Mix	31 Latino America	32 Middleburg Managers
33 Boomtown Singles	34 Starter Families	35 Sunset City Blues	36 Towns & Gowns
37 New Homesteaders	38 Middle America	39 Red, White & Blues	40 Military Quarters
41 Big Sky Families	42 New Eco-topia	43 River City, USA	44 Shotguns & Pickups
45 Single City Blues	46 Hispanic Mix	47 Inner Cities	48 Smalltown Downtown
49 Hometown Retired	50 Family Scramble	51 Southside City	52 Golden Ponds
53 Rural Industria	54 Norma Rae-Ville	55 Mines & Mills	56 Agri-Business
57 Grain Belt	58 Blue Highways	59 Rustic Elders	60 Back Country Folks
61 Scrub Pine Flats	62 Hard Scrabble		

Source: Claritas, Inc.

The description for cluster 01, Blue Blood Estates, is: "Established executives, professionals, and 'old money' heirs that live in America's wealthiest suburbs. They are accustomed to privilege and live luxuriously—one-tenth of this group's members are multimillionaires. The next affluence level is a sharp drop from this pinnacle."

Examples of clustering tasks in business and research include:

- Target marketing of a niche product for a small-capitalization business that does not have a large marketing budget
- For accounting auditing purposes, to segmentize financial behavior into benign and suspicious categories
- As a dimension-reduction tool when the data set has hundreds of attributes
- For gene expression clustering, where very large quantities of genes may exhibit similar behavior

Clustering is often performed as a preliminary step in a data mining process, with the resulting clusters being used as further inputs into a different technique downstream, such as neural networks. We discuss hierarchical and k-means clustering in Chapter 8 and Kohonen networks in Chapter 9. An application of clustering is examined in Case Study 5.

Association

The *association* task for data mining is the job of finding which attributes "go together." Most prevalent in the business world, where it is known as *affinity analysis* or *market basket analysis*, the task of association seeks to uncover rules for quantifying the relationship between two or more attributes. Association rules are of the form "If *antecedent*, then *consequent*," together with a measure of the support and confidence associated with the rule. For example, a particular supermarket may find that of the 1000 customers shopping on a Thursday night, 200 bought diapers, and of those 200 who bought diapers, 50 bought beer. Thus, the association rule would be "If buy diapers, then buy beer" with a support of $200/1000 = 20\%$ and a confidence of $50/200 = 25\%$.

Examples of association tasks in business and research include:

- Investigating the proportion of subscribers to a company's cell phone plan that respond positively to an offer of a service upgrade
- Examining the proportion of children whose parents read to them who are themselves good readers
- Predicting degradation in telecommunications networks
- Finding out which items in a supermarket are purchased together and which items are never purchased together
- Determining the proportion of cases in which a new drug will exhibit dangerous side effects

We discuss two algorithms for generating association rules, the a priori algorithm and the GRI algorithm, in Chapter 10. Association rules were utilized in Case Study 1. We examine another application of association rules in Case Study 3.

Next we examine four case studies, each of which demonstrates a particular data mining task in the context of the CRISP–DM data mining standard process.

CASE STUDY 2

PREDICTING ABNORMAL STOCK MARKET RETURNS USING NEURAL NETWORKS [20]

1. Business/Research Understanding Phase

Alan M. Safer, of California State University–Long Beach, reports that stock market trades made by insiders usually have abnormal returns. Increased profits can be made by outsiders using legal insider trading information, especially by focusing on attributes such as company size and the time frame for prediction. Safer is interested in using data mining methodology to increase the ability to predict abnormal stock price returns arising from legal insider trading.

2. Data Understanding Phase

Safer collected data from 343 companies, extending from January 1993 to June 1997 (the source of the data being the Securities and Exchange Commission). The stocks used in the study were all of the stocks that had insider records for the entire period and were in the S&P 600, S&P 400, or S&P 500 (small, medium, and large capitalization, respectively) as of June 1997. Of the 946 resulting stocks that met this description, Safer chose only those stocks that underwent at least two purchase orders per year, to assure a sufficient amount of transaction data for the data mining analyses. This resulted in 343 stocks being used for the study. The variables in the original data set include the company, name and rank of the insider, transaction date, stock price, number of shares traded, type of transaction (buy or sell), and number of shares held after the trade. To assess an insider's prior trading patterns, the study examined the previous 9 and 18 weeks of trading history. The prediction time frames for predicting abnormal returns were established as 3, 6, 9, and 12 months.

3. Data Preparation Phase

Safer decided that the company rank of the insider would not be used as a study attribute, since other research had shown it to be of mixed predictive value for predicting abnormal stock price returns. Similarly, he omitted insiders who were uninvolved with company decisions. (Note that the present author does not necessarily agree with omitting variables prior to the modeling phase, because of earlier findings of mixed predictive value. If they are indeed of no predictive value, the models will so indicate, presumably. But if there is a chance of something interesting going on, the model should perhaps be given an opportunity to look at it. However, Safer is the domain expert in this area.)

4. Modeling Phase

The data were split into a training set (80% of the data) and a validation set (20%). A neural network model was applied, which uncovered the following results:

a. Certain industries had the most predictable abnormal stock returns, including:
   - *Industry group 36:* electronic equipment, excluding computer equipment
   - *Industry Group 28:* chemical products
   - *Industry Group 37:* transportation equipment
   - *Industry Group 73:* business services

b. Predictions that looked further into the future (9 to 12 months) had increased ability to identify unusual insider trading variations than did predictions that had a shorter time frame (3 to 6 months).

c. It was easier to predict abnormal stock returns from insider trading for small companies than for large companies.

5. Evaluation Phase

Safer concurrently applied a multivariate adaptive regression spline (MARS, not covered here) model to the same data set. The MARS model uncovered many of the same findings as the neural network model, including results (a) and (b) from the modeling phase. Such a *confluence of results* is a powerful and elegant method for evaluating the quality and effectiveness of the model, analogous to getting two independent judges to concur on a decision. Data miners should strive to produce such a confluence of results whenever the opportunity arises. This is possible because often more than one data mining method may be applied appropriately to the problem at hand. If both models concur as to the results, this strengthens our confidence in the findings. If the models disagree, we should probably investigate further. Sometimes, one type of model is simply better suited to uncovering a certain type of result, but sometimes, disagreement indicates deeper problems, requiring cycling back to earlier phases.

6. Deployment Phase

The publication of Safer's findings in *Intelligent Data Analysis* [20] constitutes one method of model deployment. Now, analysts from around the world can take advantage of his methods to track the abnormal stock price returns of insider trading and thereby help to protect the small investor.

CASE STUDY 3

MINING ASSOCIATION RULES FROM LEGAL DATABASES [21]

1. Business/Research Understanding Phase

The researchers, Sasha Ivkovic and John Yearwood of the University of Ballarat, and Andrew Stranieri of La Trobe University, Australia, are interested in whether interesting and actionable association rules can be uncovered in a large data set containing information on applicants for government-funded legal aid in Australia. Because most legal data is not structured in a manner easily suited to most data mining techniques, application of knowledge discovery methods to legal data has not developed as quickly as in other areas. The researchers' goal is to improve the delivery of legal services and just outcomes in law, through improved use of available legal data.

2. Data Understanding Phase

The data are provided by Victoria Legal Aid (VLA), a semigovernmental organization that aims to provide more effective legal aid for underprivileged people in Australia. Over 380,000 applications for legal aid were collected from the 11 regional offices of VLA, spanning 1997–1999, including information on more than 300 variables. In an effort to reduce the number of variables, the researchers turned to domain experts for assistance. These experts selected seven of the most important variables for inclusion in the data set: gender, age, occupation, reason for refusal of aid, law type (e.g., civil law), decision (i.e., aid granted or not granted), and dealing type (e.g., court appearance).

3. Data Preparation Phase

The VLA data set turned out to be relatively clean, containing very few records with missing or incorrectly coded attribute values. This is in part due to the database management system used by the VLA, which performs quality checks on input data. The age variable was partitioned into discrete intervals such as "under 18," "over 50," and so on.

4. Modeling Phase

Rules were restricted to having only a single antecedent and a single consequent. Many interesting association rules were uncovered, along with many uninteresting rules, which is the typical scenario for association rule mining. One such interesting rule was: *If place of birth = Vietnam, then law type = criminal law*, with 90% confidence.

The researchers proceeded on the accurate premise that association rules are interesting if they spawn interesting hypotheses. A discussion among the researchers and experts for the reasons underlying the association rule above considered the following hypotheses:

- *Hypothesis A:* Vietnamese applicants applied for support only for criminal law and not for other types, such as family and civil law.
- *Hypothesis B:* Vietnamese applicants committed more crime than other groups.
- *Hypothesis C:* There is a lurking variable. Perhaps Vietnamese males are more likely than females to apply for aid, and males are more associated with criminal law.
- *Hypothesis D:* The Vietnamese did not have ready access to VLA promotional material.

The panel of researchers and experts concluded informally that hypothesis A was most likely, although further investigation is perhaps warranted, and no causal link can be assumed. Note, however, the intense human interactivity throughout the data mining process. Without the domain experts' knowledge and experience, the data mining results in this case would not have been fruitful.

5. Evaluation Phase

The researchers adopted a unique evaluative methodology for their project. They brought in three domain experts and elicited from them their estimates of the confidence levels for each of 144 association rules. These estimated confidence levels were then compared with the actual confidence levels of the association rules uncovered in the data set.

6. Deployment Phase

A useful Web-based application, WebAssociator, was developed, so that nonspecialists could take advantage of the rule-building engine. Users select the single antecedent and single consequent using a Web-based form. The researchers suggest that WebAssociator could be deployed as part of a judicial support system, especially for identifying unjust processes.

CASE STUDY 4

PREDICTING CORPORATE BANKRUPTCIES USING DECISION TREES [22]

1. Business/Research Understanding Phase

The recent economic crisis in East Asia has spawned an unprecedented level of corporate bankruptcies in that region and around the world. The goal of the researchers, Tae Kyung Sung from Kyonggi University, Namsik Chang from the University of Seoul, and Gunhee Lee of Sogang University, Korea, is to develop models for predicting corporate bankruptcies that maximize the interpretability of the results. They felt that interpretability was important because a negative bankruptcy prediction can itself have a devastating impact on a financial institution, so that firms that are predicted to go bankrupt demand strong and logical reasoning.

If one's company is in danger of going under, and a prediction of bankruptcy could itself contribute to the final failure, that prediction better be supported by solid "trace-able" evidence, not by a simple up/down decision delivered by a black box. Therefore, the researchers chose decision trees as their analysis method, because of the transparency of the algorithm and the interpretability of results.

2. Data Understanding Phase

The data included two groups, Korean firms that went bankrupt in the relatively stable growth period of 1991–1995, and Korean firms that went bankrupt in the economic crisis conditions of 1997–1998. After various screening procedures, 29 firms were identified, mostly in the manufacturing sector. The financial data was collected directly from the Korean Stock Exchange, and verified by the Bank of Korea and the Korea Industrial Bank.

3. Data Preparation Phase

Fifty-six financial ratios were identified by the researchers through a search of the literature on bankruptcy prediction, 16 of which were then dropped due to duplication. There remained 40 financial ratios in the data set, including measures of growth, profitability, safety/leverage, activity/efficiency, and productivity.

4. Modeling Phase

Separate decision tree models were applied to the "normal-conditions" data and the "crisis-conditions" data. As we shall learn in Chapter 6, decision tree models can easily generate rule sets. Some of the rules uncovered for the normal-conditions data were as follows:

- If the productivity of capital is greater than 19.65, predict *nonbankrupt* with 86% confidence.
- If the ratio of cash flow to total assets is greater than −5.65, predict *nonbankrupt* with 95% confidence.
- If the productivity of capital is at or below 19.65 *and* the ratio of cash flow to total assets is at or below −5.65, predict *bankrupt* with 84% confidence.

Some of the rules uncovered for the crisis-conditions data were as follows:

- If the productivity of capital is greater than 20.61, predict *nonbankrupt* with 91% confidence.
- If the ratio of cash flow to liabilities is greater than 2.64, predict *nonbankrupt* with 85% confidence.
- If the ratio of fixed assets to stockholders' equity and long-term liabilities is greater than 87.23, predict *nonbankrupt* with 86% confidence.
- If the productivity of capital is at or below 20.61, *and* the ratio of cash flow to liabilities is at or below 2.64, *and* the ratio of fixed assets to stockholders' equity and long-term liabilities is at or below 87.23, predict *bankrupt* with 84% confidence.

Cash flow and *productivity of capital* were found to be important regardless of the economic conditions. While *cash flow* is well known in the bankruptcy prediction literature, the identification of *productivity of capital* was relatively rare, which therefore demanded further verification.

5. Evaluation Phase

The researchers convened an expert panel of financial specialists, which unanimously selected *productivity of capital* as the most important attribute for differentiating firms in danger of bankruptcy from other firms. Thus, the unexpected results discovered by the decision tree model were verified by the experts.

To ensure that the model was generalizable to the population of all Korean manufacturing firms, a control sample of nonbankrupt firms was selected, and the attributes of the control sample were compared to those of the companies in the data set. It was found that the control sample's average assets and average number of employees were within 20% of the data sample.

Finally, the researchers applied multiple discriminant analysis as a performance benchmark. Many of the 40 financial ratios were found to be significant predictors of bankruptcy, and the final discriminant function included variables identified by the decision tree model.

6. Deployment Phase

There was no deployment identified per se. As mentioned earlier, deployment is often at the discretion of users. However, because of this research, financial institutions in Korea are now better aware of the predictors for bankruptcy for crisis conditions, as opposed to normal conditions.

CASE STUDY 5

PROFILING THE TOURISM MARKET USING *k*-MEANS CLUSTERING ANALYSIS [23]

1. Business/Research Understanding Phase

The researchers, Simon Hudson and Brent Ritchie, of the University of Calgary, Alberta, Canada, are interested in studying intraprovince tourist behavior in Alberta. They would like to create profiles of domestic Albertan tourists based on the decision behavior of the tourists. The overall goal of the study was to form a quantitative basis for the development of an intraprovince marketing campaign, sponsored by Travel Alberta. Toward this goal, the main objectives were to determine which factors were important in choosing destinations in Alberta, to evaluate the domestic perceptions of the "Alberta vacation product," and to attempt to comprehend the travel decision-making process.

2. Data Understanding Phase

The data were collected in late 1999 using a phone survey of 13,445 Albertans. The respondents were screened according to those who were over 18 and had traveled for leisure at least 80 kilometers for at least one night within Alberta in the past year. Only 3071 of these 13,445 completed the survey and were eligible for inclusion in the study.

3. Data Preparation Phase

One of the survey questions asked the respondents to indicate to what extent each of the factors from a list of 13 factors most influence their travel decisions. These were then considered to be variables upon which the cluster analysis was performed, and included such factors as the quality of accommodations, school holidays, and weather conditions.

4. Modeling Phase

Clustering is a natural method for generating segment profiles. The researchers chose *k*-means clustering, since that algorithm is quick and efficient as long as you know the number of clusters you expect to find. They explored between two and six cluster models before settling on a five-cluster solution as best reflecting reality. Brief profiles of the clusters are as follows:

- *Cluster 1: the young urban outdoor market.* Youngest of all clusters, equally balanced genderwise, with school schedules and budgets looming large in their travel decisions.
- *Cluster 2: the indoor leisure traveler market.* Next youngest and very female, mostly married with children, with visiting family and friends a major factor in travel plans.
- *Cluster 3: the children-first market.* More married and more children than any other cluster, with children's sports and competition schedules having great weight in deciding where to travel in Alberta.
- *Cluster 4: the fair-weather-friends market.* Second-oldest, slightly more male group, with weather conditions influencing travel decisions.
- *Cluster 5: the older, cost-conscious traveler market.* The oldest of the clusters, most influenced by cost/value considerations and a secure environment when making Alberta travel decisions.

5. Evaluation Phase

Discriminant analysis was used to verify the "reality" of the cluster categorizations, correctly classifying about 93% of subjects into the right clusters. The discriminant analysis also showed that the differences between clusters were statistically significant.

6. Deployment Phase

These study findings resulted in the launching of a new marketing campaign, "Alberta, Made to Order," based on customizing the marketing to the cluster types uncovered in the data mining. More than 80 projects were launched, through a cooperative arrangement between government and business. "Alberta, Made to Order," television commercials have now been viewed about 20 times by over 90% of adults under 55. Travel Alberta later found an increase of over 20% in the number of Albertans who indicated Alberta as a "top-of-the-mind" travel destination.

REFERENCES

1. Peter Fabris, Advanced navigation, *CIO Magazine*, May 15, 1998, `http://www.cio.com/archive/051598_mining.html`.
2. Bill Clinton, New York University speech, *Salon.com*, December 6, 2002, `http://www.salon.com/politics/feature/2002/12/06/clinton/print.html`.
3. *Mining Data to Save Children with Brain Tumors*, SPSS, Inc., `http://spss.com/success/`.
4. The Gartner Group, `www.gartner.com`.
5. David Hand, Heikki Mannila, and Padhraic Smyth, *Principles of Data Mining*, MIT Press, Cambridge, MA, 2001.
6. Peter Cabena, Pablo Hadjinian, Rolf Stadler, Jaap Verhees, and Alessandro Zanasi, *Discovering Data Mining: From Concept to Implementation*, Prentice Hall, Upper Saddle River, NJ, 1998.
7. Rachel Konrad, Data mining: Digging user info for gold, *ZDNET News*, February 7, 2001, `http://zdnet.com.com/2100-11-528032.html?legacy=zdnn`.
8. The Technology Review Ten, *MIT Technology Review*, January/February 2001.
9. Jennifer Mateyaschuk, The 1999 National IT Salary Survey: Pay up, *Information Week*, `http://www.informationweek.com/731/salsurvey.htm`.
10. The Boston Celtics, `http://www.nba.com/celtics/`.
11. Peter Gwynne, Digging for data, *Think Research*, `domino.watson.ibm.com/comm/wwwr_thinkresearch.nsf/pages/datamine296.html`.
12. John Naisbitt, *Megatrends*, 6th ed., Warner Books, New York, 1986.
13. Michael Berry and Gordon Linoff, *Data Mining Techniques for Marketing, Sales and Customer Support*, Wiley, Hoboken, NJ, 1997.
14. Michael Berry and Gordon Linoff, *Mastering Data Mining*, Wiley, Hoboken, NJ, 2000.
15. Quoted in: Mihael Ankerst, The perfect data mining tool: Interactive or automated? Report on the SIGKDD-2002 Panel, *SIGKDD Explorations*, Vol. 5, No. 1, July 2003.
16. Peter Chapman, Julian Clinton, Randy Kerber, Thomas Khabaza, Thomas Reinart, Colin Shearer, and Rudiger Wirth, *CRISP–DM Step-by-Step Data Mining Guide*, 2000, `http://www.crisp-dm.org/`.
17. Jochen Hipp and Guido Lindner, Analyzing warranty claims of automobiles: an application description following the CRISP–DM data mining process, in *Proceedings of the*

5th International Computer Science Conference (ICSC '99), pp. 31–40, Hong Kong, December 13–15, 1999, © Springer.
18. Jen Que Louie, President of Nautilus Systems, Inc. (www.nautilus-systems.com), testimony before the U.S. House of Representatives Subcommittee on Technology, Information Policy, Intergovernmental Relations, and Census, *Congressional Testimony*, March 25, 2003.
19. www.Claritas.com.
20. Alan M. Safer, A comparison of two data mining techniques to predict abnormal stock market returns, *Intelligent Data Analysis*, Vol. 7, pp. 3–13, 2003.
21. Sasha Ivkovic, John Yearwood, and Andrew Stranieri, Discovering interesting association rules from legal databases, *Information and Communication Technology Law*, Vol. 11, No. 1, 2002.
22. Tae Kyung Sung, Namsik Chang, and Gunhee Lee, Dynamics of modeling in data mining: interpretive approach to bankruptcy prediction, *Journal of Management Information Systems,* Vol. 16, No. 1, pp. 63–85, 1999.
23. Simon Hudson and Brent Richie, Understanding the domestic market using cluster analysis: a case study of the marketing efforts of Travel Alberta, *Journal of Vacation Marketing*, Vol. 8, No. 3, pp. 263–276, 2002.

EXERCISES

1. Refer to the Bank of America example early in the chapter. Which data mining task or tasks are implied in identifying "the type of marketing approach for a particular customer, based on the customer's individual profile"? Which tasks are not explicitly relevant?

2. For each of the following, identify the relevant data mining task(s):

- **a.** The Boston Celtics would like to approximate how many points their next opponent will score against them.
- **b.** A military intelligence officer is interested in learning about the respective proportions of Sunnis and Shias in a particular strategic region.
- **c.** A NORAD defense computer must decide immediately whether a blip on the radar is a flock of geese or an incoming nuclear missile.
- **d.** A political strategist is seeking the best groups to canvass for donations in a particular county.
- **e.** A homeland security official would like to determine whether a certain sequence of financial and residence moves implies a tendency to terrorist acts.
- **f.** A Wall Street analyst has been asked to find out the expected change in stock price for a set of companies with similar price/earnings ratios.

3. For each of the following meetings, explain which phase in the CRISP–DM process is represented:

- **a.** Managers want to know by next week whether deployment will take place. Therefore, analysts meet to discuss how useful and accurate their model is.
- **b.** The data mining project manager meets with the data warehousing manager to discuss how the data will be collected.
- **c.** The data mining consultant meets with the vice president for marketing, who says that he would like to move forward with customer relationship management.

d. The data mining project manager meets with the production line supervisor to discuss implementation of changes and improvements.

e. The analysts meet to discuss whether the neural network or decision tree models should be applied.

4. Discuss the need for human direction of data mining. Describe the possible consequences of relying on completely automatic data analysis tools.

5. CRISP–DM is not the only standard process for data mining. Research an alternative methodology. (*Hint:* SEMMA, from the SAS Institute.) Discuss the similarities and differences with CRISP–DM.

6. Discuss the lessons drawn from Case Study 1. Why do you think the author chose a case study where the road was rocky and the results less than overwhelming?

7. Consider the business understanding phase of Case Study 2.

a. Restate the research question in your own words.

b. Describe the possible consequences for any given data mining scenario of the data analyst not completely understanding the business or research problem.

8. Discuss the evaluation method used for Case Study 3 in light of Exercise 4.

9. Examine the association rules uncovered in Case Study 4.

a. Which association rule do you think is most useful under normal conditions? Under crisis conditions?

b. Describe how these association rules could be used to help decrease the rate of company failures in Korea.

10. Examine the clusters found in Case Study 5.

a. Which cluster do you find yourself or your relatives in?

b. Describe how you would use the information from the clusters to increase tourism in Alberta.

CHAPTER 2

DATA PREPROCESSING

Chapter 1 introduced us to data mining and the CRISP—DM standard process for data mining model development. The case studies we looked at in Chapter 1 gave us an idea of how businesses and researchers apply phase 1 in the data mining process, *business understanding* or *research understanding*. We saw examples of how businesses and researchers first enunciate project objectives, then translate these objectives into the formulation of a data mining problem definition, and finally, prepare a preliminary strategy for achieving these objectives.

Here in Chapter 2 we examine the next two phases of the CRISP—DM standard process, *data understanding* and *data preparation*. We show how to evaluate the quality of the data, clean the raw data, deal with missing data, and perform transformations on certain variables.

All of Chapter 3 is devoted to this very important aspect of the *data understanding*. The heart of any data mining project is the *modeling* phase, which we begin examining in Chapter 4.

WHY DO WE NEED TO PREPROCESS THE DATA?

Much of the raw data contained in databases is unpreprocessed, incomplete, and noisy. For example, the databases may contain:

- Fields that are obsolete or redundant
- Missing values

Discovering Knowledge in Data: An Introduction to Data Mining, By Daniel T. Larose
ISBN 0-471-66657-2

- Outliers
- Data in a form not suitable for data mining models
- Values not consistent with policy or common sense.

To be useful for data mining purposes, the databases need to undergo preprocessing, in the form of *data cleaning* and *data transformation*. Data mining often deals with data that hasn't been looked at for years, so that much of the data contains field values that have expired, are no longer relevant, or are simply missing. The overriding objective is to *minimize GIGO*: to minimize the "garbage" that gets into our model so that we can minimize the amount of garbage that our models give out.

Dorian Pyle, in his book *Data Preparation for Data Mining* [1], estimates that data preparation alone accounts for 60% of all the time and effort expanded in the entire data mining process. In this chapter we examine two principal methods for preparing the data to be mined, data cleaning, and data transformation.

DATA CLEANING

To illustrate the need to clean up data, let's take a look at some of the types of errors that could creep into even a tiny data set, such as that in Table 2.1. Let's discuss, attribute by attribute, some of the problems that have found their way into the data set in Table 2.1. The *customer ID* variable seems to be fine. What about *zip*?

Let's assume that we are expecting all of the customers in the database to have the usual five-numeral U.S. zip code. Now, customer 1002 has this strange (to American eyes) zip code of *J2S7K7*. If we were not careful, we might be tempted to classify this unusual value as an error and toss it out, until we stop to think that not all countries use the same zip code format. Actually, this is the zip code of St. Hyancinthe, Quebec, Canada, so probably represents real data from a real customer. What has evidently occurred is that a French-Canadian customer has made a purchase and put their home zip code down in the field required. Especially in this era of the North American Free Trade Agreement, we must be ready to expect unusual values in fields such as zip codes, which vary from country to country.

What about the zip code for customer 1004? We are unaware of any countries that have four-digit zip codes, such as the *6269* indicated here, so this must be an error,

TABLE 2.1 Can You Find Any Problems in This Tiny Data Set?

Customer ID	Zip	Gender	Income	Age	Marital Status	Transaction Amount
1001	10048	M	75000	C	M	5000
1002	J2S7K7	F	−40000	40	W	4000
1003	90210		10000000	45	S	7000
1004	6269	M	50000	0	S	1000
1005	55101	F	99999	30	D	3000

right? Probably not. Zip codes for the New England states begin with the numeral 0. Unless the zip code field is defined to be *character* (text) and not *numeric*, the software will probably chop off the leading zero, which is apparently what happened here. The zip code is probably *06269*, which refers to Storrs, Connecticut, home of the University of Connecticut.

The next field, *gender*, contains a missing value for customer 1003. We detail methods for dealing with missing values later in the chapter.

The income field, which we assume is measuring annual gross income, has three potentially anomalous values. First, customer 1003 is shown as having an income of \$10,000,000 per year. Although entirely possible, especially when considering the customer's zip code (*90210*, Beverly Hills), this value of income is nevertheless an *outlier*, an extreme data value. Certain statistical and data mining modeling techniques do not function smoothly in the presence of outliers; we examine methods of handling outliers later in the chapter.

Poverty is one thing, but it is rare to find an income that is negative, as our poor customer 1004 has. Unlike customer 1003's income, customer 1004's reported income of −\$40,000 lies beyond the field bounds for income and therefore must be an error. It is unclear how this error crept in, with perhaps the most likely explanation being that the negative sign is a stray data entry error. However, we cannot be sure and should approach this value cautiously, attempting to communicate with the database manager most familiar with the database history.

So what is wrong with customer 1005's income of \$99,999? Perhaps nothing; it may in fact be valid. But if all the other incomes are rounded to the nearest \$5000, why the precision with customer 1005? Often, in legacy databases, certain specified values are meant to be codes for anomalous entries, such as missing values. Perhaps *99999* was coded in an old database to mean *missing*. Again, we cannot be sure and should again refer to the "wetware."

Finally, are we clear as to which unit of measure the income variable is measured in? Databases often get merged, sometimes without bothering to check whether such merges are entirely appropriate for all fields. For example, it is quite possible that customer 1002, with the Canadian zip code, has an income measured in Canadian dollars, not U.S. dollars.

The *age* field has a couple of problems. Although all the other customers have numerical values for *age*, customer 1001's "age" of *C* probably reflects an earlier categorization of this man's age into a bin labeled *C*. The data mining software will definitely not like this categorical value in an otherwise numerical field, and we will have to resolve this problem somehow. How about customer 1004's age of 0? Perhaps there is a *newborn* male living in Storrs, Connecticut, who has made a transaction of \$1000. More likely, the age of this person is probably missing and was coded as 0 to indicate this or some other anomalous condition (e.g., refused to provide the age information).

Of course, keeping an *age* field in a database is a minefield in itself, since the passage of time will quickly make the field values obsolete and misleading. It is better to keep *date*-type fields (such as birthdate) in a database, since these are constant and may be transformed into ages when needed.

The *marital status* field seems fine, right? Maybe not. The problem lies in the meaning behind these symbols. We all think we know what these symbols mean, but are sometimes surprised. For example, if you are in search of cold water in a rest room in Montreal and turn on the faucet marked *C*, you may be in for a surprise, since the *C* stands for *chaud*, which is French for *hot*. There is also the problem of ambiguity. In Table 2.1, for example, does the *S* for customers 1003 and 1004 stand for *single* or *separated*?

The *transaction amount* field seems satisfactory as long as we are confident that we know what unit of measure is being used and that all records are transacted in this unit.

HANDLING MISSING DATA

Missing data is a problem that continues to plague data analysis methods. Even as our analysis methods gain sophistication, we continue to encounter missing values in fields, especially in databases with a large number of fields. The absence of information is rarely beneficial. All things being equal, more data is almost always better. Therefore, we should think carefully about how we handle the thorny issue of missing data.

To help us tackle this problem, we will introduce ourselves to a new data set, the *cars* data set, originally compiled by Barry Becker and Ronny Kohavi of Silicon Graphics, and available at the SGI online data repository at `www.sgi.com/tech/mlc/db`. The data set, also available on the book series Web site accompanying the text, consists of information about 261 automobiles manufactured in the 1970s and 1980s, including gas mileage, number of cylinders, cubic inches, horsepower, and so on.

Suppose, however, that some of the field values were missing for certain records. Figure 2.1 provides a peek at the first 10 records in the data set, with some of

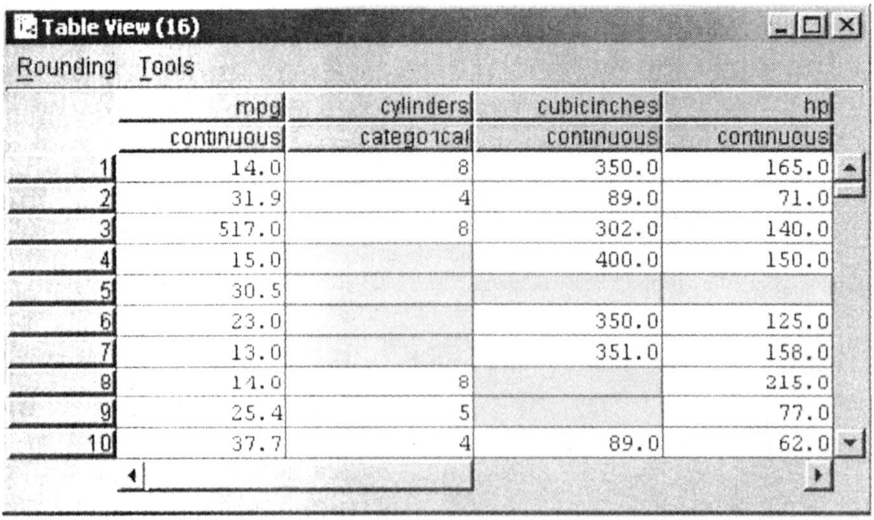

Table View (16)

Rounding Tools

	mpg	cylinders	cubicinches	hp
	continuous	categorical	continuous	continuous
1	14.0	8	350.0	165.0
2	31.9	4	89.0	71.0
3	517.0	8	302.0	140.0
4	15.0		400.0	150.0
5	30.5			
6	23.0		350.0	125.0
7	13.0		351.0	158.0
8	14.0	8		215.0
9	25.4	5		77.0
10	37.7	4	89.0	62.0

Figure 2.1 Some of our field values are missing!

the field values missing (indicated in blue). The software we will be using in this section for missing value analysis is Insightful Miner, by Insightful Corporation (`www.insightful.com`).

A common method of handling missing values is simply to omit from the analysis the records or fields with missing values. However, this may be dangerous, since the pattern of missing values may in fact be systematic, and simply deleting records with missing values would lead to a biased subset of the data. Further, it seems like a waste to omit the information in all the other fields, just because one field value is missing. Therefore, data analysts have turned to methods that would replace the missing value with a value substituted according to various criteria.

Insightful Miner offers a choice of replacement values for missing data:

1. Replace the missing value with some constant, specified by the analyst.
2. Replace the missing value with the field mean (for numerical variables) or the mode (for categorical variables).
3. Replace the missing values with a value generated at random from the variable distribution observed.

Let's take a look at the results for each of the three methods. Figure 2.2 shows the result of replacing the missing values with the constant 0.00 for the numerical variables and the label *missing* for the categorical variables. Figure 2.3 illustrates how the missing values may be replaced with the respective field means and modes. The variable *cylinders* is categorical, with mode 4, so the software replaces the missing *cylinder* values with *cylinder* = *4*. *Cubicinches*, on the other hand, is continuous (numerical), so that the software replaces the missing *cubicinches* values with *cubicinches* = 200.65, which is the mean of all 258 nonmissing values of that variable.

Isn't it nice to have the software take care of your missing data problems like this? In a way, certainly. However, don't lose sight of the fact that the software is

Table View (17)

Rounding Tools

	mpg	cylinders	cubicinches	hp
	continuous	categorical	continuous	continuous
1	14.00	8	350.00	165.00
2	31.90	4	89.00	71.00
3	517.00	8	302.00	140.00
4	15.00	Missing	400.00	150.00
5	30.50	Missing	0.00	0.00
6	23.00	Missing	350.00	125.00
7	13.00	Missing	351.00	158.00
8	14.00	8	0.00	215.00
9	25.40	5	0.00	77.00
10	37.70	4	89.00	62.00

Figure 2.2 Replacing missing field values with user-defined constants.

Table View (17)

Rounding Tools

	mpg	cylinders	cubicinches	hp
	continuous	categorical	continuous	continuous
1	14.00	8	350.00	165.00
2	31.90	4	89.00	71.00
3	517.00	8	302.00	140.00
4	15.00	4	400.00	150.00
5	30.50	4	200.65	106.53
6	23.00	4	350.00	125.00
7	13.00	4	351.00	158.00
8	14.00	8	200.65	215.00
9	25.40	5	200.65	77.00
10	37.70	4	89.00	62.00

Figure 2.3 Replacing missing field values with means or modes.

creating information on the spot, actually fabricating data to fill in the holes in the data set. Choosing the field mean as a substitute for whatever value would have been there may sometimes work out well. However, the end users and publication readers need to know that this process has taken place.

Further, the mean may not always be the best choice for what constitutes a "typical" value. For example, if many missing values are replaced with the mean, the resulting confidence levels for statistical inference will be overoptimistic, since measures of spread will be reduced artificially. It must be stressed that replacing missing values is a gamble, and the benefits must be weighed against the possible invalidity of the results.

Finally, Figure 2.4 demonstrates how Insightful Miner can replace missing values with values generated at random from the variable distribution observed. Note in Figure 2.3 how, all four of the missing *cylinder* values were replaced with the same value, *cylinder* = 4, whereas in Figure 2.4, the missing *cylinder* values were replaced with various values drawn proportionately from the distribution of *cylinder* values. In the long run, this method is probably superior to the mean substitution, since, among other reasons, the measures of center and spread should remain closer to the original.

This capacity to replace missing values with random draws from the distribution is one of the benefits of Insightful Miner. However, there is no guarantee that the resulting records would make sense. For example, the random values drawn in Figure 2.4 make sense record-wise, but it was certainly possible that record 5 could have drawn *cylinders* = 8 with something like *cubicinches* = 82, which would be a strange engine indeed! Therefore, other, more elaborate methods exist that strive to replace missing values more precisely and accurately.

For example, there are methods that ask: What would be the most likely value for this missing value given all the other attributes for a particular record? For instance, an

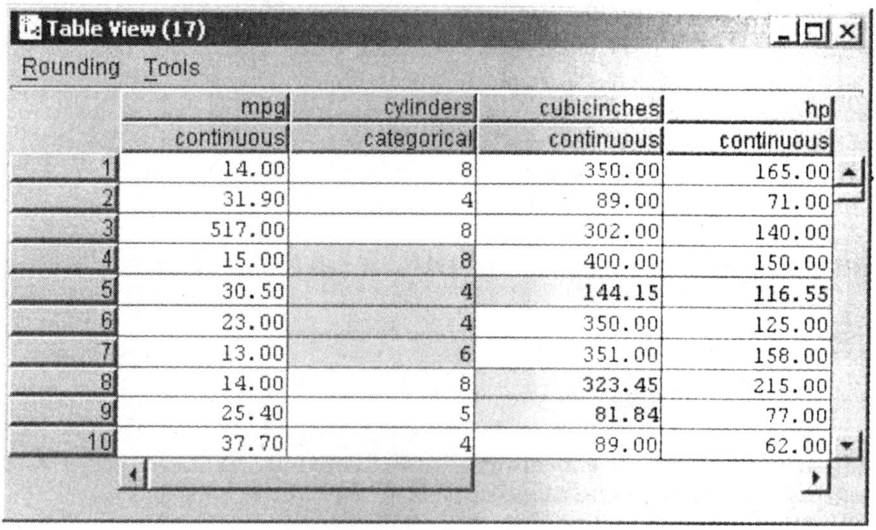

Table View (17)

Rounding Tools

	mpg	cylinders	cubicinches	hp
	continuous	categorical	continuous	continuous
1	14.00	8	350.00	165.00
2	31.90	4	89.00	71.00
3	517.00	8	302.00	140.00
4	15.00	8	400.00	150.00
5	30.50	4	144.15	116.55
6	23.00	4	350.00	125.00
7	13.00	6	351.00	158.00
8	14.00	8	323.45	215.00
9	25.40	5	81.84	77.00
10	37.70	4	89.00	62.00

Figure 2.4 Replacing missing field values with random draws from the distribution of the variable.

American car with 300 cubic inches and 150 horsepower would probably be expected to have more cylinders than a Japanese car with 100 cubic inches and 90 horsepower. For a discussion of these and other methods, including Bayesian estimation, refer to *Statistical Analysis with Missing Data* [2].

IDENTIFYING MISCLASSIFICATIONS

Let us look at an example of checking the classification labels on the categorical variables, to make sure that they are all valid and consistent. One of the functions of Insightful Miner's *missing values* node is to display a frequency distribution of the categorical variables available. For example, the frequency distribution of the categorical variable *origin*, where Insightful Miner's *missing values* node is applied to the *cars* data set, is given in Table 2.2. The frequency distribution shows five

TABLE 2.2 Notice Anything Strange about This Frequency Distribution?

Level Name	Count
USA	1
France	1
US	156
Europe	46
Japan	51

classes: USA, France, US, Europe, and Japan. However, two of the classes, USA and France, have a count of only one automobile each. What is clearly happening here is that two of the records have been classified inconsistently with respect to the origin of manufacture. To maintain consistency with the remainder of the data set, the record with origin *USA* should have been labeled *US*, and the record with origin *France* should have been labeled *Europe*.

GRAPHICAL METHODS FOR IDENTIFYING OUTLIERS

Outliers are extreme values that lie near the limits of the data range or go against the trend of the remaining data. Identifying outliers is important because they may represent errors in data entry. Also, even if an outlier is a valid data point and not in error, certain statistical methods are sensitive to the presence of outliers and may deliver unstable results. Neural networks benefit from normalization, as do algorithms that make use of distance measures, such as the k-nearest neighbor algorithm.

One graphical method for identifying outliers for numeric variables is to examine a *histogram* of the variable. Figure 2.5 shows a histogram generated of the vehicle weights from the *cars* data set. There appears to be one lonely vehicle in the extreme left tail of the distribution, with a vehicle weight in the hundreds of pounds rather than in the thousands. Examining the statistics provided by Insightful Miner, we find the minimum weight to be for a vehicle of 192.5 pounds, which is undoubtedly our little outlier in the lower tail. As 192.5 pounds is a little light for an automobile, we would tend to doubt the validity of this information. Perusal of the *weightlbs* field shows that unlike our outlier, all the other vehicles have their weight recorded in whole numbers

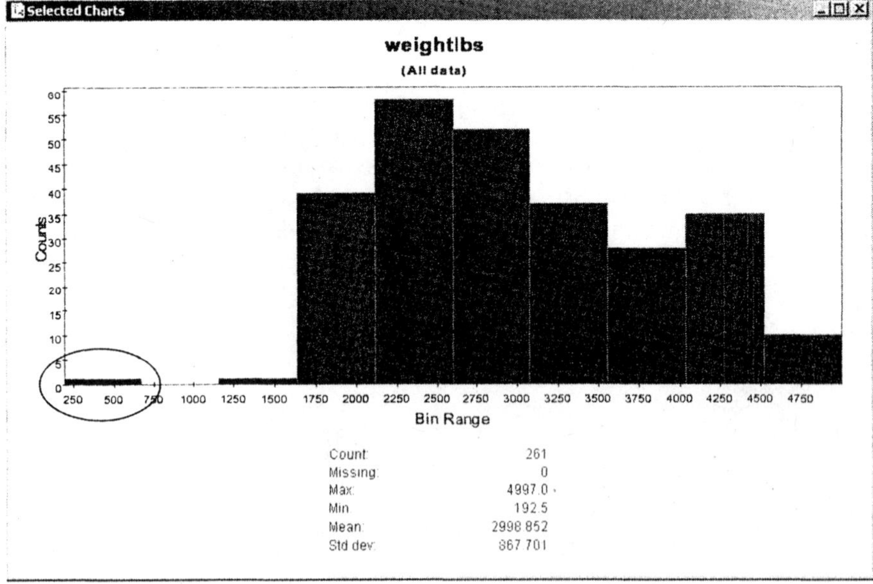

Figure 2.5 Histogram of vehicle weights: can you find the outlier?

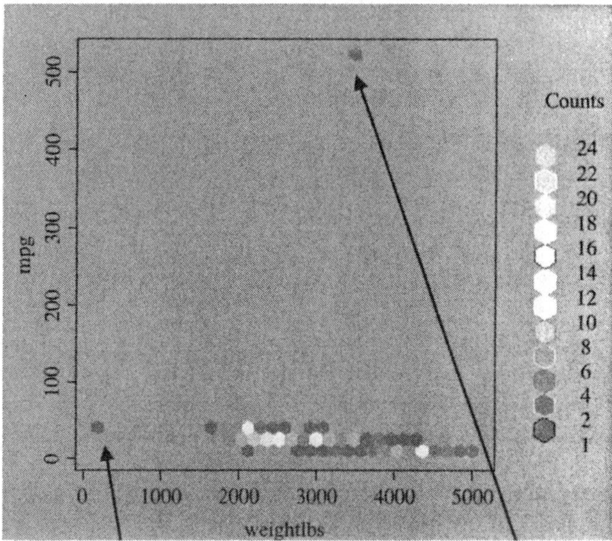

Figure 2.6 Scatter plot of *mpg* against *weightlbs* shows two outliers.

with no decimals. We can therefore surmise that perhaps the weight was originally 1925 pounds, with the decimal inserted somewhere along the line. We cannot be certain, however, and further investigation into the data sources is called for.

Sometimes two-dimensional scatter plots can help to reveal outliers in more than one variable. The scatter plot of *mpg* against *weightlbs* shown in Figure 2.6 seems to have netted two outliers. Most of the data points cluster together along the horizontal axis, except for two outliers. The one on the left is the same vehicle as that identified in Figure 2.5, weighing only 192.5 pounds. The outlier in the upper right corner is something new: a car that gets over 500 miles per gallon! Now that would have been big news at any time, especially in the energy crisis days of the 1970s when this data was abstracted. Clearly, unless this vehicle runs on dilithium crystals, we are looking at a data entry error.

We shall examine numerical methods for identifying outliers, but we need to pick up a few tools first.

DATA TRANSFORMATION

Variables tend to have ranges that vary greatly from each other. For example, if we are interested in major league baseball, players' batting averages will range from zero to less than 0.400, while the number of home runs hit in a season will range from zero to around 70. For some data mining algorithms, such differences in the ranges will lead to a tendency for the variable with greater range to have undue influence on the results.

Therefore, data miners should *normalize* their numerical variables, to standardize the scale of effect each variable has on the results. There are several techniques for *normalization*, and we shall examine two of the more prevalent methods. Let X refer to our original field value and X^* refer to the normalized field value.

Min–Max Normalization

Min–max normalization works by seeing how much greater the field value is than the minimum value min(X) and scaling this difference by the range. That is,

$$X^* = \frac{X - \min(X)}{\text{range}(X)} = \frac{X - \min(X)}{\max(X) - \min(X)}$$

For example, consider the *time-to-60* variable from the *cars* data set, which measures how long (in seconds) each automobile takes to reach 60 miles per hour. Let's find the min–max normalization for three automobiles having *times-to-60* of 8, 15.548, seconds, and 25 seconds, respectively. Refer to Figure 2.7, a histogram of the variable *time-to-60*, along with some summary statistics.

- For a "drag-racing-ready" vehicle, which takes only 8 seconds (the field minimum) to reach 60 mph, the min–max normalization is

  $$X^* = \frac{X - \min(X)}{\max(X) - \min(X)} = \frac{8 - 8}{25 - 8} = 0$$

  From this we can learn that data values which represent the minimum for the variable will have a min–max normalization value of zero.

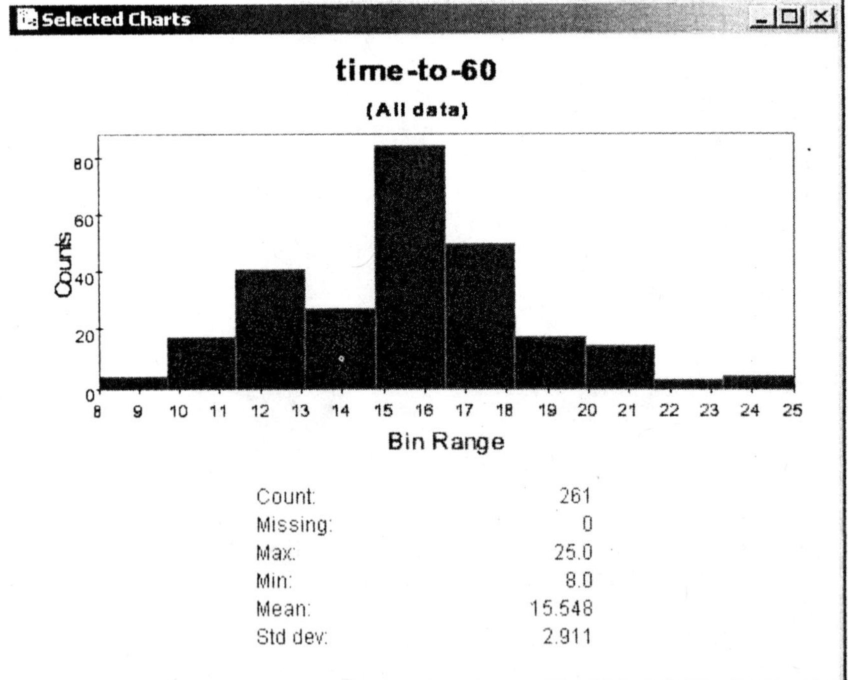

Figure 2.7 Histogram of *time-to-60*, with summary statistics.

- For an "average" vehicle (if any), which takes exactly 15.548 seconds (the variable average) to reach 60 mph, the min–max normalization is

$$X^* = \frac{X - \min(X)}{\max(X) - \min(X)} = \frac{15.548 - 8}{25 - 8} = 0.444$$

  This tells us that we may expect variables values near the center of the distribution to have a min–max normalization value near 0.5.

- For an "I'll get there when I'm ready" vehicle, which takes 25 seconds (the variable maximum) to reach 60 mph, the min–max normalization is

$$X^* = \frac{X - \min(X)}{\max(X) - \min(X)} = \frac{25 - 8}{25 - 8} = 1.0$$

  That is, data values representing the field maximum will have a min–max normalization value of 1.

To summarize, min–max normalization values will range from zero to one, unless new data values are encountered that lie outside the original range.

Z-Score Standardization

Z-score standardization, which is very widespread in the world of statistical analysis, works by taking the difference between the field value and the field mean value and scaling this difference by the standard deviation of the field values. That is,

$$X^* = \frac{X - \text{mean}(X)}{\text{SD}(X)}$$

- For the vehicle that takes only 8 seconds to reach 60 mph, the Z-score standardization is:

$$X^* = \frac{X - \text{mean}(X)}{\text{SD}(X)} = \frac{8 - 15.548}{2.911} = -2.593$$

  Thus, data values that lie below the mean will have a negative Z-score standardization.

- For an "average" vehicle (if any), which takes exactly 15.548 seconds (the variable average) to reach 60 mph, the Z-score standardization is

$$X^* = \frac{X - \text{mean}(X)}{\text{SD}(X)} = \frac{15.548 - 15.548}{2.911} = 0$$

  This tells us that variable values falling exactly on the mean will have a Z-score standardization of zero.

- For the car that takes 25 seconds to reach 60 mph, the Z-score standardization is

$$X^* = \frac{X - \text{mean}(X)}{\text{SD}(X)} = \frac{25 - 15.548}{2.911} = 3.247$$

  That is, data values that lie above the mean will have a positive Z-score standardization.

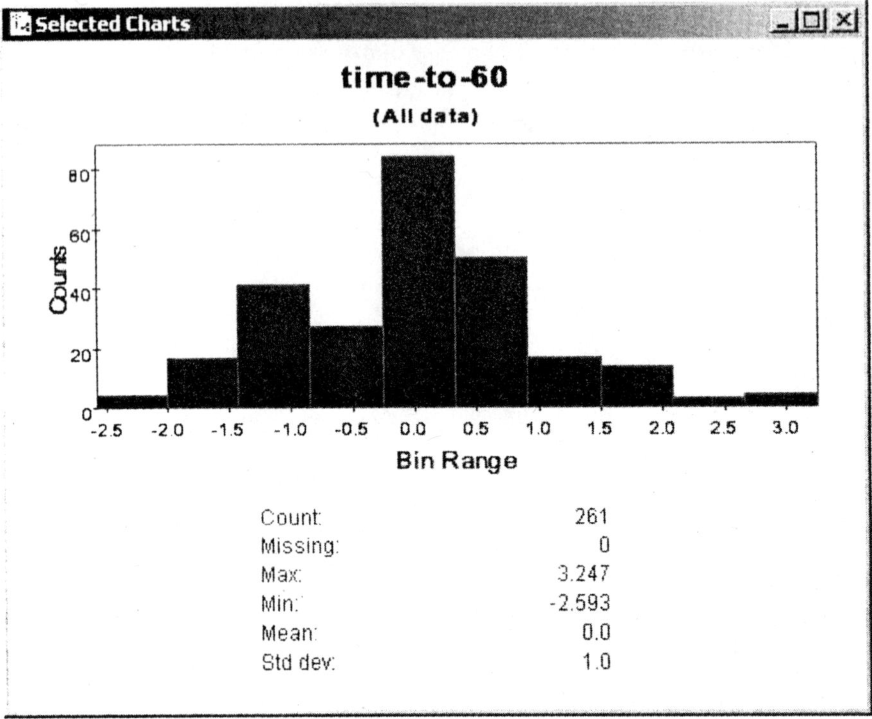

Figure 2.8 Histogram of *time-to-60* after Z-score standardization.

To summarize, Z-score standardization values will usually range between –4 and 4, with the mean value having a Z-score standardization of zero. Figure 2.8 is a histogram of the *time-to-60* variable after Insightful Miner found the Z-score standardization of each field value. Note that the distribution is centered about zero and that the minimum and maximum agree with what we found above.

NUMERICAL METHODS FOR IDENTIFYING OUTLIERS

One method of using statistics to identify outliers is to use Z-score standardization. Often, an outlier can be identified because it is much farther than 3 standard deviations from the mean and therefore has a Z-score standardization that is either less than −3 or greater than 3. Field values with Z-scores much beyond this range probably bear further investigation to verify that they do not represent data entry errors or other issues. For example, the vehicle that takes its time (25 seconds) getting to 60 mph had a Z-score of 3.247. This value is greater than 3 (although not by much), and therefore this vehicle is identified by this method as an outlier. The data analyst may wish to investigate the validity of this data value or at least suggest that the vehicle get a tune-up!

Unfortunately, the mean and standard deviation, both part of the formula for the Z-score standardization, are rather *sensitive* to the presence of outliers. That is, if an outlier is added to a data set, the values of mean and standard deviation will both be unduly affected by this new data value. Therefore, when choosing a method for evaluating outliers, it may not seem appropriate to use measures which are themselves sensitive to their presence.

Therefore, data analysts have developed more *robust* statistical methods for outlier detection, which are less sensitive to the presence of the outliers themselves. One elementary robust method is to use the *interquartile range*. The *quartiles* of a data set divide the data set into four parts, each containing 25% of the data.

- The *first quartile* (Q1) is the 25th percentile.
- The *second quartile* (Q2) is the 50th percentile, that is, the median.
- The *third quartile* (Q3) is the 75th percentile.

The *interquartile range* (IQR) is a measure of variability that is much more robust than the standard deviation. The IQR is calculated as $\text{IQR} = \text{Q3} - \text{Q1}$ and may be interpreted to represent the spread of the middle 50% of the data.

A robust measure of outlier detection is therefore defined as follows. A data value is an outlier if:

a. It is located 1.5(IQR) or more below Q1, or

b. It is located 1.5(IQR) or more above Q3.

For example, suppose that for a set of test scores, the 25th percentile was $\text{Q1} = 70$ and the 75th percentile was $\text{Q3} = 80$, so that half of all the test scores fell between 70 and 80. Then the *interquartile range*, the difference between these quartiles, was $\text{IQR} = 80 - 70 = 10$.

A test score would be robustly identified as an outlier if:

a. It is lower than $\text{Q1} - 1.5(\text{IQR}) = 70 - 1.5(10) = 55$, or

b. It is higher than $\text{Q3} + 1.5(\text{IQR}) = 80 + 1.5(10) = 95$.

In Chapter 3 we apply some basic graphical and statistical tools to help us begin to uncover simple patterns and trends in the data structure.

REFERENCES

1. Dorian Pyle, *Data Preparation for Data Mining*, Morgan Kaufmann, San Francisco, CA, 1999.
2. R. J. A. Little and D. B. Rubin, *Statistical Analysis with Missing Data*, Wiley, Hoboken, NJ, 1987.

EXERCISES

1. Describe the possible negative effects of proceeding directly to mine data that has not been preprocessed.

2. Find the mean value for the income attribute of the five customers in Table 2.1 before preprocessing. What does this number actually mean? Calculate the mean income for the three values left after preprocessing. Does this value have a meaning?

3. Which of the three methods from Figures 2.2 to 2.4 do you prefer for handling missing values?
   a. Which method is the most conservative and probably the safest, meaning that it fabricates the least amount of data? What are some drawbacks to this method?
   b. Which method would tend to lead to an underestimate of the spread (e.g., standard deviation) of the variable? What are some benefits to this method?
   c. What are some benefits and drawbacks of the method that chooses values at random from the variable distribution?
4. Make up a classification scheme that is inherently flawed and would lead to misclassification, as we find in Table 2.2: for example, classes of items bought in a grocery store.
5. Make up a data set consisting of eight scores on an exam in which one of the scores is an outlier.
   a. Find the mean score and the median score, with and without the outlier.
   b. State which measure, the mean or the median, the presence of the outlier affects more, and why. (Mean, median, and other statistics are explained in Chapter 4.)
   c. Verify that the outlier is indeed an outlier, using the IQR method.
6. Make up a data set, consisting of the heights and weights of six children, in which one of the children, but not the other, is an outlier with respect to one of the variables. Then alter this data set so that the child is an outlier with respect to both variables.
7. Using your data set from Exercise 5, find the min–max normalization of the scores. Verify that each value lies between zero and 1.

Hands-on Analysis

Use the *churn* data set at the book series Web site for the following exercises.

8. Explore whether there are missing values for any of the variables.
9. Compare the area code and state fields. Discuss any apparent abnormalities.
10. Use a graph to determine visually whether there are any outliers among the number of calls to customer service.
11. Transform the *day minutes* attribute using min–max normalization. Verify using a graph that all values lie between zero and 1.
12. Transform the *night minutes* attribute using Z-score standardization. Using a graph, describe the range of the standardized values.

CHAPTER 3

EXPLORATORY DATA ANALYSIS

HYPOTHESIS TESTING VERSUS EXPLORATORY DATA ANALYSIS

When approaching a data mining problem, a data mining analyst may already have some a priori hypotheses that he or she would like to test regarding the relationships between the variables. For example, suppose that cell-phone executives are interested in whether a recent increase in the fee structure has led to a decrease in market share. In this case, the analyst would *test* the *hypothesis* that market share has decreased and would therefore use *hypothesis-testing* procedures.

A myriad of statistical hypothesis testing procedures are available through the traditional statistical analysis literature, including methods for testing the following hypotheses:

- The Z-test for the population mean
- The t-test for the population mean
- The Z-test for the population proportion
- The Z-test for the difference in means for two populations

Discovering Knowledge in Data: An Introduction to Data Mining, By Daniel T. Larose
ISBN 0-471-66657-2

- The t-test for the difference in means for two populations
- The t-test for paired samples
- The Z-test for the difference in population proportions
- The χ^2 goodness-of-fit test for multinomial populations
- The χ^2-test for independence among categorical variables
- The analysis of variance F-test
- The t-test for the slope of the regression line

There are many other hypothesis tests throughout the statistical literature, for most conceivable situations, including time-series analysis, quality control tests, and nonparametric tests.

However, analysts do not always have a priori notions of the expected relationships among the variables. Especially when confronted with large unknown databases, analysts often prefer to use *exploratory data analysis* (EDA) or *graphical data analysis*. EDA allows the analyst to:

- Delve into the data set
- Examine the interrelationships among the attributes
- Identify interesting subsets of the observations
- Develop an initial idea of possible associations between the attributes and the target variable, if any

GETTING TO KNOW THE DATA SET

Simple (or not-so-simple) graphs, plots, and tables often uncover important relationships that could indicate fecund areas for further investigation. In Chapter 3 we use exploratory methods to delve into the *churn* data set[1] from the UCI Repository of Machine Learning Databases at the University of California, Irvine. The data set is also available at the book series Web site. In this chapter we begin by using the Clementine data mining software package from SPSS, Inc.

To begin, it is often best simply to take a look at the field values for some of the records. Figure 3.1 gives the results of using Clementine's table node for the *churn* data set, showing the attribute values for the first 10 records. *Churn*, also called *attrition*, is a term used to indicate a customer leaving the service of one company in favor of another company. The data set contains 20 variables worth of information about 3333 customers, along with an indication of whether or not that customer churned (left the company). The variables are as follows:

- *State:* categorical, for the 50 states and the District of Columbia
- *Account length:* integer-valued, how long account has been active
- *Area code:* categorical
- *Phone number:* essentially a surrogate for customer ID

- *International Plan:* dichotomous categorical, yes or no
- *VoiceMail Plan:* dichotomous categorical, yes or no
- *Number of voice mail messages:* integer-valued
- *Total day minutes:* continuous, minutes customer used service during the day
- *Total day calls:* integer-valued

Table (21 fields, 3,333 records) #1

	State	Account Length	Area Code	Phone	Intl Plan	VMail Plan	VMail Messages	Day Mins
1	KS	128	415	382-4657	no	yes	25	265.100
2	OH	107	415	371-7191	no	yes	26	161.600
3	NJ	137	415	358-1921	no	no	0	243.400
4	OH	84	408	375-9999	yes	no	0	299.400
5	OK	75	415	330-6626	yes	no	0	166.700
6	AL	118	510	391-8027	yes	no	0	223.400
7	MA	121	510	355-9993	no	yes	24	218.200
8	MO	147	415	329-9001	yes	no	0	157.000
9	LA	117	408	335-4719	no	no	0	184.500
10	WV	141	415	330-8173	yes	yes	37	258.600

Table (21 fields, 3,333 records) #1

	Day Calls	Day Charge	Eve Mins	Eve Calls	Eve Charge	Night Mins	Night Calls	Night Charge	Intl
1	110	45.070	197.400	99	16.780	244.700	91	11.010	1
2	123	27.470	195.500	103	16.620	254.400	103	11.450	1
3	114	41.380	121.200	110	10.300	162.600	104	7.320	1
4	71	50.900	61.900	88	5.260	196.900	89	8.860	
5	113	28.340	148.300	122	12.610	186.900	121	8.410	1
6	90	37.900	220.600	101	10.750	203.900	110	9.100	
7	88	37.090	348.500	108	29.620	212.600	118	9.570	
8	79	26.690	103.100	94	8.760	211.800	96	9.530	
9	97	31.370	351.600	80	29.890	215.800	90	9.710	
10	84	43.960	222.000	111	18.870	326.400	97	14.690	1

Table (21 fields, 3,333 records) #1

	Night Mins	Night Calls	Night Charge	Intl Mins	Intl Calls	Intl Charge	CustServ Calls	Churn?
1	244.700	91	11.010	10.000	3	2.700	1	False
2	254.400	103	11.450	13.700	3	3.700	1	False
3	162.600	104	7.320	12.200	5	3.290	0	False
4	196.900	89	8.860	6.600	7	1.780	2	False
5	186.900	121	8.410	10.100	3	2.730	3	False
6	203.900	118	9.180	6.300	6	1.700	0	False
7	212.600	118	9.570	7.500	7	2.030	3	False
8	211.800	96	9.530	7.100	6	1.920	0	False
9	215.800	90	9.710	8.700	4	2.350	1	False
10	326.400	97	14.690	11.200	5	3.020	0	False

Figure 3.1 Field values of the first 10 records in the *churn* data set.

- *Total day charge:* continuous, perhaps based on foregoing two variables
- *Total evening minutes:* continuous, minutes customer used service during the evening
- *Total evening calls:* integer-valued
- *Total evening charge:* continuous, perhaps based on foregoing two variables
- *Total night minutes:* continuous, minutes customer used service during the night
- *Total night calls:* integer-valued
- *Total night charge:* continuous, perhaps based on foregoing two variables
- *Total international minutes:* continuous, minutes customer used service to make international calls
- *Total international calls:* integer-valued
- *Total international charge:* continuous, perhaps based on foregoing two variables
- *Number of calls to customer service:* integer-valued

DEALING WITH CORRELATED VARIABLES

One should take care to avoid feeding correlated variables to one's data mining and statistical models. At best, using correlated variables will overemphasize one data component; at worst, using correlated variables will cause the model to become unstable and deliver unreliable results.

The data set contains three variables: *minutes*, *calls*, and *charge*. The data description indicates that the *charge* variable may be a function of *minutes* and *calls*, with the result that the variables would be correlated. We investigate using the *matrix plot* shown in Figure 3.2, which is a matrix of scatter plots for a set of

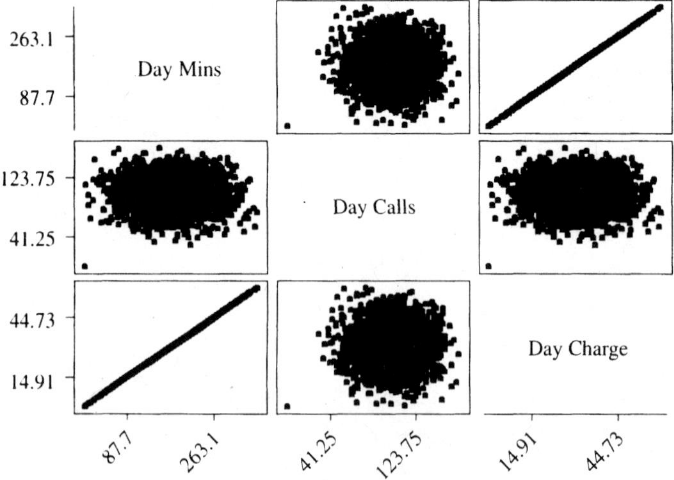

Figure 3.2 Matrix plot of *day minutes*, *day calls*, and *day charge*.

Regression Analysis: Day charge versus Day Mins

```
The regression equation is
Day Charge = 0.000613 + 0.170 Day Mins

Predictor         Coef     SE Coef          T        P
Constant     0.0006134   0.0001711       3.59    0.000
Day Mins      0.170000    0.000001  186644.31    0.000

S = 0.002864      R-Sq = 100.0%      R-Sq(adj) = 100.0%
```

Figure 3.3 Minitab regression output for *day charge* versus *day minutes*.

numeric variables. The matrix plot comes courtesy of Minitab, a widely used statistical package.

There does not seem to be any relationship between *day minutes* and *day calls* or between *day calls* and *day charge*. This we find to be rather odd, as one may have expected that as the number of calls increased, the number of minutes would tend to increase (and similarly for charge), resulting in a positive correlation between these fields. However, the graphical evidence does not support this, nor do the correlations, which are $r = 0.07$ for both relationships (from Minitab, not shown).

On the other hand, there is a perfect linear relationship between *day minutes* and *day charge*, indicating that *day charge* is a simple linear function of *day minutes* only. Using Minitab's regression tool (Figure 3.3), we find that we may express this function as the estimated regression equation: "*Day charge* equals 0.000613 plus 0.17 times *day minutes*." This is essentially a flat-rate model, billing 17 cents per minute for day use. Note from Figure 3.3 that the R-squared statistic is precisely 1, indicating a perfect linear relationship.

Since *day charge* is correlated perfectly with *day minutes*, we should eliminate one of the two variables. We do so, choosing arbitrarily to eliminate *day charge* and retain *day minutes*. Investigation of the *evening*, *night*, and *international* components reflected similar findings, and we thus also eliminate *evening charge*, *night charge*, and *international charge*. Note that had we proceeded to the modeling phase without first uncovering these correlations, our data mining and statistical models may have returned incoherent results, due in the multiple regression domain, for example, to multicollinearity. We have therefore reduced the number of predictors from 20 to 16 by eliminating redundant variables. A further benefit of doing so is that the dimensionality of the solution space is reduced, so that certain data mining algorithms may more efficiently find the globally optimal solution.

EXPLORING CATEGORICAL VARIABLES

One of the primary reasons for performing exploratory data analysis is to investigate the variables, look at histograms of the numeric variables, examine the distributions of the categorical variables, and explore the relationships among sets of variables. On the other hand, our overall objective for the data mining project as a whole (not just the EDA phase) is to develop a model of the type of customer likely to churn

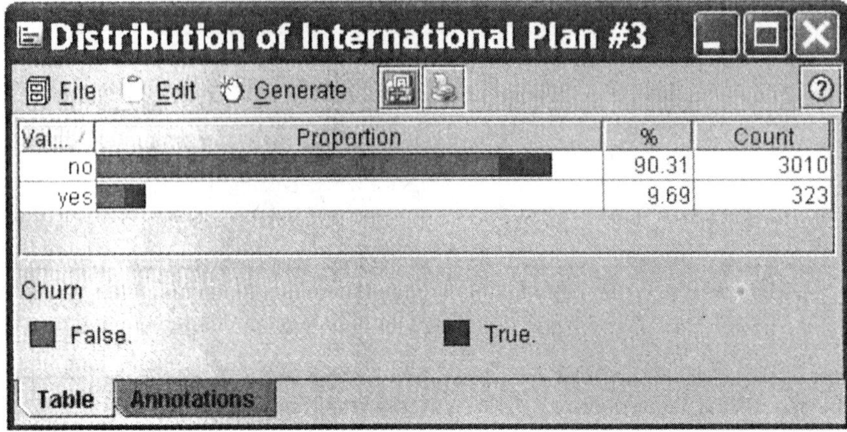

Figure 3.4 Comparison bar chart of churn proportions by International Plan participation.

(jump from your company's service to another company's service). Today's software packages allow us to become familiar with the variables while beginning to see which variables are associated with churn. In this way we can explore the data while keeping an eye on our overall goal. We begin by considering the categorical variables.

For example, Figure 3.4 shows a comparison of the proportion of churners (red) and nonchurners (blue) among customers who either had selected the International Plan (yes, 9.69% of customers) or had not selected it (no, 90.31% of customers). The graphic appears to indicate that a greater proportion of International Plan holders are churning, but it is difficult to be sure.

To increase the contrast and better discern whether the proportions differ, we can ask the software (in this case, Clementine) to provide same-size bars for each category. In Figure 3.5 we see a graph of the very same information as in Figure 3.4, except that the bar for the *yes* category has been stretched out to be the same length as the bar for the *no* category. This allows us to better discern whether the churn proportions differ

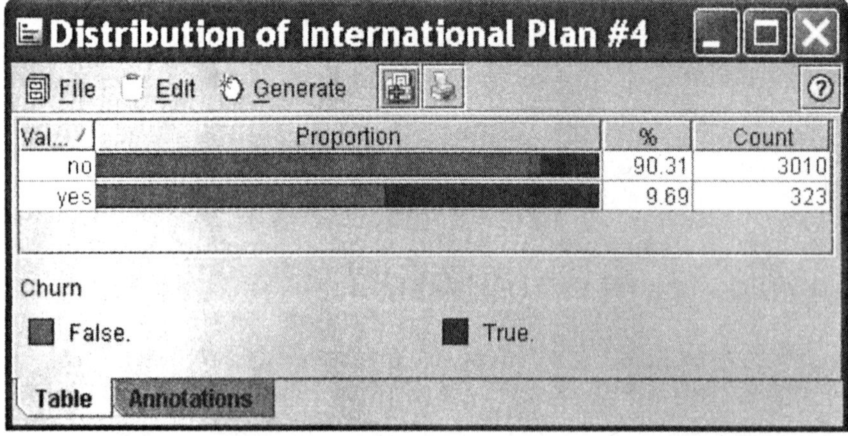

Figure 3.5 Comparison bar chart of churn proportions by International Plan participation, with equal bar length.

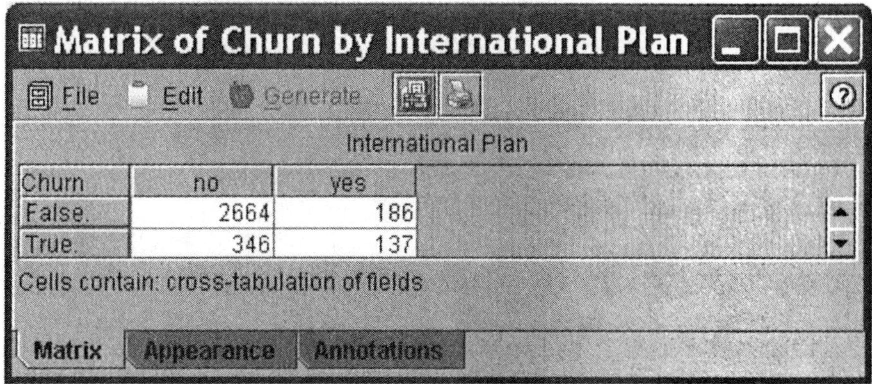

Figure 3.6 Cross-tabulation of International Plan with churn.

among the categories. Clearly, those who have selected the International Plan have a greater chance of leaving the company's service than do those who do not have the International Plan.

The graphics tell us that International Plan holders tend to churn more frequently, but they do not *quantify* the relationship. To quantify the relationship between International Plan holding and churning, we may use cross-tabulations, since both variables are categorical. Figure 3.6 shows Clementine's cross-tabulation. Note that the counts in the first column add up to the total number of nonselectors of the International Plan from Figure 3.4, $2664 + 346 = 3010$; similarly for the second column. The first row in Figure 3.6 shows the counts of those who did not churn, while the second row shows the counts of those who did churn. So the data set contains $346 + 137 = 483$ churners compared to $2664 + 186 = 2850$ nonchurners; that is, $483/(483 + 2850) = 14.5\%$ of the customers in this data set are churners.

Note that $137/(137 + 186) = 42.4\%$ of the International Plan holders churned, compared with only $346/(346 + 2664) = 11.5\%$ of those without the International Plan. Customers selecting the International Plan are more than three times as likely to leave the company's service than those without the plan.

This EDA on the International Plan has indicated that:

1. Perhaps we should investigate what it is about the International Plan that is inducing customers to leave!
2. We should expect that whatever data mining algorithms we use to predict churn, the model will probably include whether or not the customer selected the International Plan.

Let us now turn to the VoiceMail Plan. Figure 3.7 shows in a bar graph with equalized lengths that those who do not have the VoiceMail Plan are more likely to churn than those who do have the plan. (The numbers in the graph indicate proportions and counts of those who do and do not have the VoiceMail Plan, without reference to churning.)

Again, we may quantify this finding by using cross-tabulations, as in Figure 3.8. First of all, $842 + 80 = 922$ customers have the VoiceMail Plan, while $2008 + 403 = 2411$ do not. We then find that $403/2411 = 16.7\%$ of those without the VoiceMail Plan

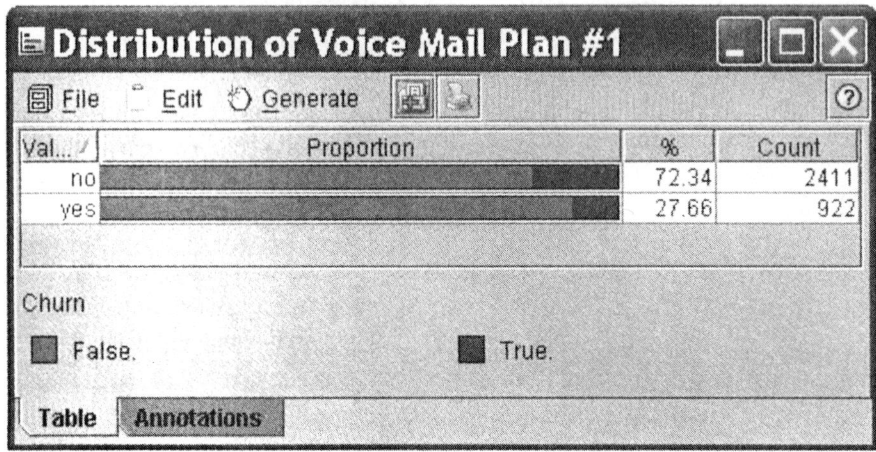

Figure 3.7 Those without the VoiceMail Plan are more likely to churn.

are churners, compared to $80/922 = 8.7\%$ of customers who do have the VoiceMail Plan. Thus, customers without the VoiceMail Plan are nearly twice as likely to churn as customers with the plan.

This EDA on the VoiceMail Plan has indicated that:

1. Perhaps we should enhance the VoiceMail Plan further or make it easier for customers to join it, as an instrument for increasing customer loyalty.
2. We should expect that whatever data mining algorithms we use to predict churn, the model will probably include whether or not the customer selected the VoiceMail Plan. Our confidence in this expectation is perhaps not quite as the high as that for the International Plan.

We may also explore the *two-way interactions* among categorical variables with respect to churn. For example, Figure 3.9 shows a pair of horizontal bar charts for

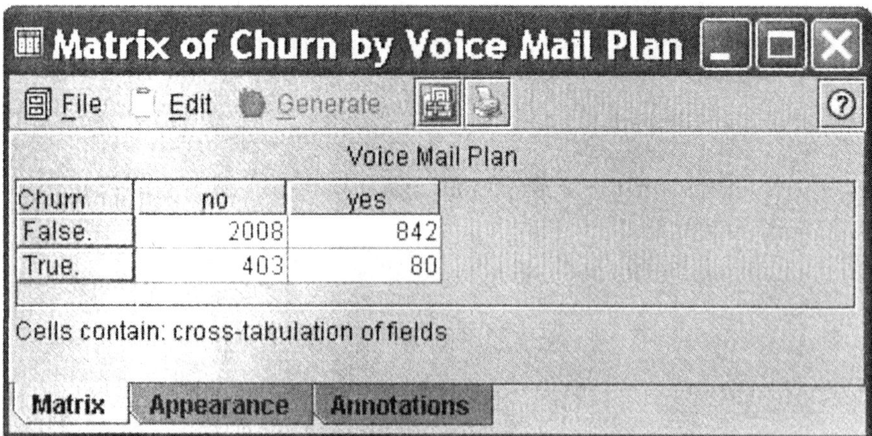

Figure 3.8 Cross-tabulation of VoiceMail Plan with churn.

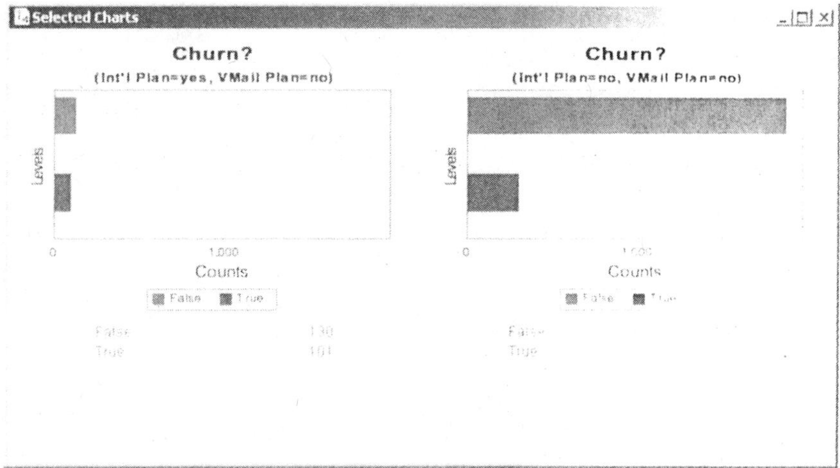

Figure 3.9 Bar charts of customers who churned, without VoiceMail Plan, subsetted by International Plan selection.

customers who did not select the VoiceMail Plan (*Vmail Plan* = *no*). The bar chart on the right contains customers who did not select the International Plan either, while the bar chart on the left contains customers who did select the International Plan.

Note that there are many more customers who have neither plan ($1878 + 302 = 2180$) than have the International Plan only ($130 + 101 = 231$). More important, among customers without the VoiceMail Plan, the proportion of churners is greater for those who do have the International Plan ($101/231 = 44\%$) than for those who don't ($302/2180 = 14\%$).

Next, Figure 3.10 shows a pair of horizontal bar charts for customers who did select the VoiceMail Plan (*Vmail Plan* = *yes*). There are many more customers who

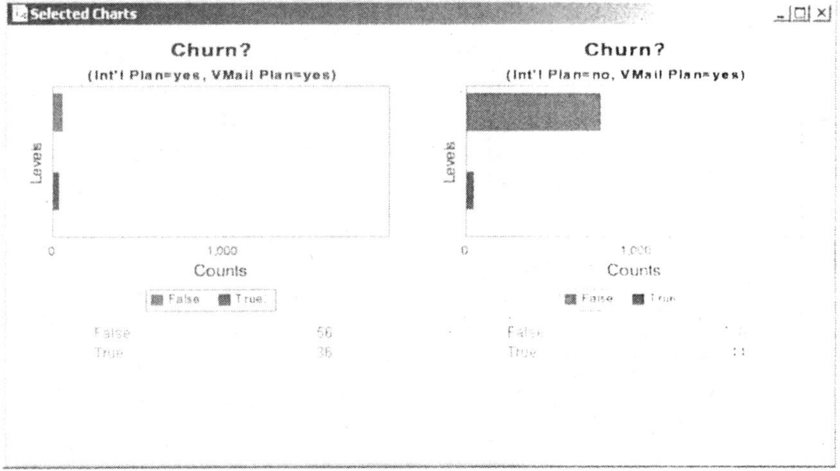

Figure 3.10 Bar charts of customers who churned, with VoiceMail Plan, subsetted by International Plan selection.

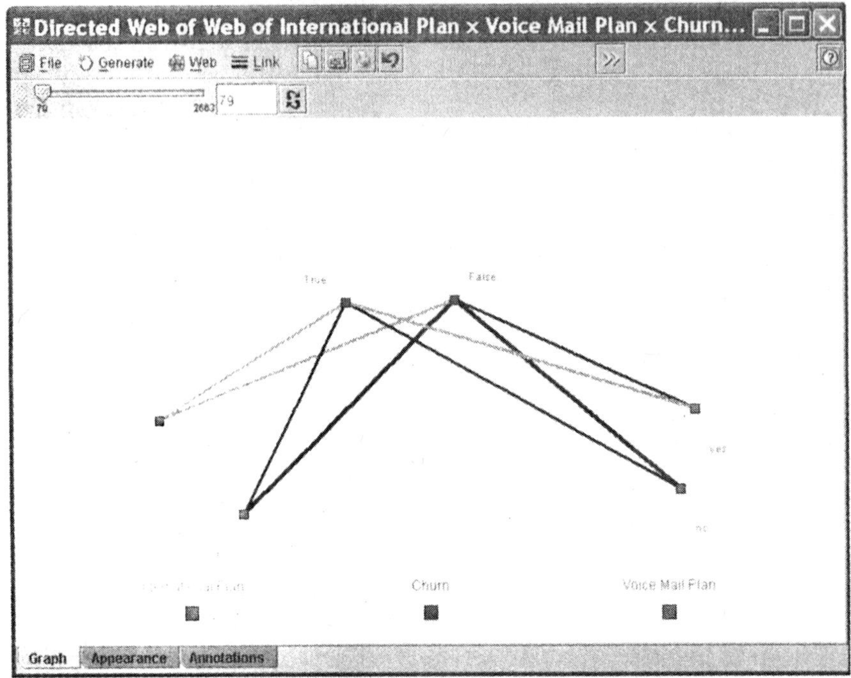

Figure 3.11 Directed web graph supports earlier findings.

have the VoiceMail Plan only ($786 + 44 = 830$) than those who have both plans ($56 + 36 = 92$). Again, however, among customers with the VoiceMail Plan, the proportion of churners is much greater for those who also select the International Plan ($36/92 = 39\%$) than for those who don't ($44/830 = 5\%$). Note that there is no interaction among the categorical variables. That is, International Plan holders have greater churn regardless of whether or not they are VoiceMail Plan adopters.

Finally, Figure 3.11 shows a Clementine *directed web graph* of the relationships between International Plan holders, VoiceMail Plan holders, and churners. Compare the edges (lines) connecting the VoiceMail Plan = Yes nodes to the Churn = True and Churn = False nodes. The edge connecting to the Churn = False node is heavier, indicating that a greater proportion of VoiceMail Plan holders will choose not to churn. This supports our earlier findings.

USING EDA TO UNCOVER ANOMALOUS FIELDS

Exploratory data analysis will sometimes uncover strange or anomalous records or fields which the earlier data cleaning phase may have missed. Consider, for example, the *area code* field in the present data set. Although the area codes contain numerals, they can also be used as categorical variables, since they can classify customers according to geographical location. We are intrigued by the fact that the area code field contains only three different values for all the records—408, 415, and 510—all three of which are in California, as shown by Figure 3.12.

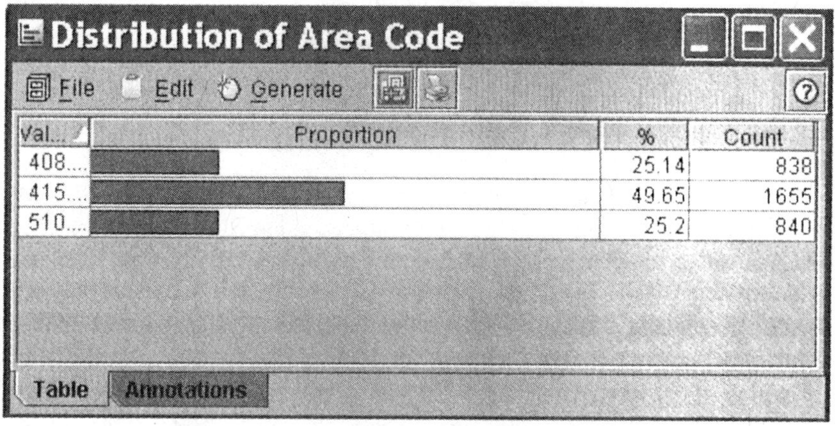

Distribution of Area Code

File Edit Generate

Val...	Proportion	%	Count
408....		25.14	838
415....		49.65	1655
510....		25.2	840

Table Annotations

Figure 3.12 Only three area codes for all records.

Now, this would not be anomalous if the records indicated that the customers all lived in California. However, as shown in the cross-tabulation in Figure 3.13 (only up to Florida, to save space), the three area codes seem to be distributed more or less evenly across all the states and the District of Columbia. It is possible that domain experts might be able to explain this type of behavior, but it is also possible that the field just contains bad data.

We should therefore be wary of this area code field, perhaps going so far as not to include it as input to the data mining models in the next phase. On the other hand, it may be the *state* field that is in error. Either way, further communication

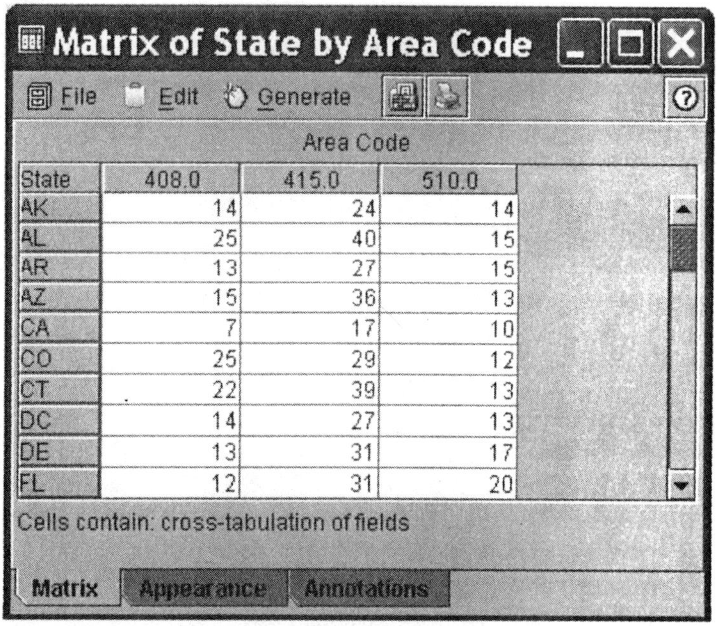

Matrix of State by Area Code

File Edit Generate

Area Code

State	408.0	415.0	510.0
AK	14	24	14
AL	25	40	15
AR	13	27	15
AZ	15	36	13
CA	7	17	10
CO	25	29	12
CT	22	39	13
DC	14	27	13
DE	13	31	17
FL	12	31	20

Cells contain: cross-tabulation of fields

Matrix Appearance Annotations

Figure 3.13 Anomaly: three area codes distributed across all 50 states.

with someone familiar with the data history, or a domain expert, is called for before inclusion of these variables in the data mining models.

EXPLORING NUMERICAL VARIABLES

Next, we turn to an exploration of the numerical predictive variables. We begin with numerical summary measures, including minimum and maximum; measures of center, such as mean, median, and mode; and measures of variability, such as standard deviation. Figure 3.14 shows these summary measures for some of our numerical variables. We see, for example, that the minimum *account length* is one month, the maximum is 243 months, and the mean and median are about the same, at around 101 months, which is an indication of symmetry. Notice that several variables show this evidence of symmetry, including *all* the *minutes*, *charge*, and *call* fields.

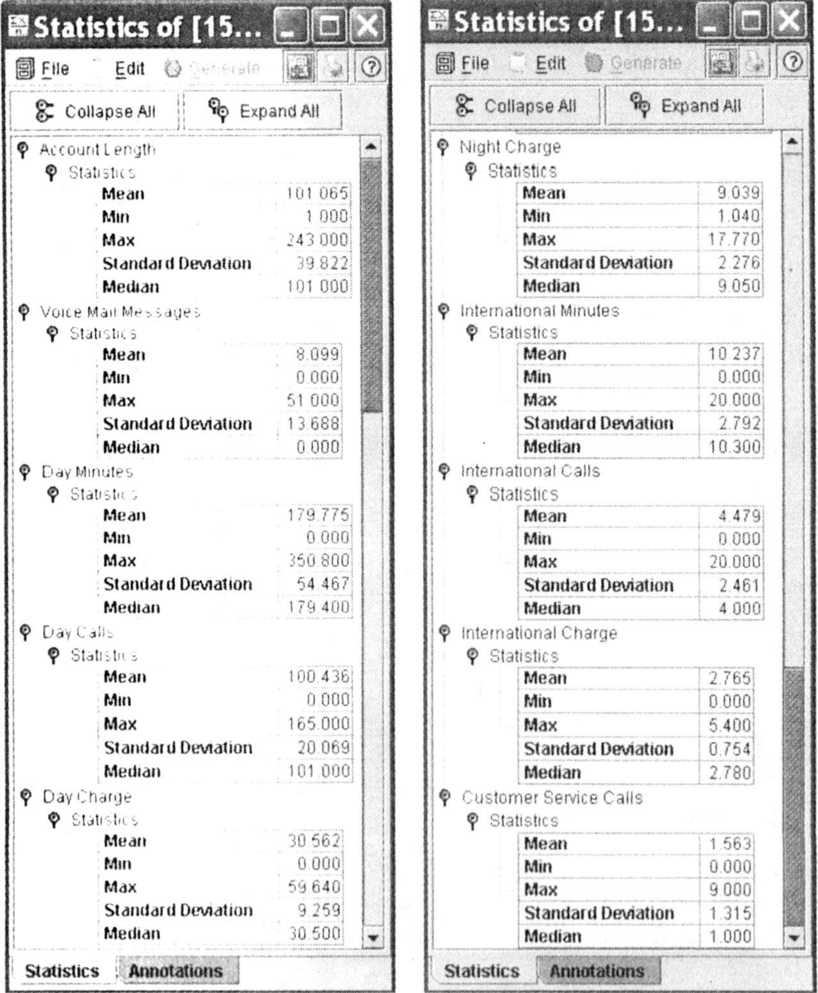

Figure 3.14 Summary statistics for several numerical variables.

Fields not showing evidence of symmetry include *voice mail messages* and *customer service calls*. The median for *voice mail messages* is zero, indicating that at least half of all customers had no voice mail messages. This results, of course, from fewer than half of the customers selecting the VoiceMail Plan, as we saw above. The mean of *customer service calls* (1.563) is greater than the median (1.0), indicating some right-skewness, as also indicated by the maximum number of customer service calls being nine.

As mentioned earlier, retaining correlated variables will, at best, overemphasize a certain predictive component at the expense of others, and at worst, cause instability in the model, leading to potentially nonsensical results. Therefore, we need to check for the correlation among our numerical variables. Figure 3.15 shows the correlations for two of the variables, *customer service calls* and *day charge*, with all of the other numerical variables. Note that all the correlations are shown as weak (this categorization is user-definable), except for the correlation between *day charge* and *day minutes*,

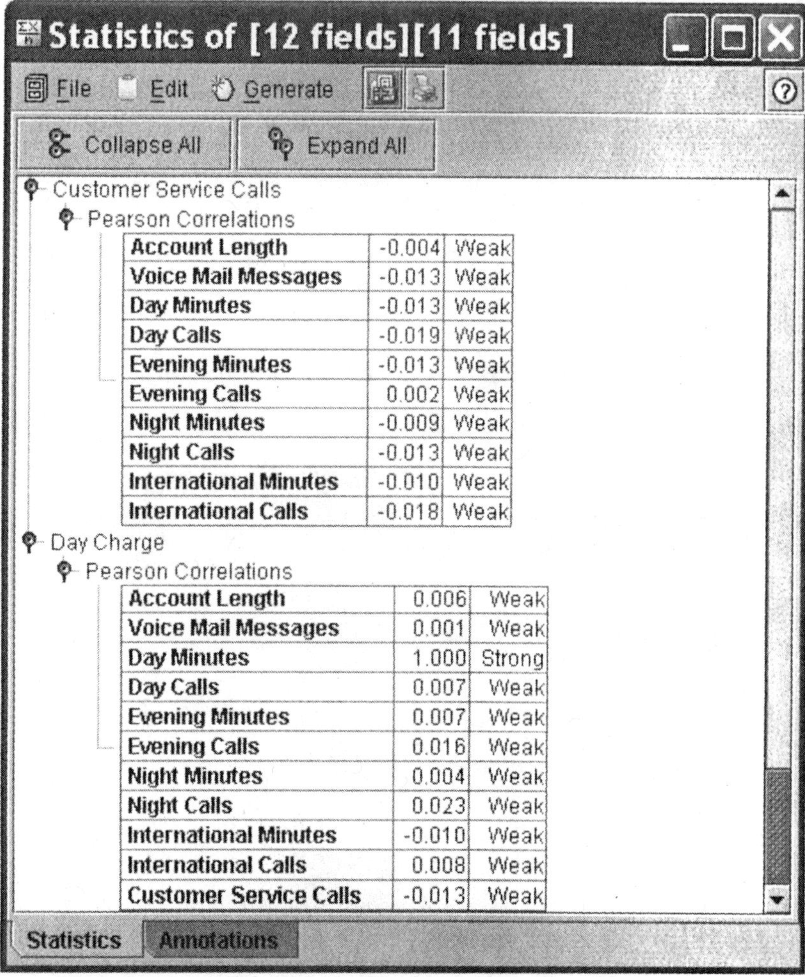

Field	Correlation	Strength
Account Length	-0.004	Weak
Voice Mail Messages	-0.013	Weak
Day Minutes	-0.013	Weak
Day Calls	-0.019	Weak
Evening Minutes	-0.013	Weak
Evening Calls	0.002	Weak
Night Minutes	-0.009	Weak
Night Calls	-0.013	Weak
International Minutes	-0.010	Weak
International Calls	-0.018	Weak

Field	Correlation	Strength
Account Length	0.006	Weak
Voice Mail Messages	0.001	Weak
Day Minutes	1.000	Strong
Day Calls	0.007	Weak
Evening Minutes	0.007	Weak
Evening Calls	0.016	Weak
Night Minutes	0.004	Weak
Night Calls	0.023	Weak
International Minutes	-0.010	Weak
International Calls	0.008	Weak
Customer Service Calls	-0.013	Weak

Figure 3.15 Correlations for *customer service calls* and *day charge*.

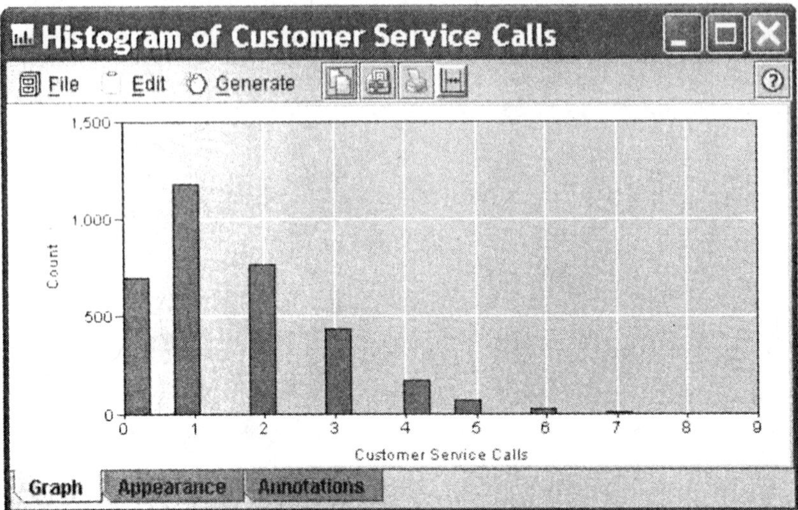

Figure 3.16 Histogram of customer service calls.

which is $r = 1.0$, the perfect linear relationship we discussed above. We checked for all pairwise correlations, and found all weak correlations once the *charge* fields were removed (not shown).

We turn next to graphical analysis of our numerical variables. We show three examples of histograms, which are useful for getting an overall look at the distribution of numerical variables, for the variable *customer service calls*. Figure 3.16 is a histogram of customer service calls, with no overlay, indicating that the distribution is right-skewed, with a mode at one call.

However, this gives us no indication of any relationship with churn, for which we must turn to Figure 3.17, the same histogram of customer service calls, this time with

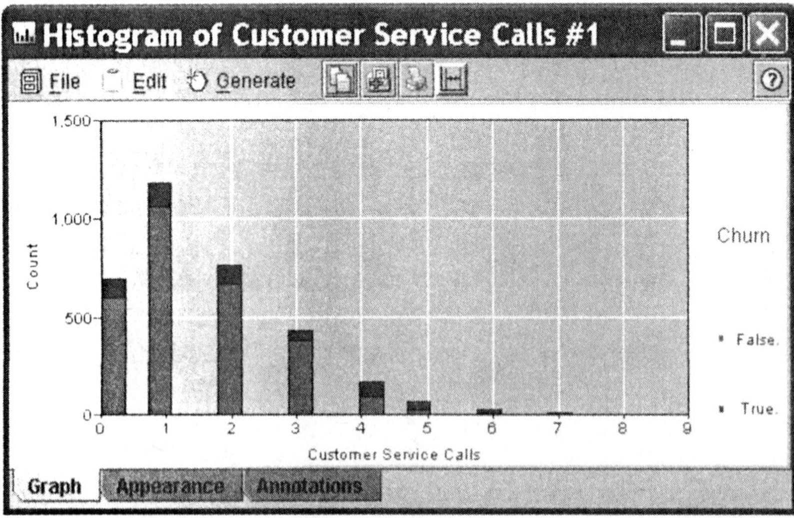

Figure 3.17 Histogram of customer service calls, with churn overlay.

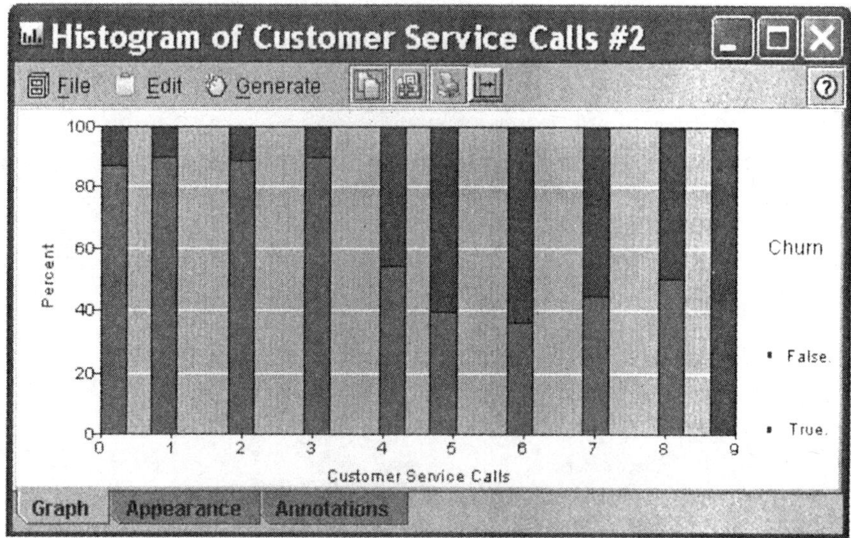

Figure 3.18 Normalized histogram of customer service calls, with churn overlay.

churn overlay. Figure 3.17 hints that the proportion of churn may be greater for higher numbers of customer service calls, but it is difficult to discern this result unequivocally. We therefore turn to a *normalized histogram*, where every rectangle has the same height and width, as shown in Figure 3.18. Note that the *proportions* of churners versus nonchurners in Figure 3.18 is exactly the same as in Figure 3.17; it is just that "stretching out" the rectangles that have low counts enables better definition and contrast. The pattern now becomes crystal clear. Customers who have called customer service three or fewer times have a markedly lower churn rate (dark part of the rectangle) than that of customers who have called customer service four or more times.

This EDA on the customer service calls has indicated that:

1. We should track carefully the number of customer service calls made by each customer. By the third call, specialized incentives should be offered to retain customer loyalty.
2. We should expect that whatever data mining algorithms we use to predict churn, the model will probably include the number of customer service calls made by the customer.

Examining Figure 3.19, we see that the normalized histogram of *day minutes* indicates that very high day users tend to churn at a higher rate. Therefore:

1. We should carefully track the number of day minutes used by each customer. As the number of day minutes passes 200, we should consider special incentives.
2. We should investigate why heavy day users are tempted to leave.
3. We should expect that our eventual data mining model will include *day minutes* as a predictor of churn.

Figure 3.20 shows a slight tendency for customers with higher *evening minutes* to churn. Based solely on the graphical evidence, however, we cannot conclude

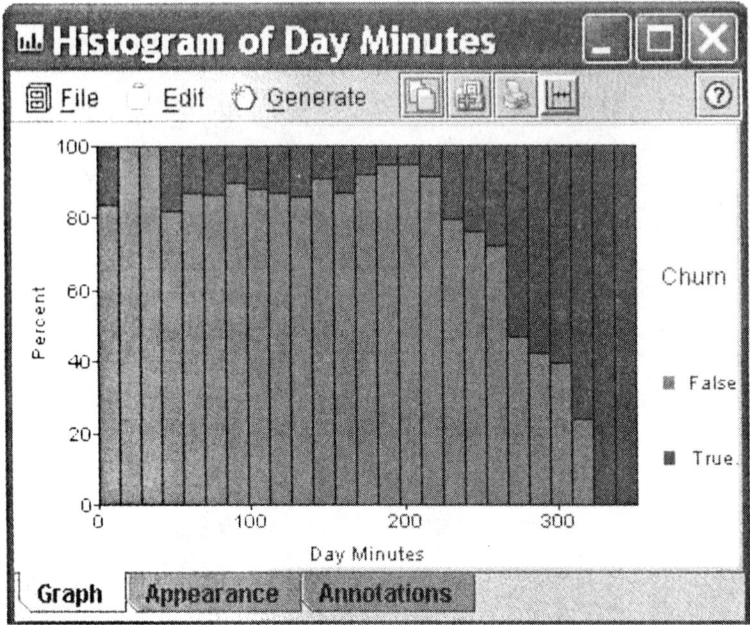

Figure 3.19 Customers with high day minutes tend to churn at a higher rate.

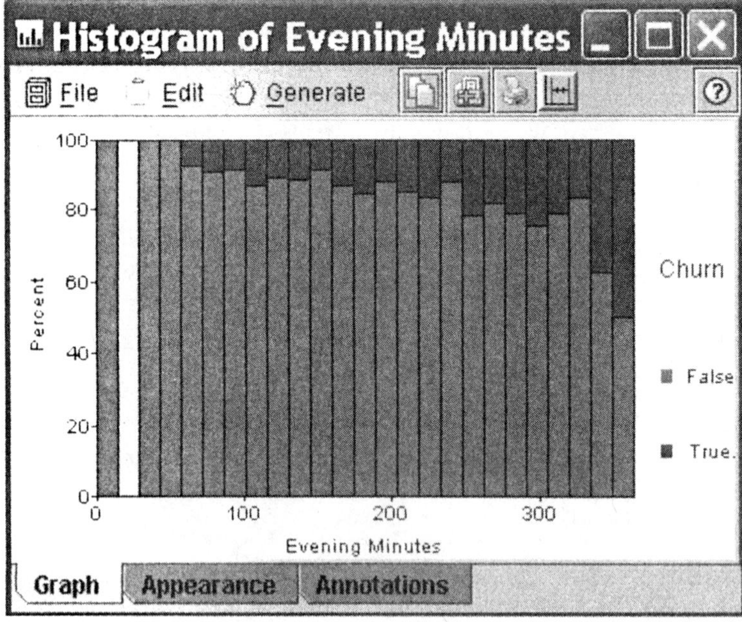

Figure 3.20 Slight tendency for customers with higher evening minutes to churn at a higher rate.

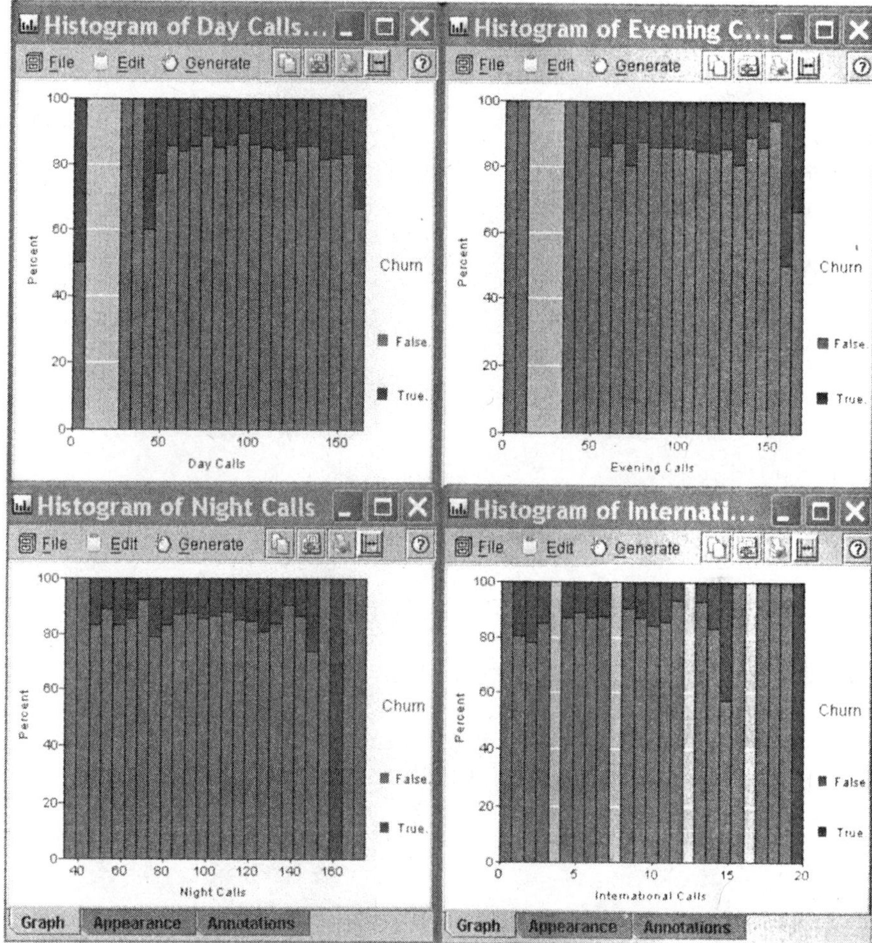

Figure 3.21 No association of churn with *day calls*, *evening calls*, *night calls*, or *international calls*.

beyond a reasonable doubt that such an effect exists. Therefore, we shall hold off on formulating policy recommendations on evening cell-phone use until our data mining models offer firmer evidence that the putative effect is in fact present.

Finally, Figures 3.21 and 3.22 indicate that there is no obvious association between churn and any of the remaining numerical variables in the data set. Figure 3.21 shows histograms of the four *calls* variables, *day*, *evening*, *night*, and *international calls*, with a churn overlay. Figure 3.22 shows histograms of *night minutes*, *international minutes*, *account length*, and *voice mail messages*, with a churn overlay. The high variability in churn proportions in the right tails of some of the histograms reflects the small sample counts in those regions.

Based on the lack of evident association between *churn* and the variables in Figures 3.21 and 3.22, we will not necessarily expect the data mining models to

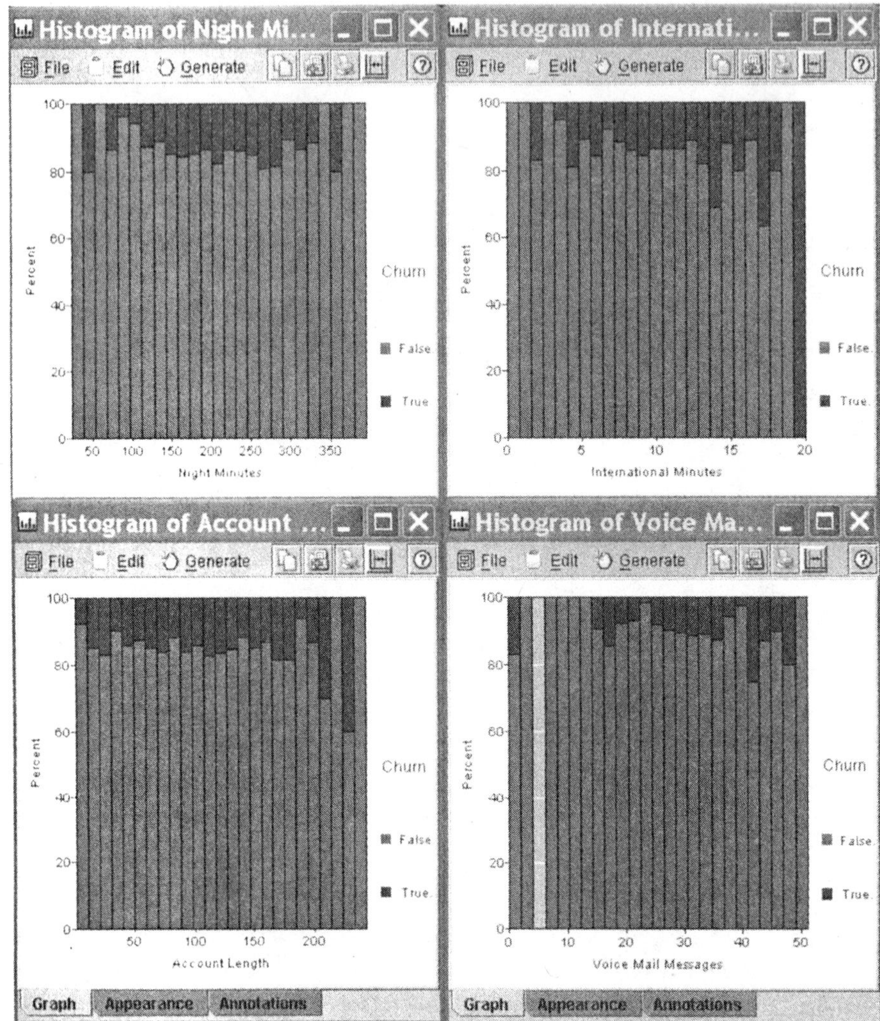

Figure 3.22 No association of churn with *night minutes, international minutes, account length*, or *voice mail messages*.

uncover valuable predictive information using these variables. We should, nevertheless, retain them as input variables for the data mining models. The reason for retaining these variables is that actionable associations may still exist for identifiable subsets of the records, and they may be involved in higher-dimension associations and interactions. In any case, unless there is a good reason (such as strong correlation) for eliminating the variable prior to modeling, we should probably allow the modeling process to identify which variables are predictive and which are not.

An exception to this situation is if there are so many fields that algorithm performance is degraded. In this case, one may consider setting aside temporarily variables

TABLE 3.1 Summary of Exploratory Findings Thus Far

Variable	Disposition
State	Anomalous. Omitted from model.
Account length	No obvious relation with churn, but retained.
Area code	Anomalous. Omitted from model.
Phone number	Surrogate for ID. Omitted from model.
International Plan	Predictive of churn. Retained.
VoiceMail Plan	Predictive of churn. Retained.
Number of voice mail messages	No obvious relation with churn, but retained.
Total day minutes	Predictive of churn. Retained.
Total day calls	No obvious relation with churn, but retained.
Total day charge	Function of *minutes*. Omitted from model.
Total evening minutes	May be predictive of churn. Retained.
Total evening calls	No obvious relation with churn, but retained.
Total evening charge	Function of *minutes*. Omitted from model.
Total night minutes	No obvious relation with churn, but retained.
Total night calls	No obvious relation with churn, but retained.
Total night charge	Function of *minutes*. Omitted from model.
Total international minutes	No obvious relation with churn, but retained.
Total international calls	No obvious relation with churn, but retained.
Total international charge	Function of *minutes*. Omitted from model.
Customer service calls	Predictive of churn. Retained.

with no obvious association with the target, until analysis with more promising variables is undertaken. Also in this case, dimension-reduction techniques should be applied, such as principal components analysis [2].

Table 3.1 summarizes our exploratory findings so far. We have examined each of the variables and have taken a preliminary look at their relationship with *churn*.

EXPLORING MULTIVARIATE RELATIONSHIPS

We turn next to an examination of possible multivariate associations of numerical variables with churn, using two- and three-dimensional scatter plots. Figure 3.23 is a scatter plot of *customer service calls* versus *day minutes* (note Clementine's incorrect reversing of this order in the plot title; the y-variable should always be the first named). Consider the partition shown in the scatter plot, which indicates a high-churn area in the upper left section of the graph and another high-churn area in the right of the graph. The high-churn area in the upper left section of the graph consists of customers who have a combination of a high number of customer service calls and a low number of day minutes used. Note that this group of customers could not have been identified had we restricted ourselves to univariate exploration (exploring variable by single variable). This is because of the *interaction* between the variables.

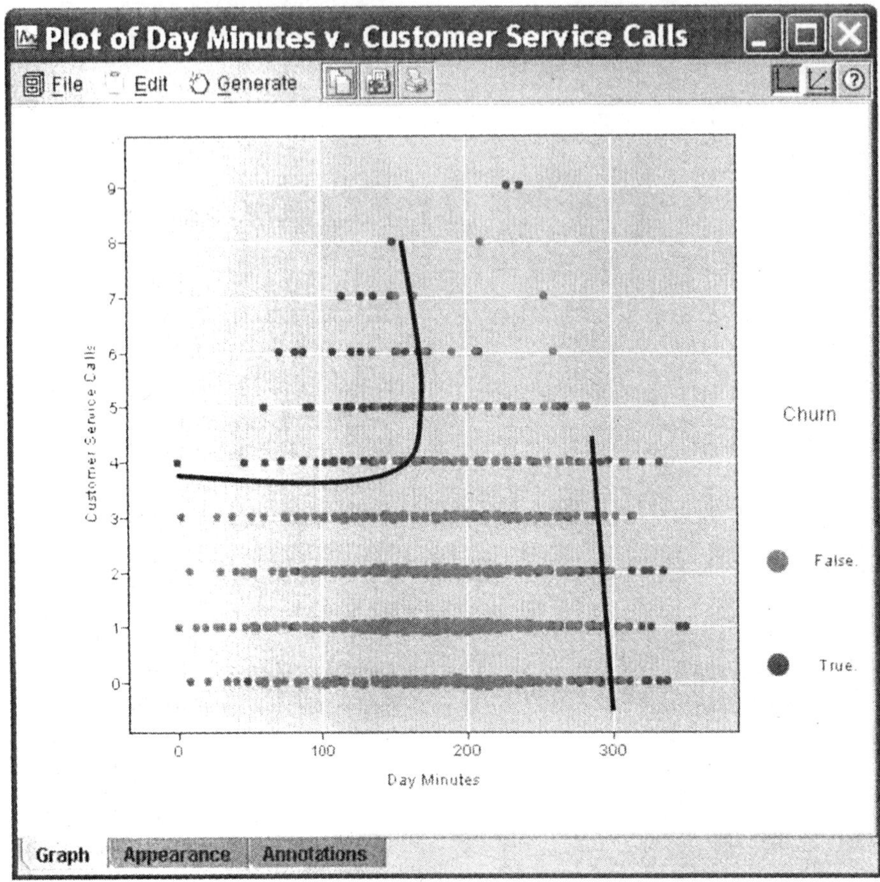

Figure 3.23 Scatter plot of *customer service calls* versus *day minutes*.

In general, customers with higher numbers of customer service calls tend to churn at a higher rate, as we learned earlier in the univariate analysis. However, Figure 3.23 shows that of these customers with high numbers of customer service calls, those who also have high day minutes are somewhat "protected" from this high churn rate. The customers in the upper right of the scatter plot exhibit a lower churn rate than that of those in the upper left.

Contrast this situation with the other high-churn area on the right (to the right of the straight line). Here, a higher churn rate is shown for those with high day minutes, *regardless* of the number of customer service calls, as indicated by the near-verticality of the partition line. In other words, these high-churn customers are the same ones as those identified in the univariate histogram in Figure 3.19.

Sometimes, three-dimensional scatter plots can be helpful as well. Figure 3.24 is an example of a plot of day minutes versus evening minutes versus customer service calls, with a churn overlay. The scroll buttons on the sides rotate the display so that the points may be examined in a three-dimensional environment.

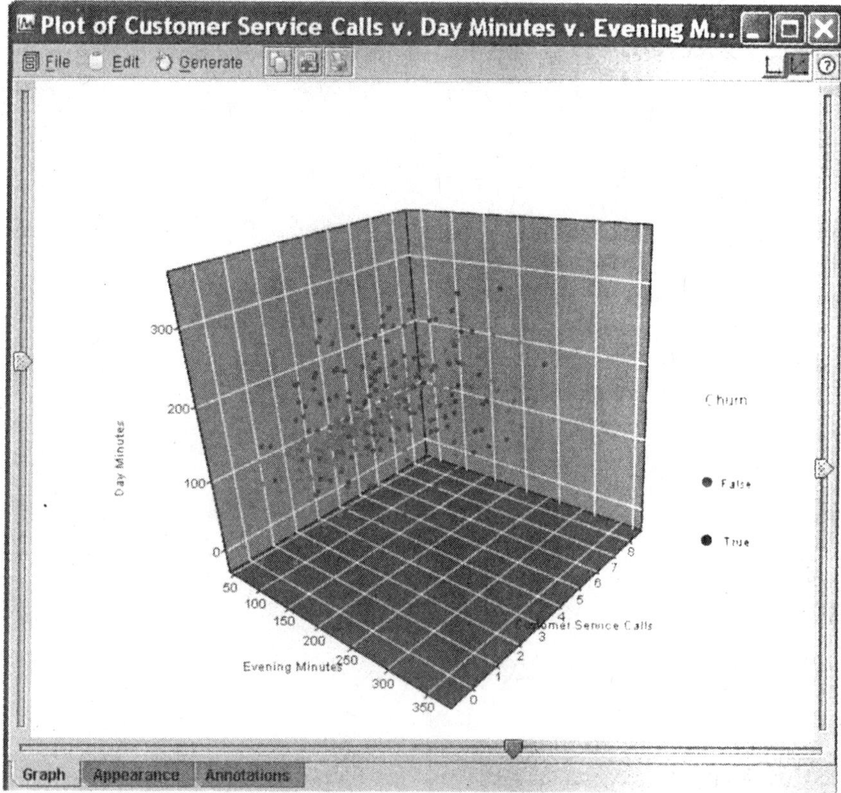

Figure 3.24 Three-dimensional scatter plot of *day minutes* versus *evening minutes* versus *customer service calls*, with a churn overlay.

SELECTING INTERESTING SUBSETS OF THE DATA FOR FURTHER INVESTIGATION

We may use scatter plots (or histograms) to identify interesting subsets of the data, in order to study these subsets more closely. In Figure 3.25 we see that customers with high *day minutes* and high *evening minutes* are more likely to churn. But how can we quantify this? Clementine allows the user to click and drag a select box around data points of interest, and select them for further investigation. Here we selected the records within the rectangular box in the upper right. (A better method would be to allow the user to select polygons besides rectangles.)

The *churn* distribution for this subset of records is shown in Figure 3.26. It turns out that over 43% of the customers who have both high *day minutes* and high *evening minutes* are churners. This is approximately three times the churn rate of the overall customer base in the data set. Therefore, it is recommended that we consider how we can develop strategies for keeping our heavy-use customers happy so that they do not leave the company's service, perhaps through discounting the higher levels of minutes used.

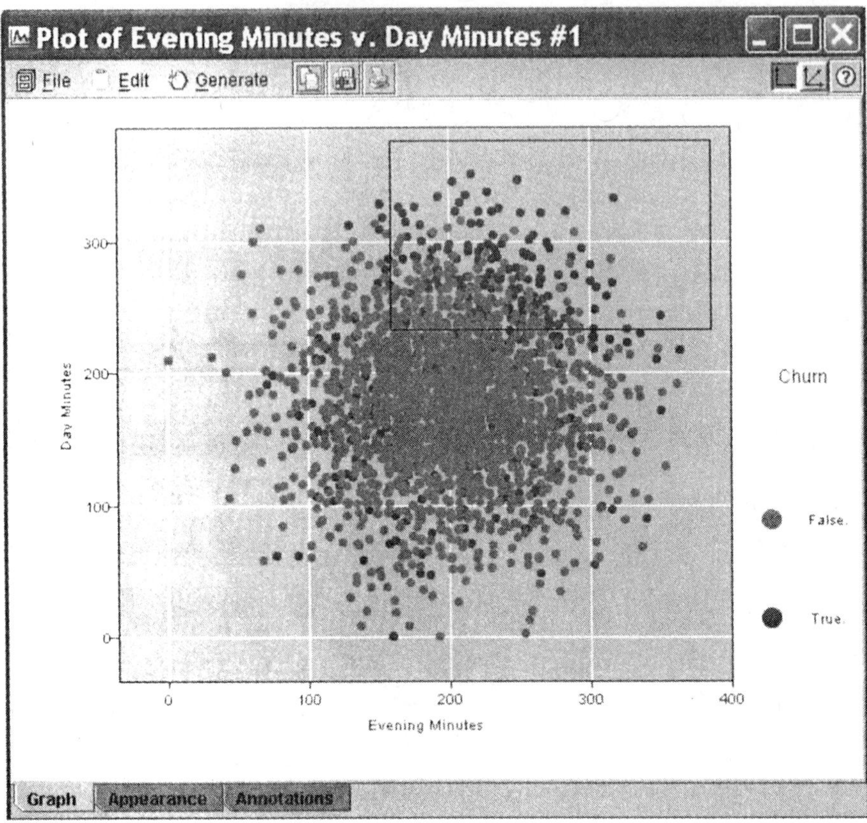

Figure 3.25 Selecting an interesting subset of records for further investigation.

BINNING

Binning (also called *banding*) refers to the categorization of numerical or categorical variables into a manageable set of classes which are convenient for analysis. For example, the number of *day minutes* could be categorized (binned) into three classes: *low*, *medium*, and *high*. The categorical variable *state* could be binned into

Distribution of Churn

File Edit Generate

Value	Proportion	%	Count
False		56.46	249
True		43.54	192

Table Annotations

Figure 3.26 Over 43% of customers with high day and evening minutes churn.

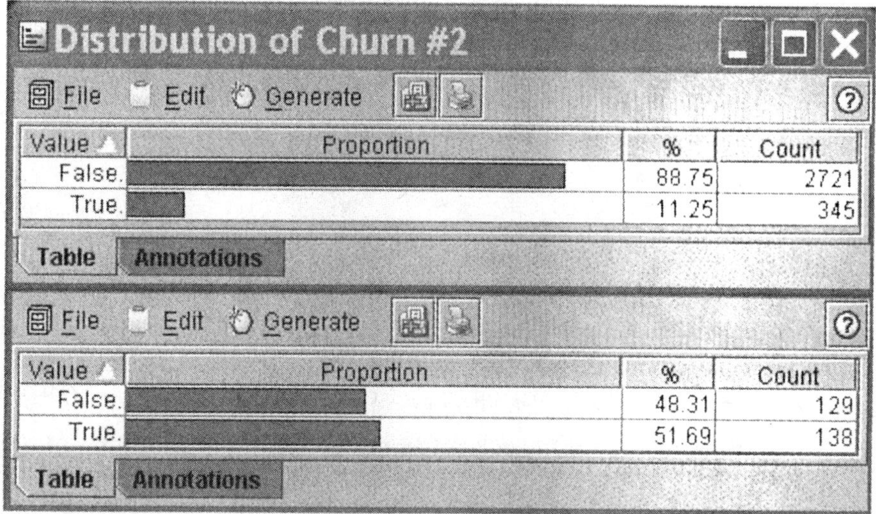

Figure 3.27 Churn rate for customers with low (top) and high (bottom) customer service calls.

a new variable, *region*, where California, Oregon, Washington, Alaska, and Hawaii would be put in the *Pacific* category, and so on. Properly speaking, binning is a data preparation activity as well as an exploratory activity.

There are various strategies for binning numerical variables. One approach is to make the classes of equal width, analogous to equal-width histograms. Another approach is to try to equalize the number of records in each class. You may consider yet another approach, which attempts to partition the data set into identifiable groups of records, which, with respect to the target variable, have behavior similar to that for other records in the same class.

For example, recall Figure 3.18, where we saw that customers with fewer than four calls to customer service had a lower churn rate than that of customers who had four or more calls to customer service. We may therefore decide to bin the *customer service calls* variable into two classes, *low* and *high*. Figure 3.27 shows that the churn rate for customers with a low number of calls to customer service is 11.25%, whereas the churn rate for customers with a high number of calls to customer service is 51.69%, more than four times higher.

SUMMARY

Let us consider some of the insights we have gained into the *churn* data set through the use of exploratory data analysis.

- The four *charge* fields are linear functions of the *minute* fields, and should be omitted.
- The *area code* field and/or the *state* field are anomalous, and should be omitted until further clarification is obtained.

- The correlations among the remaining predictor variables are weak, allowing us to retain them all for any data mining model.

Insights with respect to *churn*:

- Customers with the International Plan tend to churn more frequently.
- Customers with the VoiceMail Plan tend to churn less frequently.
- Customers with four or more *customer service calls* churn more than four times as often as do the other customers.
- Customers with high *day minutes* and *evening minutes* tend to churn at a higher rate than do the other customers.
- Customers with both high *day minutes* and high *evening minutes* churn about three times more than do the other customers.
- Customers with low *day minutes* and high *customer service calls* churn at a higher rate than that of the other customers.
- There is no obvious association of *churn* with the variables *day calls*, *evening calls*, *night calls*, *international calls*, *night minutes*, *international minutes*, *account length*, or *voice mail messages*.

Note that we have not applied any data mining algorithms yet on this data set, such as decision tree or neural network algorithms. Yet we have gained considerable insight into the attributes that are associated with customers leaving the company, simply by careful application of exploratory data analysis. These insights can easily be formulated into actionable recommendations, so that the company can take action to lower the churn rate among its customer base.

REFERENCES

1. C. L. Blake and C. J. Merz, *Churn Data Set*, UCI Repository of Machine Learning Databases, `http://www.ics.uci.edu/~mlearn/MLRepository.html`. University of California, Department of Information and Computer Science, Irvine, CA, 1998.
2. Daniel Larose, *Data Mining Methods and Models*, Wiley-Interscience, Hoboken, NJ (to appear 2005).

EXERCISES

1. Describe the possible consequences of allowing correlated variables to remain in the model.

  a. How can we determine whether correlation exists among our variables?

  b. What steps can we take to remedy the situation? Apart from the methods described in the text, think of some creative ways of dealing with correlated variables.

  c. How might we investigate correlation among categorical variables?

2. For each of the following descriptive methods, state whether it may be applied to categorical data, continuous numerical data, or both.

  a. Bar charts

  b. Histograms

  c. Summary statistics

d. Cross-tabulations

e. Correlation analysis

f. Scatter plots (two- or three-dimensional)

g. Web graphs

h. Binning

3. Why do we need to perform exploratory data analysis? Why shouldn't we simply proceed directly to the modeling phase and start applying our high-powered data mining software?

4. Make up a fictional data set (attributes with no records is fine) with a pair of anomalous attributes. Describe how EDA would help to uncover the anomaly.

5. Describe the benefits and drawbacks of using normalized histograms. Should we ever use a normalized histogram without reporting it as such? Why not?

6. Describe how scatter plots can uncover patterns in two dimensions that would be invisible from one-dimensional EDA.

7. Describe the benefits and drawbacks of the three methods of binning described in the text. Which methods require little human interaction? Which method does warrant human supervision? Which method might conceivably be used to mislead the public?

Hands-on Analysis

Use the *adult* data set at the book series Web site for the following exercises. The target variable is *income*, and the goal is to classify income based on the other variables.

8. Which variables are categorical and which are continuous?

9. Using software, construct a table of the first 10 records of the data set, to get a feel for the data.

10. Investigate whether there are any correlated variables.

11. For each of the categorical variables, construct a bar chart of the variable, with an overlay of the target variable. Normalize if necessary.

a. Discuss the relationship, if any, each of these variables has with the target variables.

b. Which variables would you expect to make a significant appearance in any data mining classification model that we work with?

12. For each pair of categorical variables, construct a cross-tabulation. Discuss your salient results.

13. (If your software supports this.) Construct a web graph of the categorical variables. Fine tune the graph so that interesting results emerge. Discuss your findings.

14. Report on whether anomalous fields exist in this data set, based on your EDA, which fields these are, and what we should do about it.

15. Report the mean, median, minimum, maximum, and standard deviation for each of the numerical variables.

16. Construct a histogram of each numerical variable, with an overlay of the target variable *income*. Normalize if necessary.

a. Discuss the relationship, if any, each of these variables has with the target variables.

b. Which variables would you expect to make a significant appearance in any data mining classification model we work with?

17. For each pair of numerical variables, construct a scatter plot of the variables. Discuss your salient results.

18. Based on your EDA so far, identify interesting subgroups of records within the data set that would be worth further investigation.

19. Apply binning to one of the numerical variables. Do it such as to maximize the effect of the classes thus created (following the suggestions in the text). Now do it such as to minimize the effect of the classes, so that the difference between the classes is diminished. Comment.

20. Refer to Exercise 19. Apply the other two binning methods (equal width and equal number of records) to the variable. Compare the results and discuss the differences. Which method do you prefer?

21. Summarize your salient EDA findings from Exercises 19 and 20 just as if you were writing a report.

CHAPTER 4

STATISTICAL APPROACHES TO ESTIMATION AND PREDICTION

DATA MINING TASKS IN *DISCOVERING KNOWLEDGE IN DATA*

In Chapter 1 we were introduced to the six data mining tasks:

- Description
- Estimation
- Prediction
- Classification
- Clustering
- Association

Discovering Knowledge in Data: An Introduction to Data Mining, By Daniel T. Larose
ISBN 0-471-66657-2

TABLE 4.1 Data Mining Tasks in *Discovering Knowledge in Data*

Task	We Learn about This Task in
Description	Chapter 3: Exploratory Data Analysis
Estimation	Chapter 4: Statistical Approaches to Estimation and Prediction
Prediction	Chapter 4: Statistical Approaches to Estimation and Prediction
Classification	Chapter 5: k-Nearest Neighbor Algorithm
	Chapter 6: Decision Trees
	Chapter 7: Neural Networks
Clustering	Chapter 8: Hierarchical and k-Means Clustering
	Chapter 9: Kohonen Networks
Association	Chapter 10: Association Rules

In the description task, analysts try to find ways to describe patterns and trends lying within the data. Descriptions of patterns and trends often suggest possible explanations for such patterns and trends, as well as possible recommendations for policy changes. This description task can be accomplished capably with exploratory data analysis, as we saw in Chapter 3. Data mining methods that perform the description task well are association rules and decision tree models. Table 4.1 provides an outline of where in this book we learn about each of the data mining tasks.

Of course, the data mining methods are not restricted to one task only, which results in a fair amount of overlap among data mining methods and tasks. For example, decision trees may be used for classification, estimation, or prediction. Therefore, Table 4.1 should not be considered as a definitive partition of the tasks, but rather as a general outline of how we are introduced to the tasks and the methods used to accomplish them.

STATISTICAL APPROACHES TO ESTIMATION AND PREDICTION

If estimation and prediction are considered to be data mining tasks, statistical analysts have been performing data mining for over a century. In this chapter we examine some of the more widespread and traditional methods of estimation and prediction, drawn from the world of statistical analysis. Our outline for the chapter is as follows. We begin by examining univariate methods, statistical estimation, and prediction methods that analyze one variable at a time. These methods include point estimation and confidence interval estimation. Next we consider simple linear regression, where the relationship between two numerical variables is investigated. Finally, we examine multiple regression, where the relationship between a response variable and a set of predictor variables is modeled linearly.

UNIVARIATE METHODS: MEASURES OF CENTER AND SPREAD

Consider our roles as data miners. We have been presented with a data set with which we are presumably unfamiliar. We have completed the data understanding and data preparation phases and have gathered some descriptive information using exploratory data analysis. Next, we would like to perform univariate estimation and prediction, using numerical field summaries.

Suppose that we are interested in estimating where the center of a particular variable lies, as measured by one of the numerical *measures of center*, the most common of which are the mean, median, and mode. Measures of center are a special case of *measures of location*, numerical summaries that indicate *where* on a number line a certain characteristic of the variable lies. Examples of measures of location are percentiles and quantiles.

The *mean* of a variable is simply the average of the valid values taken by the variable. To find the mean, simply add up all the field values and divide by the sample size. Here we introduce a bit of notation. The sample mean is denoted as $\overline{x}$ ("*x-bar*") and is computed as $\overline{x} = \sum x/n$, where $\sum$ (capital sigma, the Greek letter "S," for "*s*ummation") represents "sum all the values," and n represents the sample size. For example, suppose that we are interested in estimating where the center of the *customer service calls* variable lies from the *churn* data set explored in Chapter 3. Clementine supplies us with the statistical summaries shown in Figure 4.1. The mean number of customer service calls for this sample of $n = 3333$ customers is given as $\overline{x} = 1.563$.

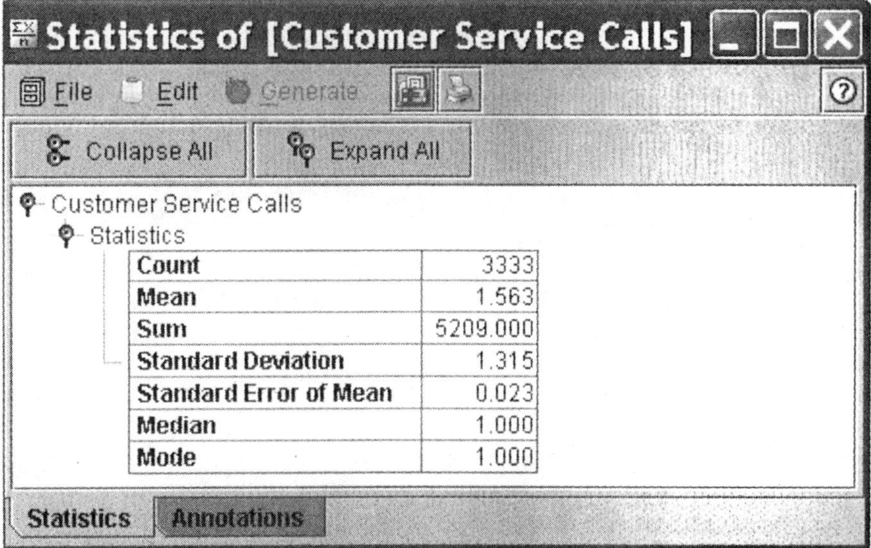

Figure 4.1 Statistical summaries of *customer service calls*.

Using the *sum* and the *count* statistics, we can verify that

$$\bar{x} = \frac{\sum x}{n} = \frac{5209}{3333} = 1.563$$

For variables that are not extremely skewed, the mean is usually not too far from the variable center. However, for extremely skewed data sets, the mean becomes less representative of the variable center. Also, the mean is sensitive to the presence of outliers. For this reason, analysts sometimes prefer to work with alternative measures of center, such as the *median*, defined as the field value in the middle when the field values are sorted into ascending order. The median is resistant to the presence of outliers. Other analysts may prefer to use the *mode*, which represents the field value occurring with the greatest frequency. The mode may be used with either numerical or categorical data, but is not always associated with the variable center.

Note that measures of center do not always concur as to where the center of the data set lies. In Figure 4.1, the median is 1.0, which means that half of the customers made at least one customer service call; the mode is also 1.0, which means that the most frequent number of customer service calls was 1. The median and mode agree. However, the mean is 1.563, which is 56.3% higher than the other measures. This is due to the mean's sensitivity to the right-skewness of the data.

Measures of location are not sufficient to summarize a variable effectively. In fact, two variables may have the very same values for the mean, median, and mode, and yet have different natures. For example, suppose that stock portfolio A and stock portfolio B contained five stocks each, with the price/earnings (P/E) ratios as shown in Table 4.2. The portfolios are distinctly different in terms of P/E ratios. Portfolio A includes one stock that has a very small P/E ratio and another with a rather large P/E ratio. On the other hand, portfolio B's P/E ratios are more tightly clustered around the mean. But despite these differences, the mean, median, and mode of the portfolio's, P/E ratios are precisely the same: The mean P/E ratio is 10, the median is 11, and the mode is 11 for each portfolio.

Clearly, these measures of center do not provide us with a complete picture. What is missing are *measures of spread* or *measures of variability*, which will describe how spread out the data values are. Portfolio A's P/E ratios are more spread out than those of portfolio B, so the measures of variability for portfolio A should be larger than those of B.

TABLE 4.2 Price/Earnings Ratios for Five Stocks in Each of Two Portfolios

Stock Portfolio A	Stock Portfolio B
1	7
11	8
11	11
11	11
16	13

Typical measures of variability include the *range* (maximum – minimum), the standard deviation, the mean absolute deviation, and the interquartile range. The sample *standard deviation* is perhaps the most widespread measure of variability and is defined by

$$s = \sqrt{\frac{\sum (x - \bar{x})^2}{n - 1}}$$

Because of the squaring involved, the standard deviation is sensitive to the presence of outliers, leading analysts to prefer other measures of spread, such as the mean absolute deviation, in situations involving extreme values.

The standard deviation can be interpreted as the "typical" distance between a field value and the mean, and most field values lie within two standard deviations of the mean. From Figure 4.1 we can state that the number of customer service calls made by most customers lies within $2(1.315) = 2.63$ of the mean of 1.563 calls. In other words, most of the number of customer service calls lie within the interval $(-1.067, 4.193)$, that is, $(0, 4)$. This can be verified by examining the histogram of customer service calls in Figure 3.16.

A more complete discussion of measures of location and variability can be found in any introductory statistics textbook, such as Johnson and Kuby [1].

STATISTICAL INFERENCE

In statistical analysis, estimation and prediction are elements of the field of *statistical inference*. Statistical inference consists of methods for estimating and testing hypotheses about population characteristics based on the information contained in the sample. A *population* is the collection of *all* elements (persons, items, or data) of interest in a particular study.

For example, presumably, the cell phone company does not want to restrict its actionable results to the sample of 3333 customers from which it gathered the data. Rather, it would prefer to deploy its churn model to *all* of its present and future cell phone customers, which would therefore represent the population. A *parameter* is a characteristic of a population, such as the mean number of customer service calls of all cell phone customers.

A *sample* is simply a subset of the population, preferably a representative subset. If the sample is not representative of the population, that is, if the sample characteristics deviate systematically from the population characteristics, *statistical inference should not be applied.* A *statistic* is a characteristic of a sample, such as the mean number of customer service calls of the 3333 customers in the sample (1.563).

Note that the values of population parameters are *unknown* for most interesting problems. Specifically, the value of the population mean is usually unknown. For example, we do not know the true mean number of customer service calls to be made by all of the company's cell phone customers. To represent their unknown nature, population parameters are often denoted with Greek letters. For example, the population mean is symbolized using the Greek lowercase letter μ (mu), which is the Greek letter for "m" ("mean").

The value of the population mean number of customer service calls μ is unknown for a variety of reasons, including the fact that the data may not yet have been collected or warehoused. Instead, data analysts would use *estimation*. For example, they would estimate the unknown value of the population mean μ by obtaining a sample and computing the sample mean $\bar{x}$, which would be used to estimate μ. Thus, we would estimate the mean number of customer service calls for all customers to be 1.563, since this is the value of our observed sample mean.

An important *caveat* is that estimation is valid only as long as the sample is truly representative of the population. For example, in the *churn* data set, the company would presumably implement policies to improve customer service and decrease the churn rate. These policies would, hopefully, result in the true mean number of customer service calls falling to a level lower than 1.563.

Analysts may also be interested in proportions, such as the proportion of customers who churn. The sample proportion p is the statistic used to measure the unknown value of the population proportion π. For example, in Chapter 3 we found that the proportion of churners in the data set was $p = 0.145$, which could be used to estimate the true proportion of churners for the population of all customers, keeping in mind the caveats above.

Point estimation refers to the use of a single known value of a statistic to estimate the associated population parameter. The observed value of the statistic is called the *point estimate*. We may summarize estimation of the population mean, standard deviation, and proportion using Table 4.3.

Estimation need not be restricted to the parameters in Table 4.3. Any statistic observed from sample data may be used to estimate the analogous parameter in the population. For example, we may use the sample maximum to estimate the population maximum, or we could use the sample 27th percentile to estimate the population 27th percentile. *Any* sample characteristic is a statistic, which, under the appropriate circumstances, can be used to estimate its appropriate parameter.

More specifically, for example, we could use the sample churn proportion of customers who did select the VoiceMail Plan, but did not select the International Plan, and who made three customer service calls to estimate the population churn proportion of all such customers. Or, we could use the sample 99th percentile of day minutes used for customers without the VoiceMail Plan to estimate the population 99th percentile of day minutes used for all customers without the VoiceMail Plan.

TABLE 4.3 Use Observed Sample Statistics to Estimate Unknown Population Parameters

	Sample Statistic	. . . Estimates . . .	Population Parameter
Mean	$\bar{x}$	$\longrightarrow$	μ
Standard deviation	s	$\longrightarrow$	σ
Proportion	p	$\longrightarrow$	π

HOW CONFIDENT ARE WE IN OUR ESTIMATES?

Let's face it: Anyone can make estimates. Crystal ball gazers will be happy (for a price) to provide you with an estimate of the parameter in which you are interested. The question is: *How confident can we be in the accuracy of the estimate*?

Do you think that the population mean number of customer service calls made by all of the company's customers is exactly the same as the sample mean $\bar{x} = 1.563$? Probably not. In general, since the sample is a subset of the population, inevitably the population contains more information than the sample about any given characteristic. Hence, unfortunately, our point estimates will nearly always "miss" the target parameter by a certain amount, and thus be in error by this amount, which is probably, though not necessarily, small.

This distance between the observed value of the point estimate and the unknown value of its target parameter is called *sampling error*, defined as |statistic − parameter|. For example, the sampling error for the mean is $|\bar{x} - \mu|$, the distance (always positive) between the observed sample mean and the unknown population mean. Since the true values of the parameter are usually unknown, the value of the sampling error is usually unknown in real-world problems. In fact, for continuous variables, the probability that the observed value of a point estimate exactly equals its target parameter is precisely zero. This is because probability represents area above an interval for continuous variables, and there is no area above a point.

Point estimates have no measure of confidence in their accuracy; there is no probability statement associated with the estimate. All we know is that the estimate is probably close to the value of the target parameter (small sampling error) but that possibly it may be far away (large sampling error). In fact, point estimation has been likened to a dart thrower, throwing darts with infinitesimally small tips (the point estimates) toward a vanishingly small bull's-eye (the target parameter). Worse, the bull's-eye is hidden, and the thrower will never know for sure how close the darts are coming to the target.

The dart thrower could perhaps be forgiven for tossing a beer mug in frustration rather than a dart. But wait! Since the beer mug has width, there does indeed exist a positive probability that some portion of the mug has hit the hidden bull's-eye. We still don't know for sure, but we can have a certain degree of confidence that the target has been hit. Very roughly, the beer mug represents our next estimation method, *confidence intervals*.

CONFIDENCE INTERVAL ESTIMATION

A *confidence interval estimate* of a population parameter consists of an interval of numbers produced by a point estimate, together with an associated *confidence level* specifying the probability that the interval contains the parameter. Most confidence intervals take the general form

$$\text{point estimate} \pm \text{margin of error}$$

where the margin of error is a measure of the precision of the interval estimate. Smaller margins of error indicate greater precision. For example, the *t-interval* for the population mean is given by

$$\bar{x} \pm t_{\alpha/2}(s/\sqrt{n})$$

where the sample mean $\bar{x}$ is the point estimate and the quantity $t_{\alpha/2}(s/\sqrt{n})$ represents the margin of error. The t-interval for the mean may be used when either the population is normal or the sample size is large.

Under what conditions will this confidence interval provide precise estimation? That is, when will the margin of error $t_{\alpha/2}(s/\sqrt{n})$ be small? The quantity $s/\sqrt{n}$ represents the standard error of the sample mean (the standard deviation of the sampling distribution of $\bar{x}$) and is small whenever the sample size is large or the sample variability is small. The multiplier $t_{\alpha/2}$ is associated with the sample size and the confidence level (usually 90 to 99%) specified by the analyst, and is smaller for lower confidence levels. Since we cannot influence the sample variability directly and we hesitate to lower our confidence level, we must turn to increasing the sample size should we seek to provide more precise confidence interval estimation.

Usually, finding a large sample size is not a problem for many data mining scenarios. For example, using the statistics in Figure 4.1, we can find the 95% t-interval for the mean number of customer service calls for all customers as follows:

$$\begin{gathered}\bar{x} \pm t_{\alpha/2}(s/\sqrt{n})\\ 1.563 \pm 1.96(1.315/\sqrt{3333})\\ 1.563 \pm 0.045\\ (1.518,\ 1.608)\end{gathered}$$

We are 95% confident that the population mean number of customer service calls for all customers falls between 1.518 and 1.608 calls. Here, the margin of error is 0.045 customer service calls, which is fairly precise for most applications.

However, data miners are often called upon to estimate the behavior of specific subsets of customers instead of the entire customer base, as in the example above. For example, suppose that we are interested in estimating the mean number of customer service calls for customers who have both the International Plan and the VoiceMail Plan and who have more than 220 day minutes. This considerably restricts the sample size, as shown in Figure 4.2.

There are only 28 customers in the sample who have both plans and who logged more than 220 minutes of day use. The point estimate for the population mean number of customer service calls for all such customers is the sample mean 1.607. We may find the 95% t-confidence interval estimate as follows:

$$\begin{gathered}\bar{x} \pm t_{\alpha/2}(s/\sqrt{n})\\ 1.607 \pm 2.048(1.892/\sqrt{28})\\ 1.607 \pm 0.732\\ (0.875,\ 2.339)\end{gathered}$$

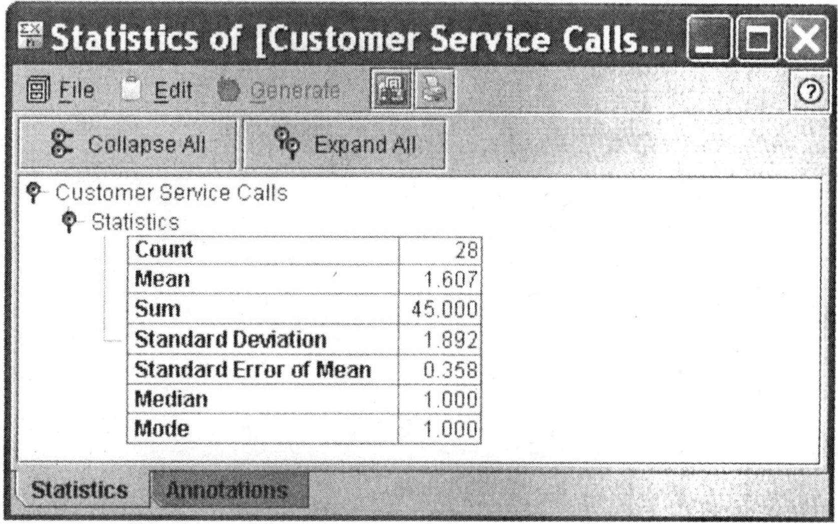

Figure 4.2 Summary statistics of customers with both the International Plan and VoiceMail Plan and with more than 200 day minutes.

We are 95% confident that the population mean number of customer service calls for all customers who have both plans and who have more than 220 minutes of day use falls between 0.875 and 2.339 calls. The margin of error for this specific subset of customers is 0.732, which indicates that our estimate of the mean number of customer service calls for this subset of customers is much less precise than for the customer base as a whole.

Confidence interval estimation can be applied to any desired target parameter. The most widespread interval estimates are for the population mean, the population standard deviation, and the population proportion of successes.

BIVARIATE METHODS: SIMPLE LINEAR REGRESSION

So far we have discussed estimation measures for one variable at a time. Analysts, however, are often interested in bivariate methods of estimation, for example, using the value of one variable to estimate the value of a different variable.

To help us learn about regression methods for estimation and prediction, let us get acquainted with a new data set, *cereals*. The *cereals* data set, included at the book series Web site courtesy of the *Data and Story Library* [2], contains nutrition information for 77 breakfast cereals and includes the following variables:

- Cereal name
- Cereal manufacturer
- Type (hot or cold)
- Calories per serving
- Grams of protein

- Grams of fat
- Milligrams of sodium
- Grams of fiber
- Grams of carbohydrates
- Grams of sugars
- Milligrams of potassium
- Percentage of recommended daily allowance of vitamins (0% 25%, or 100%)
- Weight of one serving
- Number of cups per serving
- Shelf location (1 = bottom, 2 = middle, 3 = top)
- Nutritional rating, calculated by *Consumer Reports*

Table 4.4 provides a peek at the eight of these fields for the first 16 cereals. We are interested in estimating the nutritional *rating* of a cereal given its *sugar* content. Figure 4.3 shows a scatter plot of the nutritional rating versus the sugar content for the 77 cereals, along with the least-squares regression line.

The regression line is written in the form $\hat{y} = b_0 + b_1 x$, called the *regression equation* or the *estimated regression equation* (ERE), where:

- $\hat{y}$ is the estimated value of the response variable
- b_0 is the *y-intercept* of the regression line
- b_1 is the *slope* of the regression line
- b_0 and b_1, together, are called the *regression coefficients*

TABLE 4.4 Excerpt from *Cereals* Data Set: Eight Fields, First 16 Cereals

Cereal Name	Manuf.	Sugars	Calories	Protein	Fat	Sodium	Rating
100% Bran	N	6	70	4	1	130	68.4030
100% Natural Bran	Q	8	120	3	5	15	33.9837
All-Bran	K	5	70	4	1	260	59.4255
All-Bran Extra Fiber	K	0	50	4	0	140	93.7049
Almond Delight	R	8	110	2	2	200	34.3848
Apple Cinnamon Cheerios	G	10	110	2	2	180	29.5095
Apple Jacks	K	14	110	2	0	125	33.1741
Basic 4	G	8	130	3	2	210	37.0386
Bran Chex	R	6	90	2	1	200	49.1203
Bran Flakes	P	5	90	3	0	210	53.3138
Cap'n'Crunch	Q	12	120	1	2	220	18.0429
Cheerios	G	1	110	6	2	290	50.7650
Cinnamon Toast Crunch	G	9	120	1	3	210	19.8236
Clusters	G	7	110	3	2	140	40.4002
Cocoa Puffs	G	13	110	1	1	180	22.7364

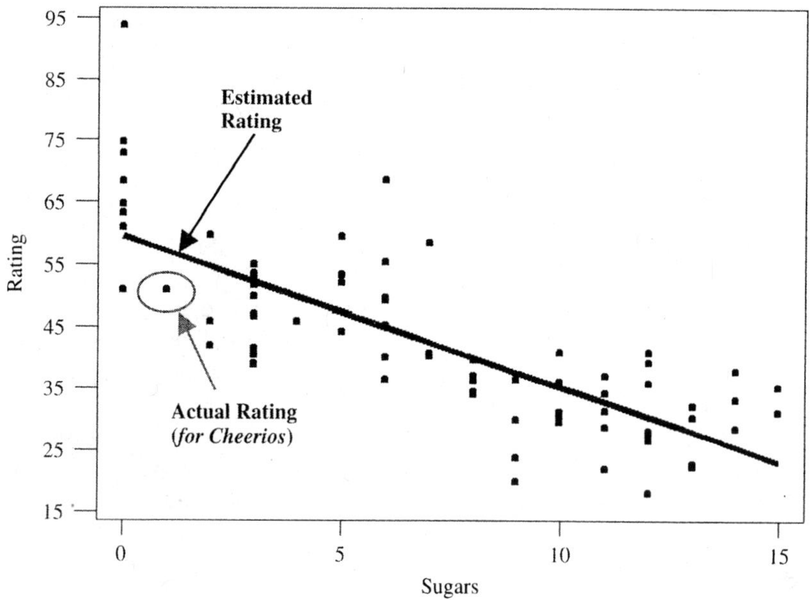

Figure 4.3 Scatter plot of nutritional rating versus sugar content for 77 cereals.

In this case the ERE is given as $\hat{y} = 59.4 - 2.42(sugars)$, so that $b_0 = 59.4$ and $b_1 = -2.42$. This estimated regression equation can then be interpreted as: "The estimated cereal rating equals 59.4 minus 2.42 times the sugar content in grams." The regression line and the ERE are used as a *linear approximation* of the relationship between the x (predictor) and y (response) variables, that is, between sugar content and nutritional rating. We can use the regression line or the ERE to make estimates or predictions.

For example, suppose that we are interested in estimating the nutritional rating for a new cereal (not in the original data) that contains $x = 1$ gram of sugar. Using the ERE, we find the estimated nutritional rating for a cereal with 1 gram of sugar to be $\hat{y} = 59.4 - 2.42(1) = 56.98$. Note that this estimated value for the nutritional rating lies directly on the regression line, at the location ($x = 1$, $\hat{y} = 56.98$), as shown in Figure 4.3. In fact, for any given value of x (sugar content), the estimated value for y (nutritional rating) lies precisely on the regression line.

Now, there is one cereal in our data set that does have a sugar content of 1 gram, Cheerios. Its nutrition rating, however, is 50.765, not 56.98 as we estimated above for the new cereal with 1 gram of sugar. Cheerios' point in the scatter plot is located at ($x = 1$, $y = 50.765$), within the oval in Figure 4.3. Now, the upper arrow in Figure 4.3 is pointing to a location on the regression line directly above the Cheerios point. This is where the regression equation predicted the nutrition rating to be for a cereal with a sugar content of 1 gram. The prediction was too high by $56.98 - 50.765 = 6.215$ rating points, which represents the vertical distance from the Cheerios data point to the regression line. This vertical distance of 6.215 rating points, in general $(y - \hat{y})$, is known variously as the *prediction error*, *estimation error*, or *residual*.

We of course seek to minimize the overall size of our prediction errors. *Least-squares regression* works by choosing the unique regression line that minimizes the sum of squared residuals over all the data points. There are alternative methods of choosing the line that best approximates the linear relationship between the variables, such as median regression, although least squares remains the most common method.

The y-intercept b_0 is the location on the y-axis where the regression line intercepts the y-axis, that is, the estimated value for the response variable when the predictor variable equals zero. Now, in many regression situations, a value of zero for the predictor variable would not make sense. For example, suppose that we were trying to predict elementary school student weight (y) based on student height (x). The meaning of *height* = 0 is unclear, so that the denotative meaning of the y-intercept would not make interpretive sense in this case.

However, for our data set, a value of zero for the sugar content does make sense, as several cereals contain zero grams of sugar. Therefore, for our data set, the y-intercept $b_0 = 59.4$ simply represents the estimated nutritional rating for cereals with zero sugar content. Note that none of the cereals containing zero grams of sugar have this estimated nutritional rating of exactly 59.4. The actual ratings, along with the prediction errors, are shown in Table 4.5. Note that all the predicted ratings are the same, since all these cereals had identical values for the predictor variable ($x = 0$).

The slope of the regression line indicates the estimated change in y per unit increase in x. We interpret $b_1 = -2.42$ to mean the following: "For each increase of 1 gram in sugar content, the estimated nutritional rating decreases by 2.42 rating points." For example, cereal A with 5 more grams of sugar than cereal B would have an estimated nutritional rating $5(2.42) = 12.1$ ratings points lower than cereal B.

The correlation coefficient r for *rating* and *sugars* is -0.76, indicating that the nutritional rating and the sugar content are negatively correlated. It is not a coincidence that both r and b_1 are both negative. In fact, the correlation coefficient r and the regression slope b_1 always have the same sign.

TABLE 4.5 Actual Ratings, Predicted Ratings, and Prediction Errors for Cereals with Zero Grams of Sugar

Cereal	Actual Rating	Predicted Rating	Prediction Error
Quaker Oatmeal	50.8284	59.4	−8.5716
All-Bran with Extra Fiber	93.7049	59.4	34.3049
Cream of Wheat (Quick)	64.5338	59.4	5.1338
Puffed Rice	60.7561	59.4	1.3561
Puffed Wheat	63.0056	59.4	3.6056
Shredded Wheat	68.2359	59.4	8.8359
Shredded Wheat 'n'Bran	74.4729	59.4	15.0729
Shredded Wheat Spoon Size	72.8018	59.4	13.4018

DANGERS OF EXTRAPOLATION

Suppose that a new cereal (say, the Chocolate Frosted Sugar Bombs loved by Calvin, the comic strip character written by Bill Watterson) arrives on the market with a very high sugar content of 30 grams per serving. Let us use our estimated regression equation to estimate the nutritional rating for Chocolate Frosted Sugar Bombs: $\hat{y} = 59.4 - 2.42(sugars) = 59.4 - 2.42(30) = -13.2$. In other words, Calvin's cereal has so much sugar that its nutritional rating is actually a negative number, unlike any of the other cereals in the data set (minimum = 18) and analogous to a student receiving a negative grade on an exam. What is going on here?

The negative estimated nutritional rating for Chocolate Frosted Sugar Bombs is an example of the dangers of *extrapolation*. Analysts should confine the estimates and predictions made using the ERE to values of the predictor variable contained within the range of the values of x in the data set. For example, in the *cereals* data set, the lowest sugar content is zero grams and the highest is 15 grams, so that predictions of nutritional rating for any value of x (sugar content) between zero and 15 grams would be appropriate. However, *extrapolation*, making predictions for x-values lying outside this range, can be dangerous, since we do not know the nature of the relationship between the response and predictor variables outside this range.

Extrapolation should be avoided if possible. If predictions outside the given range of x must be performed, the end user of the prediction needs to be informed that no x-data is available to support such a prediction. The danger lies in the possibility that the relationship between x and y, which may be linear within the range of x in the data set, may no longer be linear outside these bounds.

Consider Figure 4.4. Suppose that our data set consisted only of the data points in black but that the true relationship between x and y consisted of both the black

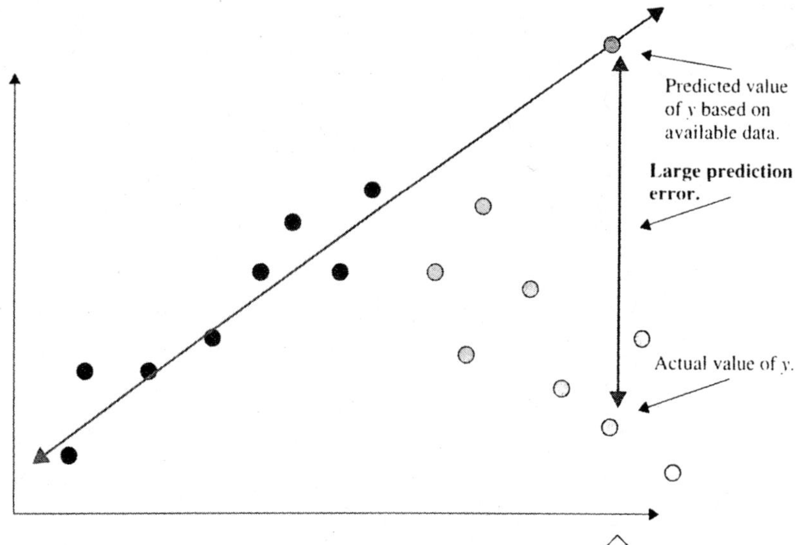

Figure 4.4 Dangers of extrapolation.

(observed) and the gray (unobserved) points. Then, a regression line based solely on the available (black dot) data would look approximately similar to the regression line indicated. Suppose that we were interested in predicting the value of y for an x-value located at the triangle. The prediction based on the available data would then be represented by the dot on the regression line indicated by the upper arrow. Clearly, this prediction has failed spectacularly, as shown by the vertical line indicating the huge prediction error. Of course, since the analyst would be completely unaware of the hidden data, he or she would hence be oblivious to the massive scope of the error in prediction. Policy recommendations based on such erroneous predictions could certainly have costly results.

CONFIDENCE INTERVALS FOR THE MEAN VALUE OF *y* GIVEN *x*

Thus far, we have discussed point estimates for values of the response variable for a given value of the predictor variable. Of course, point estimates in this context suffer the same drawbacks as point estimates in the univariate case, notably the lack of a probability statement associated with their accuracy. We may therefore have recourse to confidence intervals for the mean value of y for a given value of x.

The confidence interval for the mean value of y for a given value of x is as follows:

$$\text{point estimate} \pm \text{margin of error} = \hat{y}_p \pm t_{\alpha/2}(s)\sqrt{\frac{1}{n} + \frac{(x_p - \bar{x})^2}{\sum (x_i - \bar{x})^2}}$$

where

$$\begin{aligned}
x_p &= \text{the particular value of } x \text{ for which the prediction is being made} \\
\hat{y}_p &= \text{the point estimate of } y \text{ for a particular value of } x \\
t_{\alpha/2} &= \text{a multiplier associated with the sample size and confidence level} \\
s &= \sqrt{\text{MSE}} = \sqrt{\text{SSE}/n - 1} = \text{the standard error of the estimate} \\
\text{SSE} &= \text{the sum of squared residuals}
\end{aligned}$$

We look at an example of this type of confidence interval below, but first we are introduced to a new type of interval, the prediction interval.

PREDICTION INTERVALS FOR A RANDOMLY CHOSEN VALUE OF *y* GIVEN *x*

Have you ever considered that it is "easier" to predict the mean value of a variable than it is to predict a randomly chosen value of that variable? For example, baseball buffs perusing the weekly batting average statistics will find that the team batting averages (which are the means of all the team's players) are more closely bunched together than are the batting averages of the individual players. An estimate of the team batting average will therefore be more precise than an estimate of a randomly chosen member of that team for the same level of confidence.

Exam scores provide another example. It is not unusual for a randomly selected student's score to exceed 95, say, but it is quite unusual for the class average to be that high. This anecdotal evidence reflects the smaller variability associated with the mean (class average) of a variable rather than a randomly selected value (individual score) of that variable. Therefore, it is "easier" to predict the class average on an exam than it is to predict a randomly chosen student's score.

In many situations, data miners are more interested in predicting an individual value rather than the mean of all the values, given x. For example, an analyst may be more interested in predicting the credit score for a particular credit applicant rather than predicting the mean credit score of all similar applicants. Or, a geneticist may be interested in the expression of a particular gene rather than the mean expression of all similar genes.

Prediction intervals are used to estimate the value of a randomly chosen value of y, given x. Clearly, this is a more difficult task than estimating the mean, resulting in intervals of greater width (lower precision) than confidence intervals for the mean with the same confidence level. The prediction interval for a randomly chosen value of y for a given value of x is as follows:

$$\text{point estimate} \pm \text{margin of error} = \hat{y}_p \pm t_{\alpha/2}\,(s)\sqrt{1 + \frac{1}{n} + \frac{(x_p - \bar{x})^2}{\sum (x_i - \bar{x})^2}}$$

Note that this formula is precisely the same as the formula for the confidence interval for the mean value of y, given x, except for the presence of the "1+" inside the square root. This ensures that the prediction interval is always wider than the analogous confidence interval.

Minitab supplies us with the regression output shown in Figure 4.5 for predicting *nutrition rating* based on *sugar content*. We also asked Minitab to calculate the confidence interval for the mean of all nutrition ratings when the sugar content equals 1 gram. Let's examine this output for a moment.

- The estimated regression equation is given first: $\hat{y} = 59.4 - 2.42(sugars)$.
- Then the regression coefficients are displayed, under *coef*: $b_0 = 59.4$ and $b_1 = -2.42$.
- Under *SE coef* are found the standard errors of the coefficients, which are a measure of the variability of the coefficients.
- Under T are found the t-test statistics for the hypothesis test.
- Under P are found the p-values of these hypothesis tests for the coefficients. A small p-value (usually <0.05) indicates that the particular coefficient differs significantly from zero.
- S, the standard error of the estimate, indicates a measure of the size of the "typical" error in prediction.
- *R-squared* is a measure of how closely the linear regression model fits the data, with values closer to 90 to 100% indicating a very nice fit.

Regression Analysis: Rating versus Sugars

```
The regression equation is
Rating = 59.4 - 2.42 Sugars

Predictor      Coef    SE Coef       T       P
Constant     59.444      1.951   30.47   0.000
Sugars      -2.4193     0.2376  -10.18   0.000

S = 9.162     R-Sq = 58.0%    R-Sq(adj) = 57.5%

Analysis of Variance

Source            DF         SS        MS        F       P
Regression         1     8701.7    8701.7   103.67   0.000
Residual Error    75     6295.1      83.9
Total             76    14996.8

Unusual Observations
Obs    Sugars   Rating        Fit     SE Fit    Residual    St Resid
  2       0.0    93.70      59.44       1.95       34.26       3.83R
 32       6.0    68.40      44.93       1.07       23.48       2.58R

R denotes an observation with a large standardized residual

Predicted Values for New Observations

New Obs      Fit     SE Fit           95.0% CI                95.0% PI
1          57.02       1.75   (   53.53,     60.52)  (   38.44,     75.61)

Values of Predictors for New Observations

New Obs     Sugars
1             1.00
```

Figure 4.5 Minitab regression output.

Minitab identifies two *unusual observations*, cereal 2 (All-Bran with Extra Fiber) and cereal 32 (100% Bran), which have large positive residuals, indicating that the nutrition rating was unexpectedly high, given their sugar level.

Finally, near the bottom, we find the information regarding the confidence and prediction intervals for a new cereal containing 1 gram of sugar.

- *Fit* is nothing but the point estimate of the nutritional rating for a cereal with 1 gram of sugar: $\hat{y} = 59.444 - 2.4193(1) = 57.02$. (The difference from the 56.98 in the Cheerios example is due simply to our earlier rounding of the coefficient values.)
- *SE fit* is a measure of the variability of the point estimate.
- The 95% confidence interval for the mean nutritional rating of all cereals containing 1 gram of sugar is (53.53, 60.52).
- The 95% prediction interval for the nutritional rating of a randomly chosen cereal containing 1 gram of sugar is (38.44, 75.61).

Note that as expected, the prediction interval is wider than the confidence interval, reflecting the greater challenge of estimating a particular y value rather than the mean y value for a given value of x.

MULTIPLE REGRESSION

Suppose that a linear relationship exists between a predictor variable and a response variable but that we ignored the relationship and used only the univariate measures associated with the response variable (e.g., mean, median) to predict new cases. This would be a waste of information, and such univariate measures would on average be far less precise estimators of new values of the predictor variable than the regression model would have provided.

Now, most data mining applications enjoy a wealth (indeed, a superfluity) of data, with some data sets including hundreds of variables, many of which may have a linear relationship with the target (response) variable. *Multiple regression modeling* provides an elegant method of describing such relationships. Multiple regression models provide improved precision for estimation and prediction, analogous to the improved precision of regression estimates over univariate estimates.

To illustrate the use of multiple regression modeling using the *cereals* data set, we shall attempt to reconstruct the formula used by *Consumer Reports* for the nutritional rating of the cereals. We begin exploring the relationships between the response *rating* and the predictors *calories, protein, fat, sodium, fiber, carbohydrates, sugars, potassium,* and *vitamins*, by using Minitab draftman's plots, which plot a response variable against several predictor variables, shown here with an estimated regression line superimposed.

From Figures 4.6 and 4.7, we would expect that protein, fiber, and potassium would be positively correlated with a higher nutritional rating, while fat, sodium, sugars, and surprisingly, vitamins are negatively correlated with a higher nutritional rating. Carbohydrates seem to be uncorrelated with nutritional rating. We can verify these graphical findings with the correlation coefficients for all the variables, shown in the

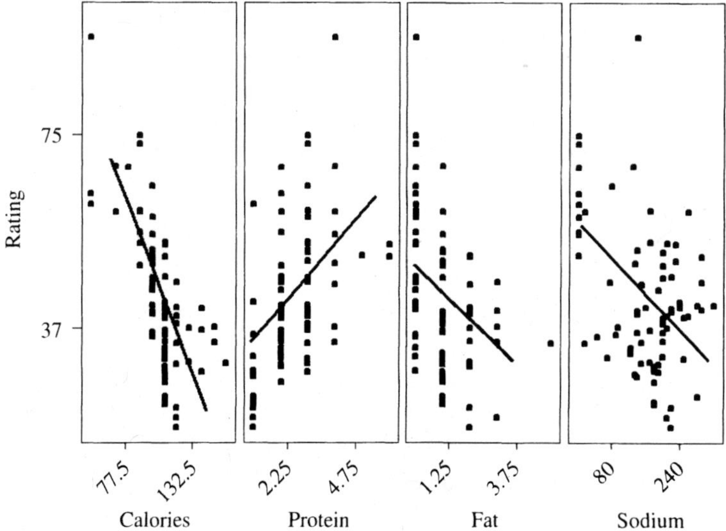

Figure 4.6 Draftman's plot of *rating* versus *calories, protein, fat,* and *sodium.*

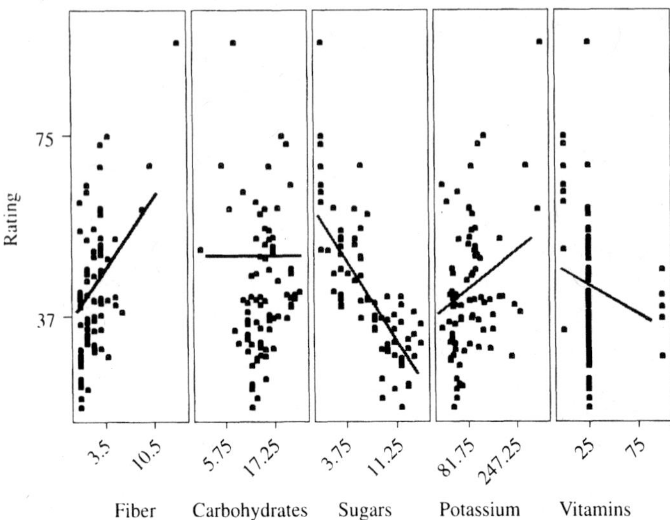

Figure 4.7 Draftman's plot of *rating* versus *fiber, carbohydrates, sugars, potassium,* and *vitamins*.

Table 4.6. The first column (in bold) shows the correlation coefficients of the predictor variables with *rating*. As expected, *protein, fiber,* and *potassium* are positively correlated with *rating*, whereas *calories, fat, sodium,* and *vitamins* are negatively correlated.

Data analysts need to guard against *multicollinearity*, a condition where some of the predictor variables are correlated with each other. Multicollinearity leads to instability in the solution space, leading to possible incoherent results. Even if such instability is avoided, inclusion of variables that are highly correlated tends to overemphasize a particular component of the model, since the component is essentially being double counted. Here, *potassium* is very highly correlated with *fiber* ($r = 0.905$). Although more sophisticated methods exist for handling correlated variables, such as principal components analysis, in this introductory example we simply omit *potassium* as a predictor.

TABLE 4.6 Correlation Coefficients for All Variables

	Rating	Calories	Protein	Fat	Sodium	Fiber	Carbohydrates	Sugars	Potassium
Calories	−0.689								
Protein	0.471	0.019							
Fat	−0.409	0.499	0.208						
Sodium	−0.401	0.301	−0.055	−0.005					
Fibre	0.577	−0.291	0.506	0.026	−0.071				
Carbos	0.050	0.255	−0.125	−0.315	0.357	−0.357			
Sugars	−0.762	0.564	−0.324	0.257	0.096	−0.137	−0.351		
Potass	0.380	−0.067	0.549	0.193	−0.033	0.905	−0.354	0.22	
Vitamins	−0.241	0.265	0.007	−0.031	0.361	−0.036	0.257	0.122	0.021

VERIFYING MODEL ASSUMPTIONS

Before a model can be implemented, the requisite model assumptions must be verified. Using a model whose assumptions are not verified is like building a house whose foundation may be cracked. Making predictions using a model where the assumptions are violated may lead to erroneous and overoptimistic results, with costly consequences when deployed.

These assumptions—linearity, independence, normality, and constant variance —may be checked using a normality plot of the residuals (Figure 4.8), and a plot of the standardized residuals against the fitted (predicted) values (Figure 4.9). One evaluates a normality plot by judging whether systematic deviations from linearity exist in the plot, in which case one concludes that the data values plotted (the residuals in this case) are not drawn from the particular distribution (the normal distribution in this case). We do not detect systematic deviations from linearity in the normal plot of the standardized residuals, and thereby conclude that our normality assumption is intact.

The plot of the residuals versus the fits (Figure 4.9) is examined for discernible patterns. If obvious curvature exists in the scatter plot, the linearity assumption is violated. If the vertical spread of the points in the plot is systematically nonuniform, the constant variance assumption is violated. We detect no such patterns in Figure 4.9 and therefore conclude that the linearity and constant variance assumptions are intact for this example.

The independence assumption makes sense for this data set, since we would not expect that the rating for one particular cereal would depend on the rating for another cereal. Time-dependent data can be examined for order independence using a runs test or a plot of the residuals versus ordering.

After thus checking that the assumptions are not violated, we may therefore proceed with the multiple regression analysis. Minitab provides us with the multiple regression output shown in Figure 4.10.

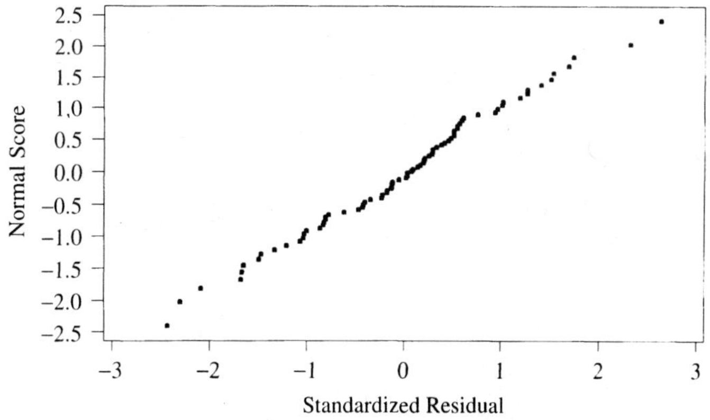

Figure 4.8 Normal plot of the residuals.

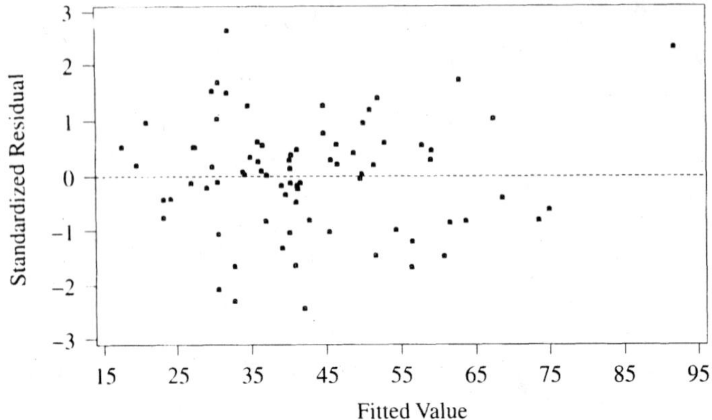

Figure 4.9 Plot of standardized residuals versus fitted (predicted values).

Let us examine these very interesting results carefully. The estimated regression equation is as follows:

> The estimated nutritional rating equals 55.9
> minus 0.225 times the number of calories
> plus 2.88 times the grams of protein
> minus 2.00 times the grams of fat
> minus 0.0546 times the milligrams of sodium
> plus 2.57 times the grams of fiber

```
The regression equation is
Rating = 55.9 - 0.225 Calories + 2.88 Protein - 2.00 Fat - 0.0546 Sodium
           + 2.57 Fiber + 1.08 Carbos - 0.823 Sugars - 0.0514 Vitamins

Predictor         Coef     SE Coef         T        P
Constant       55.9047      0.8421     66.39    0.000
Calories      -0.22456     0.01551    -14.48    0.000
Protein         2.8824      0.1626     17.73    0.000
Fat            -2.0048      0.1857    -10.80    0.000
Sodium       -0.054647    0.001609    -33.96    0.000
Fiber          2.57151     0.06505     39.53    0.000
Carbos         1.07504     0.06093     17.64    0.000
Sugars        -0.82343     0.06189    -13.31    0.000
Vitamins     -0.051422    0.005802     -8.86    0.000

S = 1.015        R-Sq = 99.5%      R-Sq(adj) = 99.5%

Analysis of Variance

Source             DF          SS          MS          F        P
Regression          8     14926.8      1865.8    1811.92    0.000
Residual Error     68        70.0         1.0
Total              76     14996.8
```

Figure 4.10 Minitab multiple regression output.

plus 1.08 times the grams of carbohydrates

minus 0.823 times the grams of sugar

minus 0.0514 times the percent RDA of vitamins

This is the equation we may use to perform point estimation and prediction for the nutritional rating of new cereals. For example, suppose that there is a new cereal with 80 calories, 2 grams of protein, no fat, no sodium, 3 grams of fiber, 16 grams of carbohydrates, no sugars, and 0% RDA of vitamins (similar to Shredded Wheat). Then the predicted nutritional rating is 55.9 − 0.225(80) + 2.88(2) − 2.00(0) − 0.0546(0) + 2.57(3) + 1.08(16) − 0.823(0) − 0.0514(0) = 68.62 using the unrounded coefficients provided by *minitab*. This prediction is remarkably close to the actual nutritional rating for Shredded Wheat of 68.2359, so that the prediction error is $y - \hat{y} = 68.2359 - 68.62 = -0.3841$.

Of course, point estimates have drawbacks, so analogous to the simple linear regression case, we can find confidence intervals and prediction intervals in multiple regression as well. We can find a 95% confidence interval for the mean nutritional rating of all such cereals (with characteristics similar to those of Shredded Wheat: 80 calories, 2 grams of protein, etc.), to be (67.914, 69.326). Also, a 95% prediction interval for the nutritional rating of a randomly chosen cereal with characteristics similar to those of Shredded Wheat is (66.475, 70.764). As before, the prediction interval is wider than the confidence interval.

Here follow further comments on the multiple regression results given in Figure 4.10. The R^2 value of 99.5% is extremely high, nearly equal to the maximum possible R^2 of 100%. This indicates that our multiple regression models accounts for nearly all of the variability in the nutritional ratings. The standard error of the estimate, s, has a value of about 1, meaning that our typical prediction error is about one point on the nutrition rating scale, and that about 95% (based on the normal distribution of the errors) of our predictions will be within two points of the actual value. Compare this with an s value of about 9 for the simple linear regression model in Figure 4.5. Using more data in our regression model has allowed us to reduce our prediction error by a factor of 9.

Note also that the p-values (under P) for all the predictor variables equal zero (actually, they are rounded to zero), indicating that each of the variables, including *carbohydrates*, belongs in the model. Recall that earlier it appeared that *carbohydrates* did not have a very high correlation with rating, so some modelers may have been tempted to eliminate *carbohydrates* from the model based on this exploratory finding. However, as we mentioned in Chapter 3, it is often best to allow variables to remain in the model even if the EDA does not show obvious association with the target. Here, *carbohydrates* was found to be a significant predictor of *rating*, *in the presence of the other predictors*. Eliminating *carbohydrates* as a predictor in the regression resulted in a point estimate for a Shredded Wheat–like cereal to have a nutritional rating of 68.805, more distant from the actual rating of 68.2359 than was the prediction that included *carbohydrates* in the model. Further, the model without *carbohydrates* had a decreased R^2 value and an s value that more than doubled, to 2.39 (not shown). Eliminating this variable due to seeming lack of association in the EDA phase would have been a mistake, reducing the functionality of model and impairing its estimation and prediction precision.

REFERENCES

1. Robert Johnson and Patricia Kuby, *Elementary Statistics*, Brooks-Cole, Toronto, Ontario, Canada, 2004.
2. *Data and Story Library*, `www.lib.stat.cmu.edu/DASL`, Carnegie Mellon University, Pittsburgh, PA.

EXERCISES

1. Explain why measures of spread are required when summarizing a data set.

2. Explain the meaning of the term *standard deviation* to a layman who has never read a statistics or data mining book.

3. Give an example from your own experience, or from newspapers, of the use of statistical inference.

4. Give an example from your own experience, or from newspapers, of the idea of sampling error.

5. What is the meaning of the term *margin of error*?

6. Discuss the relationship between the width of a confidence interval and the confidence level associated with it.

7. Discuss the relationship between the sample size and the width of a confidence interval. Which is better, a wide interval or a tight interval? Why?

8. Explain clearly why we use regression analysis and for which type of variables it is appropriate.

9. Suppose that we are interested in predicting weight of students based on height. We have run a regression analysis with the resulting estimated regression equation as follows: "The estimated weight equals (-180 pounds) plus (5 pounds times the height in inches)."

   a. Suppose that one student is 3 inches taller than another student. What is the estimated difference in weight?

   b. Suppose that a given student is 65 inches tall. What is the estimated weight?

   c. Suppose that the regression equation above was based on a sample of students ranging in height from 60 to 75 inches. Now estimate the height of a 48-inch-tall student. Comment.

   d. Explain clearly the meaning of the 5 in the equation above.

   e. Explain clearly the meaning of the -180 in the equation above.

Hands-On Analysis

Use the *cereals* data set included, at the book series Web site, for the following exercises. Use regression to estimate *rating* based on *fiber* alone.

10. What is the estimated regression equation?

11. Explain clearly the value of the slope coefficient you obtained in the regression.

12. What does the value of the y-intercept mean for the regression equation you obtained? Does it make sense in this example?

13. What would be a typical prediction error obtained from using this model to predict *rating*? Which statistic are you using to measure this? What could we do to lower this estimated prediction error?

14. How closely does our model fit the data? Which statistic are you using to measure this?

15. Find a point estimate for the rating for a cereal with a fiber content of 3 grams.

16. Find a 95% confidence interval for the true mean rating for all cereals with a fiber content of 3 grams.

17. Find a 95% prediction interval for a randomly chosen cereal with a fiber content of 3 grams.

18. Based on the regression results, what would we expect a scatter plot of *rating* versus *fiber* to look like? Why?

For the following exercises, use multiple regression to estimate *rating* based on *fiber* and *sugars*.

19. What is the estimated regression equation?

20. Explain clearly and completely the value of the coefficient for fiber you obtained in the regression.

21. Compare the R^2 values from the multiple regression and the regression done earlier in the exercises. What is going on? Will this always happen?

22. Compare the s values from the multiple regression and the regression done earlier in the exercises. Which value is preferable, and why?

CHAPTER 5

k-NEAREST NEIGHBOR ALGORITHM

SUPERVISED VERSUS UNSUPERVISED METHODS

Data mining methods may be categorized as either supervised or unsupervised. In *unsupervised methods*, no target variable is identified as such. Instead, the data mining algorithm searches for patterns and structure among all the variables. The most common unsupervised data mining method is clustering, our topic in Chapters 8 and 9. For example, political consultants may analyze congressional districts using clustering methods, to uncover the locations of voter clusters that may be responsive to a particular candidate's message. In this case, all appropriate variables (e.g., income, race, gender) would be input to the clustering algorithm, with no target variable specified, in order to develop accurate voter profiles for fund-raising and advertising purposes.

Another data mining method, which may be supervised or unsupervised, is association rule mining. In market basket analysis, for example, one may simply be

Discovering Knowledge in Data: An Introduction to Data Mining, By Daniel T. Larose
ISBN 0-471-66657-2

interested in "which items are purchased together," in which case no target variable would be identified. The problem here, of course, is that there are so many items for sale, that searching for all possible associations may present a daunting task, due to the resulting combinatorial explosion. Nevertheless, certain algorithms, such as the a priori algorithm, attack this problem cleverly, as we shall see when we cover association rule mining in Chapter 10.

Most data mining methods are *supervised methods*, however, meaning that (1) there is a particular prespecified target variable, and (2) the algorithm is given many examples where the value of the target variable is provided, so that the algorithm may learn which values of the target variable are associated with which values of the predictor variables. For example, the regression methods of Chapter 4 are supervised methods, since the observed values of the response variable y are provided to the least-squares algorithm, which seeks to minimize the squared distance between these y values and the y values predicted given the x-vector. All of the classification methods we examine in Chapters 5 to 7 are supervised methods, including decision trees, neural networks, and k-nearest neighbors.

METHODOLOGY FOR SUPERVISED MODELING

Most supervised data mining methods apply the following methodology for building and evaluating a model. First, the algorithm is provided with a *training set* of data, which includes the preclassified values of the target variable in addition to the predictor variables. For example, if we are interested in classifying *income bracket*, based on *age*, *gender*, and *occupation*, our classification algorithm would need a large pool of records, containing complete (as complete as possible) information about every field, including the target field, *income bracket*. In other words, the records in the *training set* need to be *preclassified*. A provisional data mining model is then constructed using the training samples provided in the training data set.

However, the training set is necessarily incomplete; that is, it does not include the "new" or future data that the data modelers are really interested in classifying. Therefore, the algorithm needs to guard against "memorizing" the training set and blindly applying all patterns found in the training set to the future data. For example, it may happen that all customers named "David" in a training set may be in the high-income bracket. We would presumably not want our final model, to be applied to new data, to include the pattern "If the customer's first name is David, the customer has a high income." Such a pattern is a spurious artifact of the training set and needs to be verified before deployment.

Therefore, the next step in supervised data mining methodology is to examine how the provisional data mining model performs on a *test set* of data. In the test set, a holdout data set, the values of the target variable are hidden temporarily from the provisional model, which then performs classification according to the patterns and structure it learned from the training set. The efficacy of the classifications are then evaluated by comparing them against the true values of the target variable. The provisional data mining model is then adjusted to minimize the error rate on the test set.

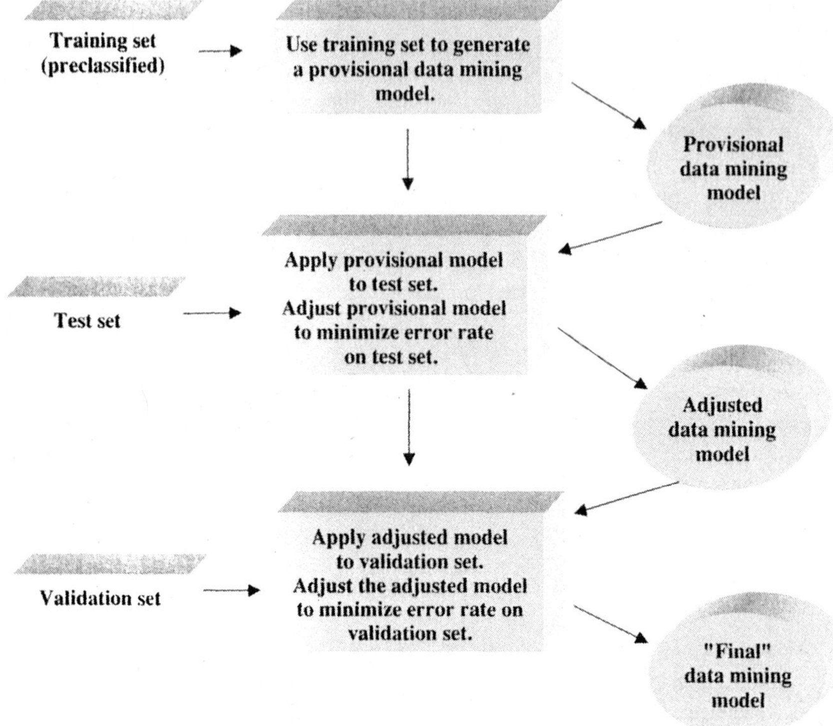

Figure 5.1 Methodology for supervised modeling.

The adjusted data mining model is then applied to a *validation* data set, another holdout data set, where the values of the target variable are again hidden temporarily from the model. The adjusted model is itself then adjusted, to minimize the error rate on the validation set. Estimates of model performance for future, unseen data can then be computed by observing various evaluative measures applied to the validation set. Such model evaluation techniques are covered in Chapter 11. An overview of this modeling process for supervised data mining is provided in Figure 5.1.

Usually, the accuracy of the provisional model is not as high on the test or validation sets as it is on the training set, often because the provisional model is *overfitting* on the training set. Overfitting results when the provisional model tries to account for every possible trend or structure in the training set, even idiosyncratic ones such as the "David" example above. There is an eternal tension in model building between model complexity (resulting in high accuracy on the training set) and generalizability to the test and validation sets. Increasing the complexity of the model in order to increase the accuracy on the training set eventually and inevitably leads to a degradation in the generalizability of the provisional model to the test and validation sets, as shown in Figure 5.2.

Figure 5.2 shows that as the provisional model begins to grow in complexity from the null model (with little or no complexity), the error rates on both the training set and the validation set fall. As the model complexity increases, the error rate on the

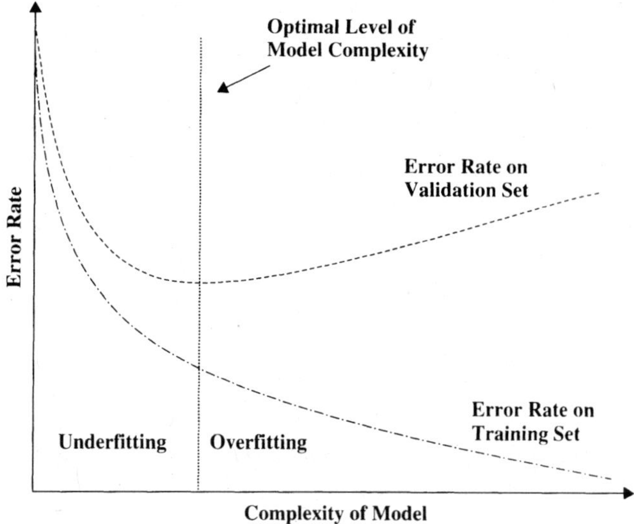

Figure 5.2 The optimal level of model complexity is at the minimum error rate on the validation set.

training set continues to fall in a monotone fashion. However, as the model complexity increases, the validation set error rate soon begins to flatten out and increase because the provisional model has memorized the training set rather than leaving room for generalizing to unseen data. The point where the minimal error rate on the validation set is encountered is the optimal level of model complexity, as indicated in Figure 5.2. Complexity greater than this is considered to be overfitting; complexity less than this is considered to be underfitting.

BIAS–VARIANCE TRADE-OFF

Suppose that we have the scatter plot in Figure 5.3 and are interested in constructing the optimal curve (or straight line) that will separate the dark gray points from the light gray points. The straight line in has the benefit of low complexity but suffers from some classification errors (points ending up on the wrong side of the line).

In Figure 5.4 we have reduced the classification error to zero but at the cost of a much more complex separation function (the curvy line). One might be tempted to adopt the greater complexity in order to reduce the error rate. However, one should be careful not to depend on the idiosyncrasies of the training set. For example, suppose that we now add more data points to the scatter plot, giving us the graph in Figure 5.5.

Note that the low-complexity separator (the straight line) need not change very much to accommodate the new data points. This means that this low-complexity separator has *low variance*. However, the high-complexity separator, the curvy line, must alter considerably if it is to maintain its pristine error rate. This high degree of change indicates that the high-complexity separator has a *high variance*.

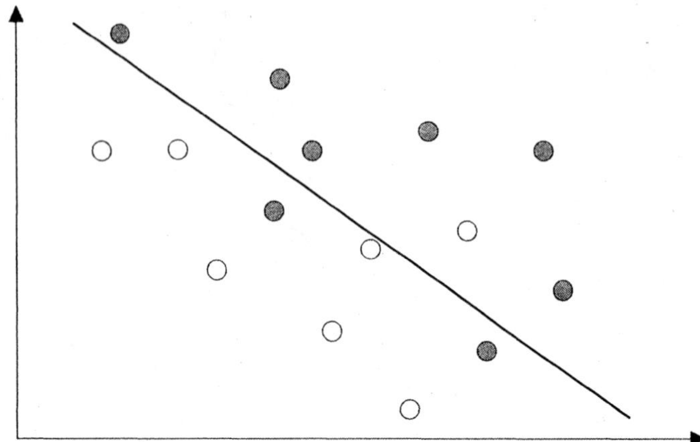

Figure 5.3 Low-complexity separator with high error rate.

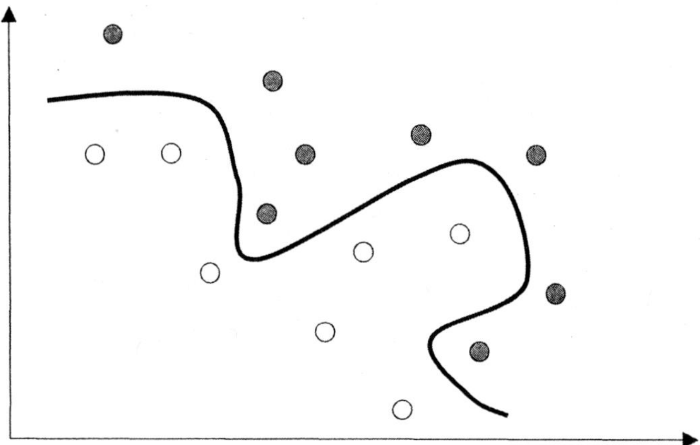

Figure 5.4 High-complexity separator with low error rate.

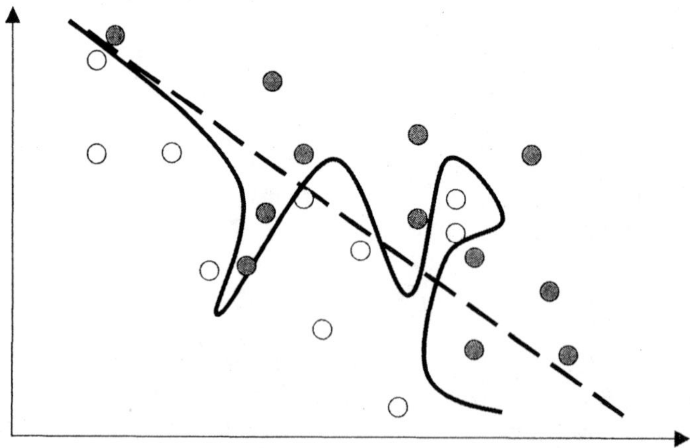

Figure 5.5 With more data: low-complexity separator need not change much; high-complexity separator needs much revision.

Even though the high-complexity model has a low *bias* (in terms of the error rate on the training set), it has a high *variance*; And even though the low-complexity model has a high *bias*, it has a low *variance*. This is what is known as the *bias–variance trade-off*. The bias–variance trade-off is another way of describing the overfitting/underfitting dilemma shown in Figure 5.2. As model complexity increases, the bias on the training set decreases but the variance increases. The goal is to construct a model in which neither the bias nor the variance is too high, but usually, minimizing one tends to increase the other.

For example, the most common method of evaluating how accurate model estimation is proceeding is to use the *mean-squared error* (MSE). Between two competing models, one may select the better model as that model with the lower MSE. Why is MSE such a good evaluative measure? Because it combines both bias and variance. The mean-squared error is a function of the estimation error (SSE) and the model complexity (e.g., degrees of freedom). It can be shown (e.g., Hand et al. [1]) that the mean-squared error can be partitioned using the following equation, which clearly indicates the complementary relationship between bias and variance:

$$\text{MSE} = \text{variance} + \text{bias}^2$$

CLASSIFICATION TASK

Perhaps the most common data mining task is that of *classification*. Examples of classification tasks may be found in nearly every field of endeavor:

- *Banking:* determining whether a mortgage application is a good or bad credit risk, or whether a particular credit card transaction is fraudulent
- *Education:* placing a new student into a particular track with regard to special needs
- *Medicine:* diagnosing whether a particular disease is present
- *Law:* determining whether a will was written by the actual person deceased or fraudulently by someone else
- *Homeland security:* identifying whether or not certain financial or personal behavior indicates a possible terrorist threat

In classification, there is a target categorical variable, (e.g., *income bracket*), which is partitioned into predetermined classes or categories, such as high income, middle income, and low income. The data mining model examines a large set of records, each record containing information on the target variable as well as a set of input or predictor variables. For example, consider the excerpt from a data set shown in Table 5.1. Suppose that the researcher would like to be able to *classify* the income bracket of persons not currently in the database, based on the other characteristics associated with that person, such as age, gender, and occupation. This task is a classification task, very nicely suited to data mining methods and techniques.

TABLE 5.1 Excerpt from Data Set for Classifying Income

Subject	Age	Gender	Occupation	Income Bracket
001	47	F	Software engineer	High
002	28	M	Marketing consultant	Middle
003	35	M	Unemployed	Low
⋮				

The algorithm would proceed roughly as follows. First, examine the data set containing both the predictor variables and the (already classified) target variable, *income bracket*. In this way, the algorithm (software) "learns about" which combinations of variables are associated with which income brackets. For example, older females may be associated with the high-income bracket. This data set is called the *training set*. Then the algorithm would look at new records for which no information about income bracket is available. Based on the classifications in the training set, the algorithm would assign classifications to the new records. For example, a 63-year-old female professor might be classified in the high-income bracket.

k-NEAREST NEIGHBOR ALGORITHM

The first algorithm we shall investigate is the *k-nearest neighbor* algorithm, which is most often used for classification, although it can also be used for estimation and prediction. *k*-Nearest neighbor is an example of *instance-based learning*, in which the training data set is stored, so that a classification for a new unclassified record may be found simply by comparing it to the most similar records in the training set. Let's consider an example.

Recall the example from Chapter 1 where we were interested in classifying the type of drug a patient should be prescribed, based on certain patient characteristics, such as the age of the patient and the patient's sodium/potassium ratio. For a sample of 200 patients, Figure 5.6 presents a scatter plot of the patients' sodium/potassium (Na/K) ratio against the patients' age. The particular drug prescribed is symbolized by the shade of the points. Light gray points indicate drug Y; medium gray points indicate drug A or X; dark gray points indicate drug B or C.

Now suppose that we have a new patient record, without a drug classification, and would like to classify which drug should be prescribed for the patient based on which drug was prescribed for other patients with similar attributes. Identified as "new patient 1," this patient is 40 years old and has a Na/K ratio of 29, placing her at the center of the circle indicated for new patient 1 in Figure 5.6. Which drug classification should be made for new patient 1? Since her patient profile places her deep into a section of the scatter plot where all patients are prescribed drug Y, we would thereby

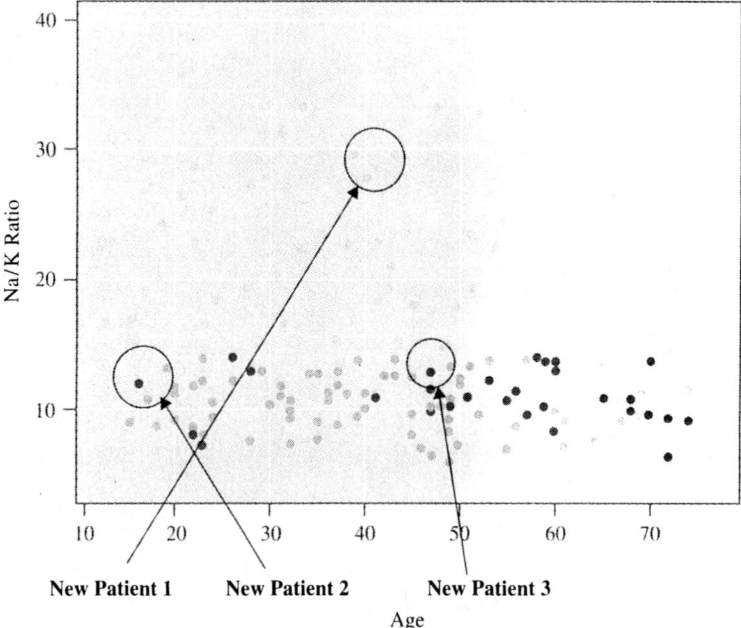

Figure 5.6 Scatter plot of sodium/potassium ratio against age, with drug overlay.

classify new patient 1 as drug Y. All of the points nearest to this point, that is, all of the patients with a similar profile (with respect to age and Na/K ratio) have been prescribed the same drug, making this an easy classification.

Next, we move to new patient 2, who is 17 years old with a Na/K ratio of 12.5. Figure 5.7 provides a close-up view of the training data points in the local neighborhood of and centered at new patient 2. Suppose we let $k = 1$ for our k-nearest neighbor algorithm, so that new patient 2 would be classified according to whichever *single* (one) observation it was closest to. In this case, new patient 2 would be classified

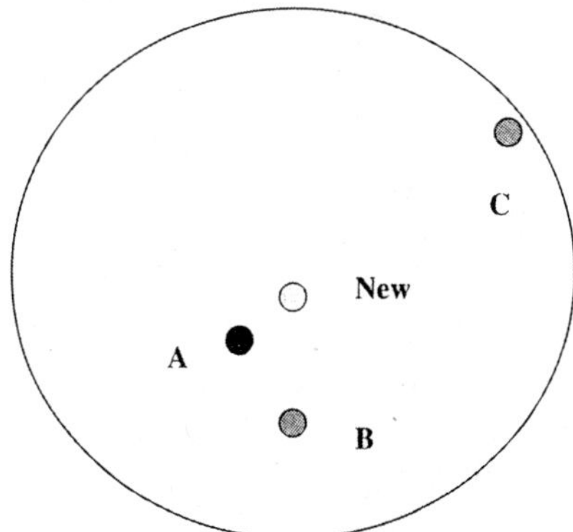

Figure 5.7 Close-up of three nearest neighbors to new patient 2.

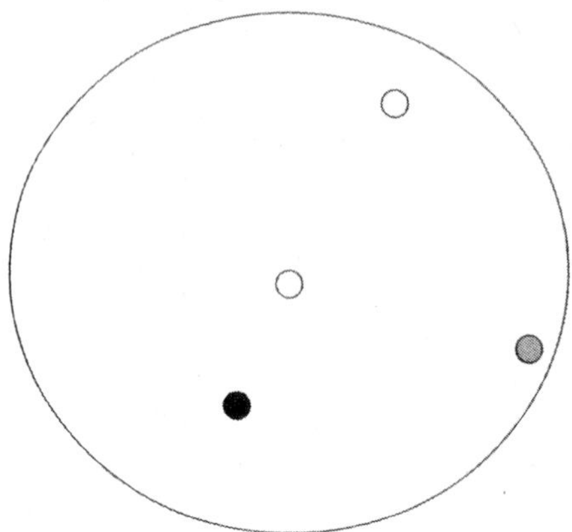

Figure 5.8 Close-up of three nearest neighbors to new patient 2.

for drugs B and C (dark gray), since that is the classification of the point closest to the point on the scatter plot for new patient 2.

However, suppose that we now let $k = 2$ for our k-nearest neighbor algorithm, so that new patient 2 would be classified according to the classification of the $k = 2$ points closest to it. One of these points is dark gray, and one is medium gray, so that our classifier would be faced with a decision between classifying new patient 2 for drugs B and C (dark gray) or drugs A and X (medium gray). How would the classifier decide between these two classifications? Voting would not help, since there is one vote for each of two classifications.

Voting would help, however, if we let $k = 3$ for the algorithm, so that new patient 2 would be classified based on the three points closest to it. Since two of the three closest points are medium gray, a classification based on voting would therefore choose drugs A and X (medium gray) as the classification for new patient 2. Note that the classification assigned for new patient 2 differed based on which value we chose for k.

Finally, consider new patient 3, who is 47 years old and has a Na/K ratio of 13.5. Figure 5.8 presents a close-up of the three nearest neighbors to new patient 3. For $k = 1$, the k-nearest neighbor algorithm would choose the dark gray (drugs B and C) classification for new patient 3, based on a distance measure. For $k = 2$, however, voting would not help. But voting would not help for $k = 3$ in this case either, since the three nearest neighbors to new patient 3 are of three different classifications.

This example has shown us some of the issues involved in building a classifier using the k-nearest neighbor algorithm. These issues include:

- How many neighbors should we consider? That is, what is k?
- How do we measure distance?
- How do we combine the information from more than one observation?

Later we consider other questions, such as:

- Should all points be weighted equally, or should some points have more influence than others?

DISTANCE FUNCTION

We have seen above how, for a new record, the k-nearest neighbor algorithm assigns the classification of the most similar record or records. But just how do we define *similar*? For example, suppose that we have a new patient who is a 50-year-old male. Which patient is more similar, a 20-year-old male or a 50-year-old female?

Data analysts define distance metrics to measure similarity. A *distance metric* or *distance function* is a real-valued function d, such that for any coordinates x, y, and z:

1. $d(x,y) \geq 0$, and $d(x,y) = 0$ if and only if $x = y$
2. $d(x,y) = d(y,x)$
3. $d(x,z) \leq d(x,y) + d(y,z)$

Property 1 assures us that distance is always nonnegative, and the only way for distance to be zero is for the coordinates (e.g., in the scatter plot) to be the same. Property 2 indicates commutativity, so that, for example, the distance from New York to Los Angeles is the same as the distance from Los Angeles to New York. Finally, property 3 is the *triangle inequality*, which states that introducing a third point can never shorten the distance between two other points.

The most common distance function is *Euclidean distance*, which represents the usual manner in which humans think of distance in the real world:

$$d_{\text{Euclidean}}(\mathbf{x},\mathbf{y}) = \sqrt{\sum_i (x_i - y_i)^2}$$

where $\mathbf{x} = x_1, x_2, \ldots, x_m$, and $\mathbf{y} = y_1, y_2, \ldots, y_m$ represent the m attribute values of two records. For example, suppose that patient A is $x_1 = 20$ years old and has a Na/K ratio of $x_2 = 12$, while patient B is $y_1 = 30$ years old and has a Na/K ratio of $y_2 = 8$. Then the Euclidean distance between these points, as shown in Figure 5.9, is

$$\begin{aligned} d_{\text{Euclidean}}(\mathbf{x},\mathbf{y}) &= \sqrt{\sum_i (x_i - y_i)^2} = \sqrt{(20-30)^2 + (12-8)^2} \\ &= \sqrt{100 + 16} = 10.77 \end{aligned}$$

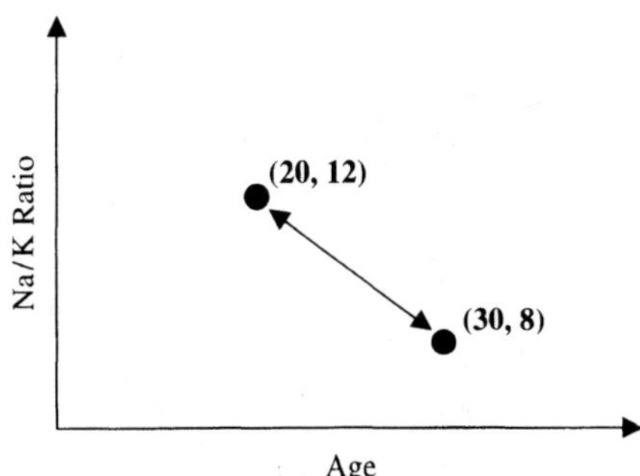

Figure 5.9 Euclidean distance.

When measuring distance, however, certain attributes that have large values, such as income, can overwhelm the influence of other attributes which are measured on a smaller scale, such as years of service. To avoid this, the data analyst should make sure to *normalize* the attribute values.

For continuous variables, the *min–max normalization* or *Z-score standardization*, discussed in Chapter 2, may be used:

Min–max normalization:

$$X^* = \frac{X - \min(X)}{\text{range}(X)} = \frac{X - \min(X)}{\max(X) - \min(X)}$$

Z-score standardization:

$$X^* = \frac{X - \text{mean}(X)}{\text{SD}(X)}$$

For categorical variables, the Euclidean distance metric is not appropriate. Instead, we may define a function, "different from," used to compare the ith attribute values of a pair of records, as follows:

$$\text{different}(x_i, y_i) = \begin{cases} 0 & \text{if } x_i = y_i \\ 1 & \text{otherwise} \end{cases}$$

where x_i and y_i are categorical values. We may then substitute different (x_i, y_i) for the ith term in the Euclidean distance metric above.

For example, let's find an answer to our earlier question: Which patient is more similar to a 50-year-old male: a 20-year-old male or a 50-year-old female? Suppose that for the *age* variable, the range is 50, the minimum is 10, the mean is 45, and the standard deviation is 15. Let patient A be our 50-year-old male, patient B the 20-year-old male, and patient C the 50-year-old female. The original variable values, along with the min–max normalization (age_{MMN}) and Z-score standardization ($\text{age}_{Z\text{score}}$), are listed in Table 5.2.

We have one continuous variable (age, x_1) and one categorical variable (gender, x_2). When comparing patients A and B, we have different $(x_2, y_2) = 0$, with different $(x_2, y_2) = 1$ for the other combinations of patients. First, let's see what happens when we forget to normalize the age variable. Then the distance between patients A and B is $\text{d(A, B)} = \sqrt{(50 - 20)^2 + 0^2} = 30$, and the distance between patients A and C is $\text{d(A,C)} = \sqrt{(20 - 20)^2 + 1^2} = 1$. We would thus conclude that the 20-year-old male is 30 times more "distant" from the 50-year-old male than the 50-year-old

TABLE 5.2 Variable Values for Age and Gender

Patient	Age	Age_{MMN}	$\text{Age}_{Z\text{score}}$	Gender
A	50	$\frac{50-10}{50} = 0.8$	$\frac{50-45}{15} = 0.33$	Male
B	20	$\frac{20-10}{50} = 0.2$	$\frac{20-45}{15} = -1.67$	Male
C	50	$\frac{50-10}{50} = 0.8$	$\frac{50-45}{15} = 0.33$	Female

female is. In other words, the 50-year-old female is 30 times more "similar" to the 50-year-old male than the 20-year-old male is. Does this seem justified to you? Well, in certain circumstances, it may be justified, as in certain age-related illnesses. But, in general, one may judge that the two men are just as similar as are the two 50-year-olds. The problem is that the *age* variable is measured on a larger scale than the Different(x_2, y_2) variable. Therefore, we proceed to account for this discrepancy by normalizing and standardizing the age values, as shown in Table 5.2.

Next, we use the min–max normalization values to find which patient is more similar to patient A. We have $d_{\text{MMN}}(\text{A,B}) = \sqrt{(0.8 - 0.2)^2 + 0^2} = 0.6$ and $d_{\text{MMN}}(\text{A,C}) = \sqrt{(0.8 - 0.8)^2 + 1^2} = 1.0$, which means that patient B is now considered to be more similar to patient A.

Finally, we use the Z-score standardization values to determine which patient is more similar to patient A. We have $d_{Z\text{score}}(\text{A,B}) = \sqrt{[0.33 - (-1.67)]^2 + 0^2} = 2.0$ and $d_{Z\text{score}}(\text{A,C}) = \sqrt{(0.33 - 0.33)^2 + 1^2} = 1.0$, which means that patient C is again closer. Using the Z-score standardization rather than the min–max standardization has reversed our conclusion about which patient is considered to be more similar to patient A. This underscores the importance of understanding which type of normalization one is using. The min–max normalization will almost always lie between zero and 1 just like the "identical" function. The Z-score standardization, however, usually takes values $-3 < z < 3$, representing a wider scale than that of the min–max normalization. Therefore, perhaps, when mixing categorical and continuous variables, the min–max normalization may be preferred.

COMBINATION FUNCTION

Now that we have a method of determining which records are most similar to the new, unclassified record, we need to establish how these similar records will combine to provide a classification decision for the new record. That is, we need a *combination function*. The most basic combination function is simple unweighted voting.

Simple Unweighted Voting

1. Before running the algorithm, decide on the value of k, that is, how many records will have a voice in classifying the new record.
2. Then, compare the new record to the k *nearest neighbors*, that is, to the k records that are of minimum distance from the new record in terms of the Euclidean distance or whichever metric the user prefers.
3. Once the k records have been chosen, then for simple unweighted voting, their distance from the new record no longer matters. It is simple one record, one vote.

We observed simple unweighted voting in the examples for Figures 5.4 and 5.5. In Figure 5.4, for $k = 3$, a classification based on simple voting would choose drugs A and X (medium gray) as the classification for new patient 2, since two of the three closest points are medium gray. The classification would then be made for drugs A and X, with *confidence* 66.67%, where the confidence level represents the count of records, with the winning classification divided by k.

On the other hand, in Figure 5.5, for $k = 3$, simple voting would fail to choose a clear winner since each of the three categories receives one vote. There would be a tie among the three classifications represented by the records in Figure 5.5, and a tie may not be a preferred result.

Weighted Voting

One may feel that neighbors that are closer or more similar to the new record should be weighted more heavily than more distant neighbors. For example, in Figure 5.5, does it seem fair that the light gray record farther away gets the same vote as the dark gray vote that is closer to the new record? Perhaps not. Instead, the analyst may choose to apply *weighted voting*, where closer neighbors have a larger voice in the classification decision than do more distant neighbors. Weighted voting also makes it much less likely for ties to arise.

In weighted voting, the influence of a particular record is inversely proportional to the distance of the record from the new record to be classified. Let's look at an example. Consider Figure 5.6, where we are interested in finding the drug classification for a new record, using the $k = 3$ nearest neighbors. Earlier, when using simple unweighted voting, we saw that there were two votes for the medium gray classification, and one vote for the dark gray. However, the dark gray record is closer than the other two records. Will this greater proximity be enough for the influence of the dark gray record to overcome that of the more numerous medium gray records?

Assume that the records in question have the values for age and Na/K ratio given in Table 5.3, which also shows the min–max normalizations for these values. Then the distances of records A, B, and C from the new record are as follows:

$$d(\text{new}, A) = \sqrt{(0.05 - 0.0467)^2 + (0.25 - 0.2471)^2} = 0.004393$$

$$d(\text{new}, B) = \sqrt{(0.05 - 0.0533)^2 + (0.25 - 0.1912)^2} = 0.58893$$

$$d(\text{new}, C) = \sqrt{(0.05 - 0.0917)^2 + (0.25 - 0.2794)^2} = 0.051022$$

The votes of these records are then weighted according to the inverse square of their distances.

One record (A) votes to classify the new record as dark gray (drugs B and C), so the weighted vote for this classification is

TABLE 5.3 Age and Na/K Ratios for Records from Figure 5.4

Record	Age	Na/K	Age_{MMN}	Na/K_{MMN}
New	17	12.5	0.05	0.25
A (dark gray)	16.8	12.4	0.0467	0.2471
B (medium gray)	17.2	10.5	0.0533	0.1912
C (medium gray)	19.5	13.5	0.0917	0.2794

$$\text{votes (dark gray)} = \frac{1}{d(\text{new},A)^2} = \frac{1}{0.004393^2} \simeq 51{,}818$$

Two records (B and C) vote to classify the new record as medium gray (drugs A and X), so the weighted vote for this classification is

$$\text{votes (medium gray)} = \frac{1}{d(\text{new},B)^2} + \frac{1}{d(\text{new},C)^2} = \frac{1}{0.058893^2} + \frac{1}{0.051022^2}$$
$$\simeq 672$$

Therefore, by the convincing total of 51,818 to 672, the weighted voting procedure would choose dark gray (drugs B and C) as the classification for a new 17-year-old patient with a sodium/potassium ratio of 12.5. Note that this conclusion reverses the earlier classification for the unweighted $k = 3$ case, which chose the medium gray classification.

When the distance is zero, the inverse would be undefined. In this case the algorithm should choose the majority classification of all records whose distance is zero from the new record.

Consider for a moment that once we begin weighting the records, there is no theoretical reason why we couldn't increase k arbitrarily so that all existing records are included in the weighting. However, this runs up against the practical consideration of very slow computation times for calculating the weights of all of the records every time a new record needs to be classified.

QUANTIFYING ATTRIBUTE RELEVANCE: STRETCHING THE AXES

Consider that not all attributes may be relevant to the classification. In decision trees (Chapter 6), for example, only those attributes that are helpful to the classification are considered. In the k-nearest neighbor algorithm, the distances are by default calculated on all the attributes. It is possible, therefore, for relevant records that are proximate to the new record in all the important variables, but are distant from the new record in unimportant ways, to have a moderately large distance from the new record, and therefore not be considered for the classification decision. Analysts may therefore consider restricting the algorithm to fields known to be important for classifying new records, or at least to blind the algorithm to known irrelevant fields.

Alternatively, rather than restricting fields a priori, the data analyst may prefer to indicate which fields are of more or less importance for classifying the target variable. This can be accomplished using a *cross-validation approach* or one based on domain expert knowledge. First, note that the problem of determining which fields are more or less important is equivalent to finding a coefficient z_j by which to multiply the jth axis, with larger values of z_j associated with more important variable axes. This process is therefore termed *stretching the axes*.

The cross-validation approach then selects a random subset of the data to be used as a training set and finds the set of values $z_1, z_2, \ldots z_m$ that minimize the classification error on the test data set. Repeating the process will lead to a more accurate set of values $z_1, z_2, \ldots z_m$. Otherwise, domain experts may be called upon to recommend a set of values for $z_1, z_2, \ldots z_m$. In this way, the k-nearest neighbor algorithm may be made more precise.

For example, suppose that either through cross-validation or expert knowledge, the Na/K ratio was determined to be three times as important as age for drug classification. Then we would have $z_{\text{Na/K}} = 3$ and $z_{\text{age}} = 1$. For the example above, the new distances of records A, B, and C from the new record would be as follows:

$$\text{d(new,A)} = \sqrt{(0.05 - 0.0467)^2 + [3(0.25 - 0.2471)]^2} = 0.009305$$

$$\text{d(new,B)} = \sqrt{(0.05 - 0.0533)^2 + [3(0.25 - 0.1912)]^2} = 0.17643$$

$$\text{d(new,C)} = \sqrt{(0.05 - 0.0917)^2 + [3(0.25 - 0.2794)]^2} = 0.09756$$

In this case, the classification would not change with the stretched axis for Na/K, remaining dark gray. In real-world problems, however, axis stretching can lead to more accurate classifications, since it represents a method for quantifying the relevance of each variable in the classification decision.

DATABASE CONSIDERATIONS

For instance-based learning methods such as the k-nearest neighbor algorithm, it is vitally important to have access to a rich database full of as many different combinations of attribute values as possible. It is especially important that rare classifications be represented sufficiently, so that the algorithm does not only predict common classifications. Therefore, the data set would need to be *balanced*, with a sufficiently large percentage of the less common classifications. One method to perform balancing is to reduce the proportion of records with more common classifications.

Maintaining this rich database for easy access may become problematic if there are restrictions on main memory space. Main memory may fill up, and access to auxiliary storage is slow. Therefore, if the database is to be used for k-nearest neighbor methods only, it may be helpful to retain only those data points that are near a classification "boundary." For example, in Figure 5.6, all records with Na/K ratio value greater than, say, 19 could be omitted from the database without loss of classification accuracy, since all records in this region are classified as light gray. New records with Na/K ratio > 19 would therefore be classified similarly.

k-NEAREST NEIGHBOR ALGORITHM FOR ESTIMATION AND PREDICTION

So far we have considered how to use the k-nearest neighbor algorithm for classification. However, it may be used for estimation and prediction as well as for continuous-valued target variables. One method for accomplishing this is called *locally weighted*

TABLE 5.4 $k = 3$ **Nearest Neighbors of the New Record**

Record	Age	Na/K	BP	Age_{MMN}	Na/K_{MMN}	Distance
New	17	12.5	?	0.05	0.25	—
A	16.8	12.4	120	0.0467	0.2471	0.009305
B	17.2	10.5	122	0.0533	0.1912	0.16783
C	19.5	13.5	130	0.0917	0.2794	0.26737

averaging. Assume that we have the same data set as the example above, but this time rather than attempting to classify the drug prescription, we are trying to estimate the systolic blood pressure reading (BP, the target variable) of the patient, based on that patient's *age* and *Na/K ratio* (the predictor variables). Assume that BP has a range of 80 with a minimum of 90 in the patient records.

In this example we are interested in estimating the systolic blood pressure reading for a 17-year-old patient with a Na/K ratio of 12.5, the same new patient record for which we earlier performed drug classification. If we let $k = 3$, we have the same three nearest neighbors as earlier, shown here in Table 5.4. Assume that we are using the $z_{\text{Na/K}} =$ three-axis-stretching to reflect the greater importance of the Na/K ratio.

Locally weighted averaging would then estimate BP as the weighted average of BP for the $k = 3$ nearest neighbors, using the same inverse square of the distances for the weights that we used earlier. That is, the estimated target value $\hat{y}$ is calculated as

$$\hat{y}_{\text{new}} = \frac{\sum_i w_i y_i}{\sum_i w_i}$$

where $w_i = 1/\text{d}(\text{new}, x_i)^2$ for existing records $x_1, x_2, \ldots, x_k$. Thus, in this example, the estimated systolic blood pressure reading for the new record would be

$$\hat{y}_{\text{new}} = \frac{\sum_i w_i y_i}{\sum_i w_i} = \frac{\frac{120}{0.009305^2} + \frac{122}{0.17643^2} + \frac{130}{0.09756^2}}{\frac{1}{0.009305^2} + \frac{1}{0.17643^2} + \frac{1}{0.09756^2}} = 120.0954.$$

As expected, the estimated BP value is quite close to the BP value in the present data set that is much closer (in the stretched attribute space) to the new record. In other words, since record A is closer to the new record, its BP value of 120 contributes greatly to the estimation of the BP reading for the new record.

CHOOSING *k*

How should one go about choosing the value of k? In fact, there may not be an obvious best solution. Consider choosing a small value for k. Then it is possible that the classification or estimation may be unduly affected by outliers or unusual observations ("noise"). With small k (e.g., $k = 1$), the algorithm will simply return the target value of the nearest observation, a process that may lead the algorithm toward overfitting, tending to memorize the training data set at the expense of generalizability.

On the other hand, choosing a value of k that is not too small will tend to smooth out any idiosyncratic behavior learned from the training set. However, if we take this too far and choose a value of k that is too large, locally interesting behavior will be overlooked. The data analyst needs to balance these considerations when choosing the value of k.

It is possible to allow the data itself to help resolve this problem, by following a cross-validation procedure similar to the earlier method for finding the optimal values $z_1, z_2, \ldots z_m$ for axis stretching. Here we would try various values of k with different randomly selected training sets and choose the value of k that minimizes the classification or estimation error.

REFERENCE

1. David Hand, Heikki Mannila, and Padhraic Smyth, 2001, *Principles of Data Mining*, MIT Press, Cambridge, MA, 2001.

EXERCISES

1. Explain the difference between supervised and unsupervised methods. Which data mining tasks are associated with unsupervised methods? Supervised? Both?

2. Describe the differences between the training set, test set, and validation set.

3. Should we strive for the highest possible accuracy with the training set? Why or why not? How about the validation set?

4. How is the bias–variance trade-off related to the issue of overfitting and underfitting? Is high bias associated with overfitting and underfitting, and why? High variance?

5. What is meant by the term *instance-based learning*?

6. Make up a set of three records, each with two numeric predictor variables and one categorical target variable, so that the classification would not change regardless of the value of k.

7. Refer to Exercise 6. Alter your data set so that the classification changes for different values of k.

8. Refer to Exercise 7. Find the Euclidean distance between each pair of points. Using these points, verify that Euclidean distance is a true distance metric.

9. Compare the advantages and drawbacks of unweighted versus weighted voting.

10. Why does the database need to be balanced?

11. The example in the text regarding using the k-nearest neighbor algorithm for estimation has the closest record, overwhelming the other records in influencing the estimation. Suggest two creative ways that we could dilute this strong influence of the closest record.

12. Discuss the advantages and drawbacks of using a small value versus a large value for k.

CHAPTER 6

DECISION TREES

CLASSIFICATION AND REGRESSION TREES

C4.5 ALGORITHM

DECISION RULES

COMPARISON OF THE C5.0 AND CART ALGORITHMS APPLIED TO REAL DATA

In this chapter we continue our examination of classification methods for data mining. One attractive classification method involves the construction of a *decision tree*, a collection of *decision nodes*, connected by *branches*, extending downward from the *root node* until terminating in *leaf nodes*. Beginning at the root node, which by convention is placed at the top of the decision tree diagram, attributes are tested at the decision nodes, with each possible outcome resulting in a branch. Each branch then leads either to another decision node or to a terminating leaf node. Figure 6.1 provides an example of a simple decision tree.

The target variable for the decision tree in Figure 6.1 is *credit risk*, with potential customers being classified as either good or bad credit risks. The predictor variables are *savings* (low, medium, and high), *assets* (low or not low), and *income* ($\leq$\$50,000 or $>$\$50,000). Here, the root node represents a decision node, testing whether each record has a low, medium, or high savings level (as defined by the analyst or domain expert). The data set is partitioned, or *split*, according to the values of this attribute. Those records with low savings are sent via the leftmost branch (*savings* = *low*) to another decision node. The records with high savings are sent via the rightmost branch to a different decision node.

The records with medium savings are sent via the middle branch directly to a leaf node, indicating the termination of this branch. Why a leaf node and not another decision node? Because, in the data set (not shown), all of the records with medium savings levels have been classified as good credit risks. There is no need for another decision node, because our knowledge that the customer has medium savings predicts good credit with 100% accuracy in the data set.

For customers with low savings, the next decision node tests whether the customer has low assets. Those with low assets are then classified as bad credit risks; the others are classified as good credit risks. For customers with high savings, the

Discovering Knowledge in Data: An Introduction to Data Mining, By Daniel T. Larose
ISBN 0-471-66657-2

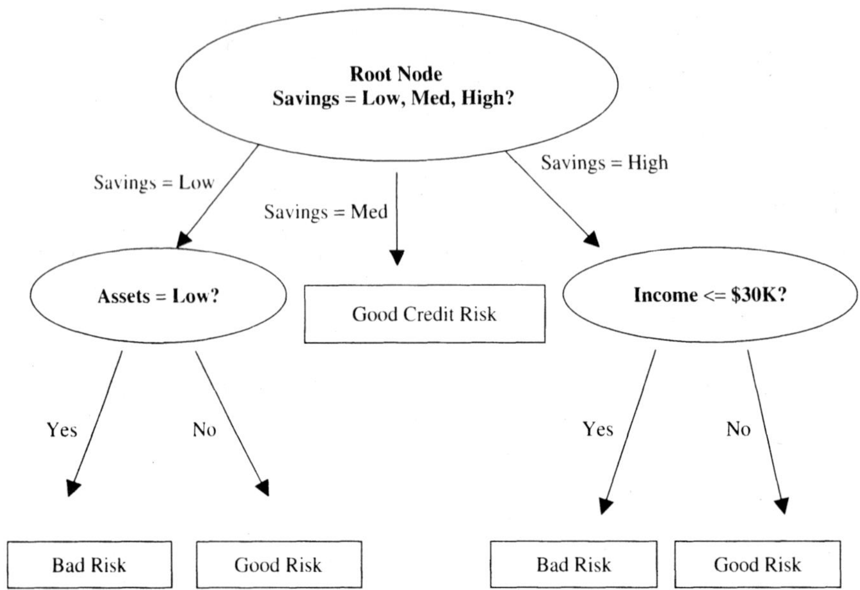

Figure 6.1 Simple decision tree.

next decision node tests whether the customer has an income of at most $30,000. Customers with incomes of $30,000 or less are then classified as bad credit risks, with the others classified as good credit risks.

When no further splits can be made, the decision tree algorithm stops growing new nodes. For example, suppose that all of the branches terminate in "pure" leaf nodes, where the target variable is unary for the records in that node (e.g., each record in the leaf node is a good credit risk). Then no further splits are necessary, so no further nodes are grown.

However, there are instances when a particular node contains "diverse" attributes (with nonunary values for the target attribute), and yet the decision tree cannot make a split. For example, suppose that we consider the records from Figure 6.1 with high savings and low income ($\leq$\$30,000). Suppose that there are five records with these values, all of which also have low assets. Finally, suppose that three of these five customers have been classified as bad credit risks and two as good credit risks, as shown in Table 6.1. In the real world, one often encounters situations such as this, with varied values for the response variable, even for exactly the same values for the predictor variables.

Here, since all customers have the same predictor values, there is no possible way to split the records according to the predictor variables that will lead to a pure leaf node. Therefore, such nodes become diverse leaf nodes, with mixed values for the target attribute. In this case, the decision tree may report that the classification for such customers is "bad," with 60% confidence, as determined by the three-fifths of customers in this node who are bad credit risks. Note that not all attributes are tested for all records. Customers with low savings and low assets, for example, are not tested with regard to income in this example.

TABLE 6.1 Sample of Records That Cannot Lead to Pure Leaf Node

Customer	Savings	Assets	Income	Credit Risk
004	High	Low	≤$30,000	Good
009	High	Low	≤$30,000	Good
027	High	Low	≤$30,000	Bad
031	High	Low	≤$30,000	Bad
104	High	Low	≤$30,000	Bad

Certain requirements must be met before decision tree algorithms may be applied:

1. Decision tree algorithms represent supervised learning, and as such require preclassified target variables. A training data set must be supplied which provides the algorithm with the values of the target variable.
2. This training data set should be rich and varied, providing the algorithm with a healthy cross section of the types of records for which classification may be needed in the future. Decision trees learn by example, and if examples are systematically lacking for a definable subset of records, classification and prediction for this subset will be problematic or impossible.
3. The target attribute classes must be discrete. That is, one cannot apply decision tree analysis to a continuous target variable. Rather, the target variable must take on values that are clearly demarcated as either belonging to a particular class or not belonging.

Why in the example above, did the decision tree choose the *savings* attribute for the root node split? Why did it not choose *assets* or *income* instead? Decision trees seek to create a set of leaf nodes that are as "pure" as possible, that is, where each of the records in a particular leaf node has the same classification. In this way, the decision tree may provide classification assignments with the highest measure of confidence available.

However, how does one measure uniformity, or conversely, how does one measure heterogeneity? We shall examine two of the many methods for measuring leaf node purity, which lead to the two leading algorithms for constructing decision trees:

- Classification and regression trees (CART) algorithm
- C4.5 algorithm

CLASSIFICATION AND REGRESSION TREES

The *classification and regression trees* (CART) method was suggested by Breiman et al. [1] in 1984. The decision trees produced by CART are strictly binary, containing exactly two branches for each decision node. CART recursively partitions the records in the training data set into subsets of records with similar values for the target attribute. The CART algorithm grows the tree by conducting for each decision node, an exhaustive search of all available variables and all possible splitting values, selecting the optimal split according to the following criteria (from Kennedy et al. [2]).

Let $\Phi(s|t)$ be a measure of the "goodness" of a candidate split s at node t, where

$$\Phi(s|t) = 2P_L P_R \sum_{j=1}^{\#\text{ classes}} |P(j|t_L) - P(j|t_R)| \tag{6.1}$$

and where

$$t_L = \text{left child node of node } t$$

$$t_R = \text{right child node of node } t$$

$$P_L = \frac{\text{number of records at } t_L}{\text{number of records in training set}}$$

$$P_R = \frac{\text{number of records at } t_R}{\text{number of records in training set}}$$

$$P(j|t_L) = \frac{\text{number of class } j \text{ records at } t_L}{\text{number of records at } t}$$

$$P(j|t_R) = \frac{\text{number of class } j \text{ records at } t_R}{\text{number of records at } t}$$

Then the optimal split is whichever split maximizes this measure $\Phi(s|t)$ over all possible splits at node t.

Let's look at an example. Suppose that we have the training data set shown in Table 6.2 and are interested in using CART to build a decision tree for predicting whether a particular customer should be classified as being a good or a bad credit risk. In this small example, all eight training records enter into the root node. Since CART is restricted to binary splits, the candidate splits that the CART algorithm would evaluate for the initial partition at the root node are shown in Table 6.3. Although *income* is a continuous variable, CART may still identify a finite list of possible splits based on the number of different values that the variable actually takes in the data

TABLE 6.2 Training Set of Records for Classifying Credit Risk

Customer	Savings	Assets	Income ($1000s)	Credit Risk
1	Medium	High	75	Good
2	Low	Low	50	Bad
3	High	Medium	25	Bad
4	Medium	Medium	50	Good
5	Low	Medium	100	Good
6	High	High	25	Good
7	Low	Low	25	Bad
8	Medium	Medium	75	Good

TABLE 6.3 Candidate Splits for t = Root Node

Candidate Split	Left Child Node, t_L	Right Child Node, t_R
1	$Savings = low$	$Savings \in \{medium, high\}$
2	$Savings = medium$	$Savings \in \{low, high\}$
3	$Savings = high$	$Savings \in \{low, medium\}$
4	$Assets = low$	$Assets \in \{medium, high\}$
5	$Assets = medium$	$Assets \in \{low, high\}$
6	$Assets = high$	$Assets \in \{low, medium\}$
7	$Income \leq \$25,000$	$Income > \$25,000$
8	$Income \leq \$50,000$	$Income > \$50,000$
9	$Income \leq \$75,000$	$Income > \$75,000$

set. Alternatively, the analyst may choose to categorize the continuous variable into a smaller number of classes.

For each candidate split, let us examine the values of the various components of the optimality measure $\Phi(s|t)$ in Table 6.4. Using these observed values, we may investigate the behavior of the optimality measure under various conditions. For example, when is $\Phi(s|t)$ large? We see that $\Phi(s|t)$ is large when both of its main components are large: $2P_L P_R$ and $\sum_{j=1}^{\text{\# classes}} |P(j|t_L) - P(j|t_R)|$.

TABLE 6.4 Values of the Components of the Optimality Measure $\Phi(s|t)$ for Each Candidate Split, for the Root Node

Split	P_L	P_R	$P(j\|t_L)$	$P(j\|t_R)$	$2P_L P_R$	$Q(s\|t)$	$\Phi(s\|t)$
1	0.375	0.625	G: .333 B: .667	G: .8 B: .2	0.46875	0.934	0.4378
2	0.375	0.625	G: 1 B: 0	G: 0.4 B: 0.6	0.46875	1.2	0.5625
3	0.25	0.75	G: 0.5 B: 0.5	G: 0.667 B: 0.333	0.375	0.334	0.1253
4	0.25	0.75	G: 0 B: 1	G: 0.833 B: 0.167	0.375	1.667	0.6248
5	0.5	0.5	G: 0.75 B: 0.25	G: 0.5 B: 0.5	0.5	0.5	0.25
6	0.25	0.75	G: 1 B: 0	G: 0.5 B: 0.5	0.375	1	0.375
7	0.375	0.625	G: 0.333 B: 0.667	G: 0.8 B: 0.2	0.46875	0.934	0.4378
8	0.625	0.375	G: 0.4 B: 0.6	G: 1 B: 0	0.46875	1.2	0.5625
9	0.875	0.125	G: 0.571 B: 0.429	G: 1 B: 0	0.21875	0.858	0.1877

Let $Q(s|t) = \sum_{j=1}^{\#\text{ classes}} |P(j|t_L) - P(j|t_R)|$. When is the component $Q(s|t)$ large? $Q(s|t)$ is large when the distance between $P(j|t_L)$ and $P(j|t_R)$ is maximized across each class (value of the target variable). In other words, this component is maximized when the proportions of records in the child nodes for each particular value of the target variable are as different as possible. The maximum value would therefore occur when for each class the child nodes are completely uniform (pure). The theoretical maximum value for $Q(s|t)$ is k, where k is the number of classes for the target variable. Since our output variable *credit risk* takes two values, *good* and *bad*, $k = 2$ is the maximum for this component.

The component $2P_LP_R$ is maximized when P_L and P_R are large, which occurs when the proportions of records in the left and right child nodes are equal. Therefore, $\Phi(s|t)$ will tend to favor balanced splits that partition the data into child nodes containing roughly equal numbers of records. Hence, the optimality measure $\Phi(s|t)$ prefers splits that will provide child nodes that are homogeneous for all classes and have roughly equal numbers of records. The theoretical maximum for $2P_LP_R$ is $2(0.5)(0.5) = 0.5$.

In this example, only candidate split 5 has an observed value for $2P_LP_R$ that reaches the theoretical maximum for this statistic, 0.5, since the records are partitioned equally into two groups of four. The theoretical maximum for $Q(s|t)$ is obtained only when each resulting child node is pure, and thus is not achieved for this data set.

The maximum observed value for $\Phi(s|t)$ among the candidate splits is therefore attained by split 4, with $\Phi(s|t) = 0.6248$. CART therefore chooses to make the initial partition of the data set using candidate split 4, assets = low versus assets $\in$ {medium, high}, as shown in Figure 6.2.

The left child node turns out to be a terminal leaf node, since both of the records that were passed to this node had *bad* credit risk. The right child node, however, is diverse and calls for further partitioning. We again compile a table of the candidate

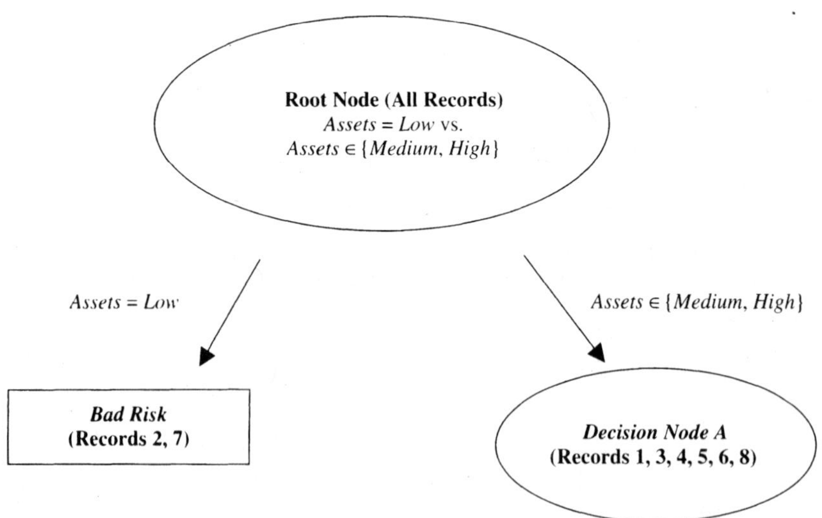

Figure 6.2 CART decision tree after initial split.

TABLE 6.5 Values of the Components of the Optimality Measure $\Phi(s|t)$ for Each Candidate Split, for Decision Node A

Split	P_L	P_R	$P(j\|t_L)$	$P(j\|t_R)$	$2P_LP_R$	$Q(s\|t)$	$\Phi(s\|t)$
1	0.167	0.833	G: 1 B: 0	G: .8 B: .2	0.2782	0.4	0.1112
2	0.5	0.5	G: 1 B: 0	G: 0.667 B: 0.333	0.5	0.6666	0.3333
3	0.333	0.667	G: 0.5 B: 0.5	G: 1 B: 0	0.4444	1	0.4444
5	0.667	0.333	G: 0.75 B: 0.25	G: 1 B: 0	0.4444	0.5	0.2222
6	0.333	0.667	G: 1 B: 0	G: 0.75 B: 0.25	0.4444	0.5	0.2222
7	0.333	0.667	G: 0.5 B: 0.5	G: 1 B: 0	0.4444	1	0.4444
8	0.5	0.5	G: 0.667 B: 0.333	G: 1 B: 0	0.5	0.6666	0.3333
9	0.167	0.833	G: 0.8 B: 0.2	G: 1 B: 0	0.2782	0.4	0.1112

splits (all are available except split 4), along with the values for the optimality measure (Table 6.5). Here two candidate splits (3 and 7) share the highest value for $\Phi(s|t)$, 0.4444. We arbitrarily select the first split encountered, split 3, savings = high versus savings $\in$ {low, medium}, for decision node A, with the resulting tree shown in Figure 6.3.

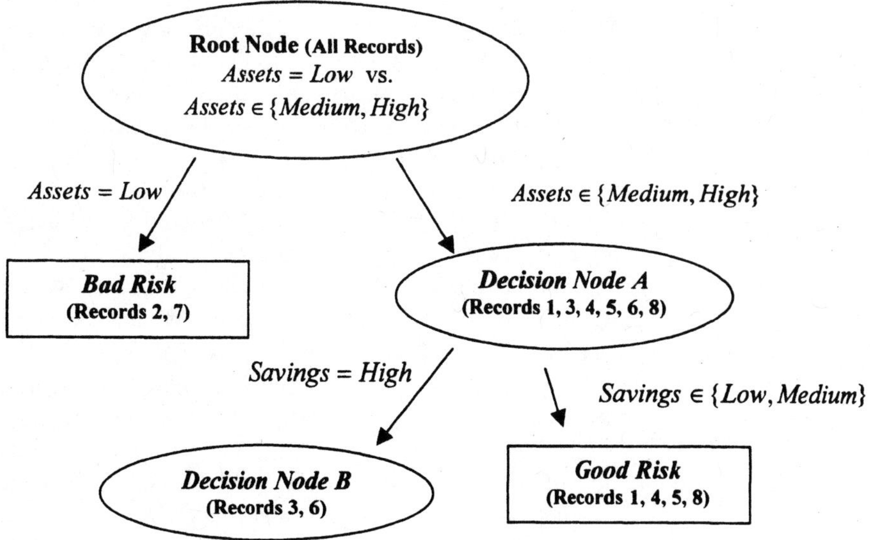

Figure 6.3 CART decision tree after decision node A split.

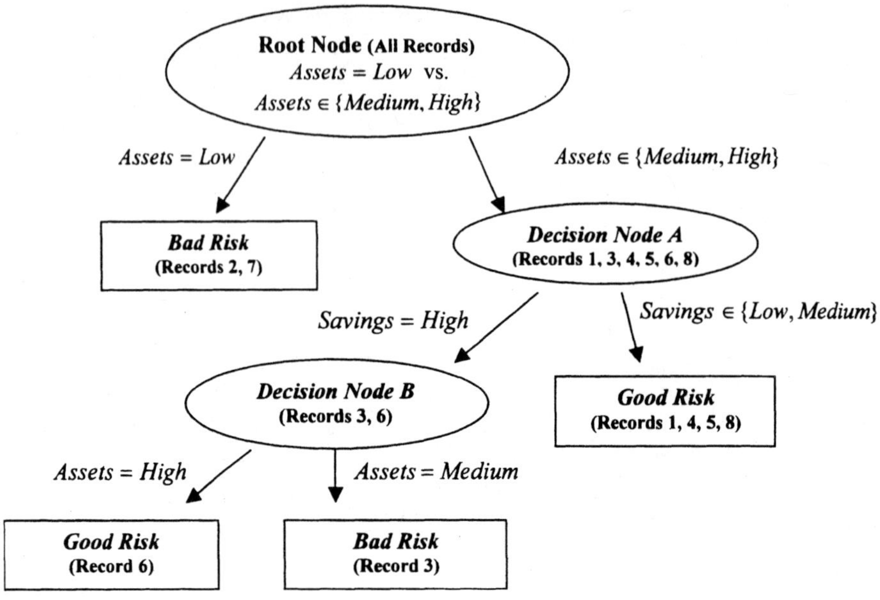

Figure 6.4 CART decision tree, fully grown form.

Since decision node *B* is diverse, we again need to seek the optimal split. Only two records remain in this decision node, each with the same value for savings (high) and income (25). Therefore, the only possible split is assets = high versus assets = medium, providing us with the final form of the CART decision tree for this example, in Figure 6.4. Compare Figure 6.4 with Figure 6.5, the decision tree generated by *Clementine*'s CART algorithm.

Let us leave aside this example now, and consider how CART would operate on an arbitrary data set. In general, CART would recursively proceed to visit each remaining decision node and apply the procedure above to find the optimal split at each node. Eventually, no decision nodes remain, and the "full tree" has been grown. However, as we have seen in Table 6.1, not all leaf nodes are necessarily homogeneous, which leads to a certain level of *classification error*.

For example, suppose that since we cannot further partition the records in Table 6.1, we classify the records contained in this leaf node as *bad credit risk*. Then the probability that a randomly chosen record from this leaf node would be classified correctly is 0.6, since three of the five records (60%) are actually classified as bad credit risks. Hence, our *classification error rate* for this particular leaf would be 0.4 or 40%, since two of the five records are actually classified as good credit risks. CART would then calculate the error rate for the entire decision tree to be the weighted average of the individual leaf error rates, with the weights equal to the proportion of records in each leaf.

To avoid memorizing the training set, the CART algorithm needs to begin pruning nodes and branches that would otherwise reduce the generalizability of the classification results. Even though the fully grown tree has the lowest error rate on the training set, the resulting model may be too complex, resulting in overfitting. As each

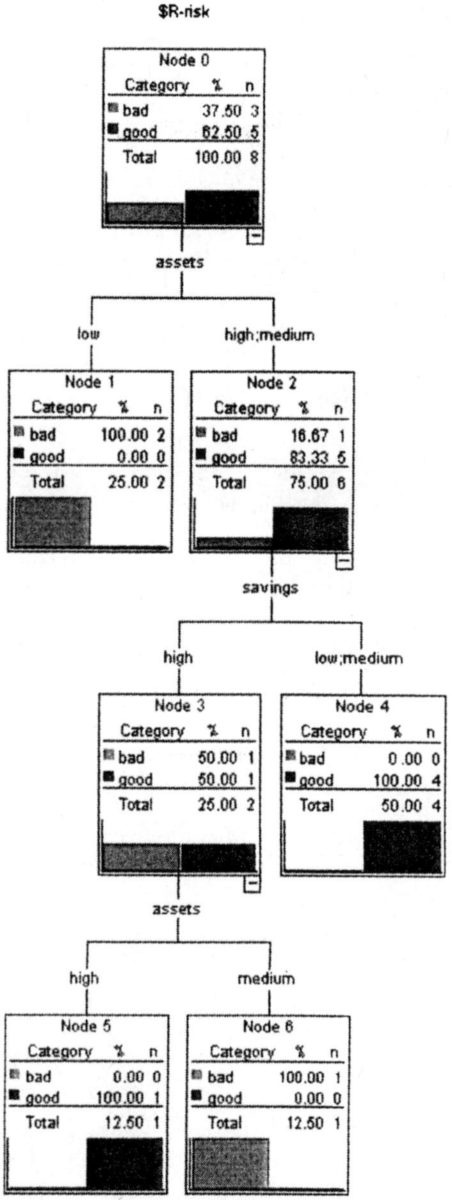

Figure 6.5 Clementine's CART decision tree.

decision node is grown, the subset of records available for analysis becomes smaller and less representative of the overall population. Pruning the tree will increase the generalizability of the results. How the CART algorithm performs tree pruning is explained in Breiman et al. [1, p. 66]. Essentially, an adjusted overall error rate is found that penalizes the decision tree for having too many leaf nodes and thus too much complexity.

C4.5 ALGORITHM

The C4.5 *algorithm* is Quinlan's extension of his own ID3 algorithm for generating decision trees [3]. Just as with CART, the C4.5 algorithm recursively visits each decision node, selecting the optimal split, until no further splits are possible. However, there are interesting differences between CART and C4.5:

- Unlike CART, the C4.5 algorithm is not restricted to binary splits. Whereas CART always produces a binary tree, C4.5 produces a tree of more variable shape.
- For categorical attributes, C4.5 by default produces a separate branch for each value of the categorical attribute. This may result in more "bushiness" than desired, since some values may have low frequency or may naturally be associated with other values.
- The C4.5 method for measuring node homogeneity is quite different from the CART method and is examined in detail below.

The C4.5 algorithm uses the concept of *information gain* or *entropy reduction* to select the optimal split. Suppose that we have a variable X whose k possible values have probabilities $p_1, p_2, \ldots, p_k$. What is the smallest number of bits, on average per symbol, needed to transmit a stream of symbols representing the values of X observed? The answer is called the *entropy of X* and is defined as

$$H(X) = -\sum_j p_j \log_2(p_j)$$

Where does this formula for entropy come from? For an event with probability p, the average amount of information in bits required to transmit the result is $-\log_2(p)$. For example, the result of a fair coin toss, with probability 0.5, can be transmitted using $-\log_2(0.5) = 1$ bit, which is a zero or 1, depending on the result of the toss. For variables with several outcomes, we simply use a weighted sum of the $\log_2(p_j)$'s, with weights equal to the outcome probabilities, resulting in the formula

$$H(X) = -\sum_j p_j \log_2(p_j)$$

C4.5 uses this concept of entropy as follows. Suppose that we have a candidate split S, which partitions the training data set T into several subsets, $T_1, T_2, \ldots, T_k$. The mean information requirement can then be calculated as the weighted sum of the entropies for the individual subsets, as follows:

$$H_S(T) = \sum_{i=1}^{k} P_i H_S(T_i) \tag{6.2}$$

where P_i represents the proportion of records in subset i. We may then define our *information gain* to be gain$(S) = H(T) - H_S(T)$, that is, the increase in information produced by partitioning the training data T according to this candidate split S. At each decision node, C4.5 chooses the optimal split to be the split that has the greatest information gain, gain(S).

TABLE 6.6 Candidate Splits at Root Node for C4.5 Algorithm

Candidate Split	Child Nodes		
1	*Savings* = *low*	*Savings* = *medium*	*Savings* = *high*
2	*Assets* = *low*	*Assets* = *medium*	*Assets* = *high*
3	*Income* ≤ \$25,000		*Income* > \$25,000
4	*Income* ≤ \$50,000		*Income* > \$50,000
5	*Income* ≤ \$75,000		*Income* > \$75,000

To illustrate the C4.5 algorithm at work, let us return to the data set in Table 6.2 and apply the C4.5 algorithm to build a decision tree for classifying credit risk, just as we did earlier using CART. Once again, we are at the root node and are considering all possible splits using all the data (Table 6.6).

Now, because five of the eight records are classified as *good credit risk*, with the remaining three records classified as *bad credit risk*, the entropy before splitting is

$$H(T) = -\sum_j p_j \log_2(p_j) = -\tfrac{5}{8}\log_2\left(\tfrac{5}{8}\right) - \tfrac{3}{8}\log_2\left(\tfrac{3}{8}\right) = 0.9544$$

We shall compare the entropy of each candidate split against this $H(T) = 0.9544$, to see which split results in the greatest reduction in entropy (or gain in information).

For candidate split 1 (*savings*), two of the records have *high* savings, three of the records have *medium* savings, and three of the records have *low* savings, so we have: $P_{\text{high}} = \frac{2}{8}$, $P_{\text{medium}} = \frac{3}{8}$, $P_{\text{low}} = \frac{3}{8}$. Of the records with *high* savings, one is a good credit risk and one is bad, giving a probability of 0.5 of choosing the record with a good credit risk. Thus, the entropy for *high* savings is $-\frac{1}{2}\log_2\left(\frac{1}{2}\right) - \frac{1}{2}\log_2\left(\frac{1}{2}\right) = 1$, which is similar to the flip of a fair coin. All three of the records with *medium* savings are good credit risks, so that the entropy for *medium* is $-\frac{3}{3}\log_2\left(\frac{3}{3}\right) - \frac{0}{3}\log_2\left(\frac{0}{3}\right) = 0$, where by convention we define $\log_2(0) = 0$.

In engineering applications, *information* is analogous to *signal*, and *entropy* is analogous to *noise*, so it makes sense that the entropy for medium savings is zero, since the signal is crystal clear and there is no noise: If the customer has medium savings, he or she is a good credit risk, with 100% confidence. The amount of information required to transmit the credit rating of these customers is zero, as long as we know that they have medium savings.

One of the records with *low* savings is a good credit risk, and two records with *low* savings are bad credit risks, giving us our entropy for *low* credit risk as $-\frac{1}{3}\log_2\left(\frac{1}{3}\right) - \frac{2}{3}\log_2\left(\frac{2}{3}\right) = 0.9183$. We combine the entropies of these three subsets, using equation (6.2) and the proportions of the subsets P_i, so that $H_{\text{savings}}(T) = \frac{2}{8}(1) + \frac{3}{8}(0) + \frac{3}{8}(0.9183) = 0.5944$. Then the information gain represented by the split on the *savings* attribute is calculated as $H(T) - H_{\text{savings}}(T) = 0.9544 - 0.5944 = 0.36$ bits.

How are we to interpret these measures? First, $H(T) = 0.9544$ means that, on average, one would need 0.9544 bit (0's or 1's) to transmit the credit risk of the eight customers in the data set. Now, $H_{\text{savings}}(T) = 0.5944$ means that the partitioning of the customers into three subsets has lowered the average bit requirement for transmitting the credit risk status of the customers to 0.5944 bits. Lower entropy is good. This *entropy reduction* can be viewed as *information gain*, so that we have gained on average $H(T) - H_{\text{savings}}(T) = 0.9544 - 0.5944 = 0.36$ bits of information by using the *savings* partition. We will compare this to the information gained by the other candidate splits, and choose the split with the largest information gain as the optimal split for the root node.

For candidate split 2 (*assets*), two of the records have *high* assets, four of the records have *medium* assets, and two of the records have *low* assets, so we have $P_{\text{high}} = \frac{2}{8}$, $P_{\text{medium}} = \frac{4}{8}$, $P_{\text{low}} = \frac{2}{8}$. Both of the records with *high* assets are classified as good credit risks, which means that the entropy for *high* assets will be zero, just as it was for *medium savings* above.

Three of the records with *medium* assets are good credit risks and one is a bad credit risk, giving us entropy $-\frac{3}{4}\log_2\left(\frac{3}{4}\right) - \frac{1}{4}\log_2\left(\frac{1}{4}\right) = 0.8113$. And both of the records with *low* assets are bad credit risks, which results in the entropy for *low* assets equaling zero. Combining the entropies of these three subsets, using equation (6.2) and the proportions of the subsets P_i, we have $H_{\text{assets}}(T) = \frac{2}{8}(0) + \frac{4}{8}(0.8113) + \frac{2}{8}(0) = 0.4057$. The entropy for the *assets* split is lower than the entropy (0.5944) for the *savings* split, which indicates that the *assets* split contains less noise and is to be preferred over the *savings* split. This is measured directly using the information gain, as follows: $H(T) - H_{\text{assets}}(T) = 0.9544 - 0.4057 = 0.5487$ bits. This information gain of 0.5487 bits is larger than that for the *savings* split of 0.36 bits, verifying that the *assets* split is preferable.

While C4.5 partitions the categorical variables differently from CART, the partitions for the numerical variables are similar. Here we have four observed values for *income*: 25,000, 50,000, 75,000, and 100,000, which provide us with three thresholds for partitions, as shown in Table 6.6. For candidate split 3 from Table 6.6, $income \leq \$25{,}000$ versus $income > \$25{,}000$, three of the records have $income \leq \$25{,}000$, with the other five records having $income > \$25{,}000$, giving us $P_{\text{income} \leq \$25{,}000} = \frac{3}{8}$, $P_{\text{income} > \$25{,}000} = \frac{5}{8}$. Of the records with $income \leq \$25{,}000$, one is a good credit risk and two are bad, giving us the entropy for $income \leq \$25{,}000$ as $-\frac{1}{3}\log_2\left(\frac{1}{3}\right) - \frac{2}{3}\log_2\left(\frac{2}{3}\right) = 0.9183$. Four of the five records with $income > \$25{,}000$ are good credit risks, so that the entropy for $income > \$25{,}000$ is $-\frac{4}{5}\log_2\left(\frac{4}{5}\right) - \frac{1}{5}\log_2\left(\frac{1}{5}\right) = 0.7219$. Combining, we find the entropy for candidate split 3 to be $H_{\text{income} \leq \$25{,}000}(T) = \frac{3}{8}(0.9183) + \frac{5}{8}(0.7219) = 0.7946$. Then the information gain for this split is $H(T) - H_{\text{income} \leq \$25{,}000}(T) = 0.9544 - 0.7946 = 0.1588$ bits, which is our poorest choice yet.

For candidate split 4, $income \leq \$50{,}000$ versus $income > \$50{,}000$, two of the five records with $income \leq \$50{,}000$ are good credit risks, and three are bad, while all three of the records with $income > \$50{,}000$ are good credit risks. This gives us the entropy for candidate split 4 as

$$H_{\text{income} \leq \$50{,}000}(T) = \frac{5}{8}\left(-\frac{2}{5}\log_2\frac{2}{5} - \frac{3}{5}\log_2\frac{3}{5}\right) + \frac{3}{8}\left(-\frac{3}{3}\log_2\frac{3}{3} - \frac{0}{3}\log_2\frac{0}{3}\right) = 0.6069$$

The information gain for this split is thus $H(T) - H_{\text{income} \leq \$50,000}(T) = 0.9544 - 0.6069 = 0.3475$, which is not as good as for *assets*. Finally, for candidate split 5, *income* $\leq$ \$75,000 versus *income* $>$ \$75,000, four of the seven records with *income* $\leq$ \$75,000 are good credit risks, and three are bad, while the single record with *income* $>$ \$75,000 is a good credit risk. Thus, the entropy for candidate split 4 is

$$H_{\text{income} \leq \$75,000}(T) = \tfrac{7}{8}\left(-\tfrac{4}{7}\log_2 \tfrac{4}{7} - \tfrac{3}{7}\log_2 \tfrac{3}{7}\right) + \tfrac{1}{8}\left(-\tfrac{1}{1}\log_2 \tfrac{1}{1} - \tfrac{0}{1}\log_2 \tfrac{0}{1}\right)$$
$$= 0.8621$$

The information gain for this split is $H(T) - H_{\text{income} \leq \$75,000}(T) = 0.9544 - 0.8621 = 0.0923$, making this split the poorest of the five candidate splits.

Table 6.7 summarizes the information gain for each candidate split at the root node. Candidate split 2, *assets*, has the largest information gain, and so is chosen for the initial split by the C4.5 algorithm. Note that this choice for an optimal split concurs with the partition preferred by CART, which split on *assets* = *low* versus *assets* = {*medium, high*}. The partial decision tree resulting from C4.5's initial split is shown in Figure 6.6.

The initial split has resulted in the creation of two terminal leaf nodes and one new decision node. Since both records with *low assets* have bad credit risk, this classification has 100% confidence, and no further splits are required. Similarly for the two records with *high assets*. However, the four records at decision node *A* (*assets* = *medium*) contain both *good* and *bad* credit risks, so that further splitting is called for.

We proceed to determine the optimal split for decision node *A*, containing records 3, 4, 5, and 8, as indicated in Table 6.8. Because three of the four records are classified as *good credit risks*, with the remaining record classified as a *bad credit*

TABLE 6.7 Information Gain for Each Candidate Split at the Root Node

Candidate Split	Child Nodes	Information Gain (Entropy Reduction)
1	*Savings* = *low* *Savings* = *medium* *Savings* = *high*	0.36 bits
2	*Assets* = *low* *Assets* = *medium* *Assets* = *high*	0.5487 bits
3	*Income* $\leq$ \$25,000 *Income* $>$ \$25,000	0.1588 bits
4	*Income* $\leq$ \$50,000 *Income* $>$ \$50,000	0.3475 bits
5	*Income* $\leq$ \$75,000 *Income* $>$ \$75,000	0.0923 bits

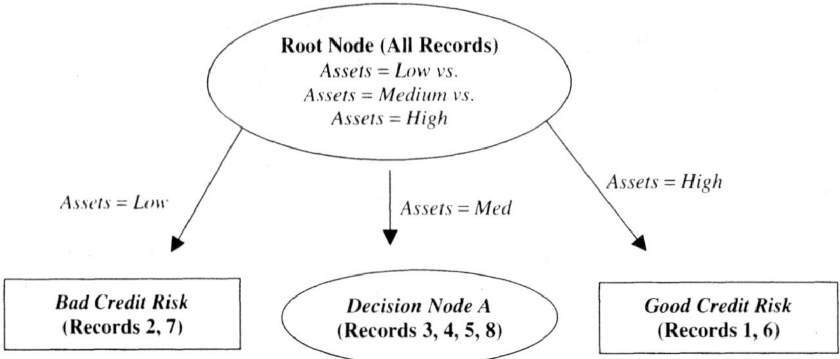

Figure 6.6 C4.5 concurs with CART in choosing *assets* for the initial partition.

risk, the entropy before splitting is

$$H(A) = -\sum_j p_j \log_2(p_j) = -\frac{3}{4}\log_2\left(\frac{3}{4}\right) - \frac{1}{4}\log_2\left(\frac{1}{4}\right) = 0.8113$$

The candidate splits for decision node A are shown in Table 6.9.

For candidate split 1, *savings*, the single record with *low* savings is a good credit risk, along with the two records with *medium* savings. Perhaps counterintuitively, the single record with *high* savings is a *bad* credit risk. So the entropy for each of these three classes equals zero, since the level of savings determines the credit risk completely. This also results in a combined entropy of zero for the *assets* split, $H_{\text{assets}}(A) = 0$, which is optimal for decision node A. The information gain for this split is thus $H(A) - H_{\text{assets}}(A) = 0.8113 - 0.0 = 0.8113$. This is, of course, the maximum information gain possible for decision node A. We therefore need not continue our calculations, since no other split can result in a greater information gain. As it happens, candidate split 3, *income* $\leq$ \$25,000 versus *income* $>$ \$25,000, also results in the maximal information gain, but again we arbitrarily select the first such split encountered, the *savings* split.

Figure 6.7 shows the form of the decision tree after the *savings* split. Note that this is the fully grown form, since all nodes are now leaf nodes, and C4.5 will grow no further nodes. Comparing the C4.5 tree in Figure 6.7 with the CART tree in Figure 6.4, we see that the $C4.5$ tree is "bushier," providing a greater breadth, while the CART tree is one level deeper. Both algorithms concur that *assets* is the most

TABLE 6.8 Records Available at Decision Node *A* for Classifying Credit Risk

Customer	Savings	Assets	Income ($1000s)	Credit Risk
3	High	Medium	25	Bad
4	Medium	Medium	50	Good
5	Low	Medium	100	Good
8	Medium	Medium	75	Good

TABLE 6.9 Candidate Splits at Decision Node *A*

Candidate Split	Child Nodes		
1	*Savings* = *low*	*Savings* = *medium*	*Savings* = *high*
3	*Income* ≤ \$25,000		*Income* > \$25,000
4	*Income* ≤ \$50,000		*Income* > \$50,000
5	*Income* ≤ \$75,000		*Income* > \$75,000

important variable (the root split) and that *savings* is also important. Finally, once the decision tree is fully grown, C4.5 engages in *pessimistic postpruning*. Interested readers may consult Kantardzic [4, p. 153].

DECISION RULES

One of the most attractive aspects of decision trees lies in their interpretability, especially with respect to the construction of *decision rules*. Decision rules can be constructed from a decision tree simply by traversing any given path from the root node to any leaf. The complete set of decision rules generated by a decision tree is equivalent (for classification purposes) to the decision tree itself. For example, from the decision tree in Figure 6.7, we may construct the decision rules given in Table 6.10.

Decision rules come in the form *if antecedent, then consequent*, as shown in Table 6.10. For decision rules, the antecedent consists of the attribute values from the branches taken by the particular path through the tree, while the consequent consists of the classification value for the target variable given by the particular leaf node.

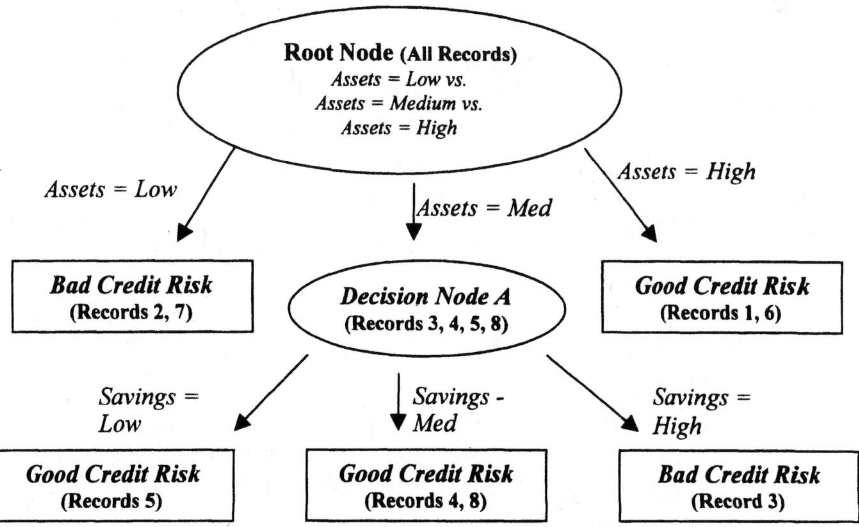

Figure 6.7 C4.5 Decision tree: fully grown form.

TABLE 6.10 Decision Rules Generated from Decision Tree in Figure 6.7

Antecedent	Consequent	Support	Confidence
If *assets* = *low*	then *bad credit risk*.	$\frac{2}{8}$	1.00
If *assets* = *high*	then *good credit risk*.	$\frac{2}{8}$	1.00
If *assets* = *medium* and *savings* = *low*	then *good credit risk*.	$\frac{1}{8}$	1.00
If *assets* = *medium* and *savings* = *medium*	then *good credit risk*.	$\frac{2}{8}$	1.00
If *assets* = *medium* and *savings* = *high*	then *bad credit risk*.	$\frac{1}{8}$	1.00

The *support* of the decision rule refers to the proportion of records in the data set that rest in that particular terminal leaf node. The *confidence* of the rule refers to the proportion of records in the leaf node for which the decision rule is true. In this small example, all of our leaf nodes are pure, resulting in perfect confidence levels of 100% = 1.00. In real-world examples, such as in the next section, one cannot expect such high confidence levels.

COMPARISON OF THE C5.0 AND CART ALGORITHMS APPLIED TO REAL DATA

Next, we apply decision tree analysis using Clementine on a real-world data set. The data set *adult* was abstracted from U.S. census data by Kohavi [5] and is available online from the University of California at Irvine Machine Learning Repository [6]. Here we are interested in classifying whether or not a person's income is less than $50,000, based on the following set of predictor fields.

- Numerical variables

  Age

  Years of education

  Capital gains

  Capital losses

  Hours worked per week

- Categorical variables

  Race

  Gender

  Work class

  Marital status

The numerical variables were normalized so that all values ranged between zero and 1. Some collapsing of low-frequency classes was carried out on the *work class* and *marital status* categories. Clementine was used to compare the C5.0 algorithm (an update of the C4.5 algorithm) with CART, examining a training set of 24,986 records. The decision tree produced by the CART algorithm is shown in Figure 6.8.

```
Marital_Status in ["Married"] [Mode: <=50K. ] (11,781)
    education-num < 0.833333333333333 [Mode: <=50K. ] (8,292)
        capital-gain < 0.0509555095550955 [Mode: <=50K. ] (7,890)
            capital-loss < 0.411730945821855 [Mode: <=50K. ] (7,611)
                education-num < 0.566666666666667 [Mode: <=50K. ] ⇨ <=50K. (1,308, 0.906)
                education-num >= 0.566666666666667 [Mode: <=50K. ] ⇨ <=50K. (6,303, 0.69)
            capital-loss >= 0.411730945821855 [Mode: >50K. ] ⇨ >50K. (279, 0.731)
        capital-gain >= 0.0509555095550955 [Mode: >50K. ] ⇨ >50K. (402, 0.975)
    education-num >= 0.833333333333333 [Mode: >50K. ] (3,489)
        capital-gain < 0.0509555095550955 [Mode: >50K. ] (2,970)
            capital-loss < 0.411845730027548 [Mode: >50K. ] (2,669)
                hours-per-week < 0.331632653061224 [Mode: <=50K. ] ⇨ <=50K. (251, 0.629)
                hours-per-week >= 0.331632653061224 [Mode: >50K. ] ⇨ >50K. (2,418, 0.649)
            capital-loss >= 0.411845730027548 [Mode: >50K. ] ⇨ >50K. (301, 0.96)
        capital-gain >= 0.0509555095550955 [Mode: >50K. ] ⇨ >50K. (519, 0.994)
Marital_Status in ["Divorced" "Never_married" "Separated" "Widowed"] [Mode: <=50K. ] ⇨ <=50K. (13,205, 0.936)
```

Figure 6.8 CART decision tree for the adult data set.

Here, the tree structure is displayed horizontally, with the root node at the left and the leaf nodes on the right. For the CART algorithm, the root node split is on *marital status*, with a binary split separating married persons from all others (*Marital_Status in [“Divorced” “Never_married” “Separated” “Widowed”]*). That is, this particular split on *marital status* maximized the CART split selection criterion [equation (6.1)]:

$$\Phi(s|t) = 2P_L P_R \sum_{j=1}^{\#\text{ classes}} \left|P(j|t_L) - P(j|t_R)\right|$$

Note that the mode classification for each branch is $\leq$50,000. The married branch leads to a decision node, with several further splits downstream. However, the nonmarried branch is a leaf node, with a classification of $\leq$50,000 for the 13,205 such records, with 93.6% confidence. In other words, of the 13,205 persons in the data set who are not presently married, 93.6% of them have incomes below \$50,000.

The root node split is considered to indicate the most important single variable for classifying income. Note that the split on the *Marital_Status* attribute is binary, as are all CART splits on categorical variables. All the other splits in the full CART decision tree shown in Figure 6.8 are on numerical variables. The next decision node is *education-num*, representing the normalized number of years of education. The split occurs at *education-num* $<$0.8333 (mode $\leq$50,000) versus *education-num* $>$0.8333 (mode $>$50,000). However, what is the actual number of years of education that the normalized value of 0.8333 represents? The normalization, carried out automatically using Insightful Miner, was of the form

$$X^* = \frac{X}{\text{range}(X)} = \frac{X}{\max(X) - \min(X)}$$

a variant of min–max normalization. Therefore, *denormalization* is required to identify the original field values. Years of education ranged from 16 (maximum) to 1 (minimum), for a range of 15. Therefore, denormalizing, we have $X = \text{range}(X) \cdot X^* = 15(0.8\overline{333}) = 12.5$. Thus, the split occurs right at 12.5 years of education. Those with at least some college education tend to have higher incomes than those who do not.

Interestingly, for both education groups, *capital gains* and *capital loss* represent the next two most important decision nodes. Finally, for the lower-education group, the last split is again on *education-num*, whereas for the higher-education group, the last split is on *hours-per-week*.

Now, will the information-gain splitting criterion and the other characteristics of the C5.0 algorithm lead to a decision tree that is substantially different from or largely similar to the tree derived using CART's splitting criteria? Compare the CART decision tree above with Clementine's C5.0 decision tree of the same data displayed in Figure 6.9.

Differences emerge immediately at the root node. Here, the root split is on the *capital-gain* attribute, with the split occurring at the relatively low normalized level of 0.0685. Since the range of capital gains in this data set is \$99,999 (maximum = 99,999, minimum = 0), this is denormalized as $X = \text{range}(X) \cdot X^* = 99{,}999(0.0685) = \$6850$. More than half of those with capital gains greater than \$6850 have incomes above \$50,000, whereas more than half of those with capital gains of less than \$6850 have incomes below \$50,000. This is the split that was chosen

```
capital-gain <= 0.068490997 [Mode: <=50K.] (23,921)
  capital-loss <= 0.41689599 [Mode: <=50K.] (23,165)
    Marital_Status = Divorced [Mode: <=50K.] ⇨ <=50K. (3,287, 0.925)
    Marital_Status = Married [Mode: <=50K.] (10,365)
      capital-gain <= 0.050131001 [Mode: <=50K.] (10,280)
      capital-gain > 0.050131001 [Mode: >50K.] (85)
    Marital_Status = Never_married [Mode: <=50K.] (8,017)
      education-num <= 0.80000001 [Mode: <=50K.] ⇨ <=50K. (6,271, 0.989)
      education-num > 0.80000001 [Mode: <=50K.] (1,746)
    Marital_Status = Separated [Mode: <=50K.] (761)
      education-num <= 0.80000001 [Mode: <=50K.] ⇨ <=50K. (668, 0.979)
      education-num > 0.80000001 [Mode: <=50K.] (93)
    Marital_Status = Widowed [Mode: <=50K.] ⇨ <=50K. (735, 0.948)
  capital-loss > 0.41689599 [Mode: >50K.] (756)
    capital-loss <= 0.453857 [Mode: >50K.] (487)
      Marital_Status = Divorced [Mode: <=50K.] ⇨ <=50K. (15, 1.0)
      Marital_Status = Married [Mode: >50K.] ⇨ >50K. (439, 0.977)
      Marital_Status = Never_married [Mode: <=50K.] ⇨ <=50K. (27, 1.0)
      Marital_Status = Separated [Mode: <=50K.] ⇨ <=50K. (4, 1.0)
      Marital_Status = Widowed [Mode: <=50K.] ⇨ <=50K. (2, 1.0)
    capital-loss > 0.453857 [Mode: <=50K.] (269)
      capital-loss <= 0.53994501 [Mode: <=50K.] (168)
      capital-loss > 0.53994501 [Mode: >50K.] (101)
capital-gain > 0.068490997 [Mode: >50K.] (1,065)
  hours-per-week <= 0.35714301 [Mode: >50K.] (92)
    age <= 0.369863 [Mode: <=50K.] ⇨ <=50K. (6, 0.833)
    age > 0.369863 [Mode: >50K.] ⇨ >50K. (86, 0.965)
  hours-per-week > 0.35714301 [Mode: >50K.] ⇨ >50K. (973, 0.99)
```

Figure 6.9 C5.0 decision tree for the adult data set.

by the information-gain criterion as the optimal split among all possible splits over all fields. Note, however, that there are 23 times more records in the low-capital-gains category than in the high-capital-gains category (23,921 versus 1065 records).

For records with lower capital gains, the second split occurs on *capital loss*, with a pattern similar to the earlier split on capital gains. Most people (23,165 records) had low capital loss, and most of these have incomes below $50,000. Most of the few (756 records) who had higher capital loss had incomes above $50,000.

For records with low capital gains and low capital loss, consider the next split, which is made on *marital status*. Note that C5.0 provides a separate branch for each field value, whereas CART was restricted to binary splits. A possible drawback of C5.0's strategy for splitting categorical variables is that it may lead to an overly bushy tree, with many leaf nodes containing few records. In fact, the decision tree displayed in Figure 6.9 is only an excerpt from the much larger tree provided by the software.

To avoid this problem, analysts may alter the algorithm's settings to require a certain minimum number of records to be passed to child decision nodes. Figure 6.10 shows a C5.0 decision tree from Clementine on the same data, this time requiring each decision node to have at least 300 records. In general, a business or research decision may be rendered regarding the minimum number of records considered to be actionable. Figure 6.10 represents the entire tree.

Again, capital gains represents the root node split, with the split occurring at the same value. This time, however, the high-capital-gains branch leads directly to a leaf node, containing 1065 records, and predicting with 98.3 confidence that the proper classification for these persons is income greater than $50,000. For the other records,

```
capital-gain <= 0.068490997 [Mode: <=50K.] (23,921)
  capital-loss <= 0.41689599 [Mode: <=50K.] (23,165)
    Marital_Status = Divorced [Mode: <=50K.] ⇨ <=50K. (3,287, 0.925)
    Marital_Status = Married [Mode: <=50K.] (10,365)
      capital-gain <= 0.050131001 [Mode: <=50K.] (10,280)
        education-num <= 0.80000001 [Mode: <=50K.] (7,611)
          capital-gain <= 0.044160001 [Mode: <=50K.] (7,564)
            capital-gain <= 0.04101 [Mode: <=50K.] ⇨ <=50K. (7,519, 0.729)
            capital-gain > 0.04101 [Mode: >50K.] ⇨ >50K. (45, 0.822)
          capital-gain > 0.044160001 [Mode: <=50K.] ⇨ <=50K. (47, 1.0)
        education-num > 0.80000001 [Mode: >50K.] (2,669)
          hours-per-week <= 0.35714301 [Mode: <=50K.] ⇨ <=50K. (330, 0.57)
          hours-per-week > 0.35714301 [Mode: >50K.] ⇨ >50K. (2,339, 0.65)
      capital-gain > 0.050131001 [Mode: >50K.] ⇨ >50K. (85, 0.953)
    Marital_Status = Never_married [Mode: <=50K.] ⇨ <=50K. (8,017, 0.967)
    Marital_Status = Separated [Mode: <=50K.] ⇨ <=50K. (761, 0.95)
    Marital_Status = Widowed [Mode: <=50K.] ⇨ <=50K. (735, 0.948)
  capital-loss > 0.41689599 [Mode: >50K.] ⇨ >50K. (756, 0.708)
capital-gain > 0.068490997 [Mode: >50K.] ⇨ >50K. (1,065, 0.983)
```

Figure 6.10 C5.0 decision tree with a required minimum number of records at each decision node.

the second split is again on the same value of the same attribute as earlier, capital loss. For high capital loss, this leads directly to a leaf node containing 756 records predicting high income with only 70.8% confidence.

For those with low capital gains and low capital loss, the third split is again marital status, with a separate branch for each field value. Note that for all values of the marital status field *except* "married," these branches lead directly to child nodes predicting income of at most $50,000 with various high values of confidence. For married persons, further splits are considered.

Although the CART and C5.0 decision trees do not agree in the details, we may nevertheless glean useful information from the broad areas of agreement between them. For example, the most important variables are clearly marital status, education, capital gains, capital loss, and perhaps hours per week. Both models agree that these fields are important, but disagree as to the ordering of their importance. Much more modeling analysis may be called for.

For a soup-to-nuts application of decision trees to a real-world data set, from data preparation through model building and decision rule generation, see Reference 7.

REFERENCES

1. Leo Breiman, Jerome Friedman, Richard Olshen, and Charles Stone, *Classification and Regression Trees*, Chapman & Hall/CRC Press, Boca Raton, FL, 1984.
2. Ruby L. Kennedy, Yuchun Lee, Benjamin Van Roy, Christopher D. Reed, and Richard P. Lippman, *Solving Data Mining Problems through Pattern Recognition*, Pearson Education, Upper Saddle River, NJ, 1995.
3. J. Ross Quinlan, *C4.5: Programs for Machine Learning*, Morgan Kaufmann, San Francisco, CA, 1992.
4. Mehmed Kantardzic, *Data Mining: Concepts, Models, Methods, and Algorithms*, Wiley-Interscience, Hoboken, NJ, 2003.
5. Ronny Kohavi, Scaling up the accuracy of naive Bayes classifiers: A decision tree hybrid, *Proceedings of the 2nd International Conference on Knowledge Discovery and Data Mining*, Portland, OR, 1996.
6. C. L. Blake and C. J. Merz, UCI Repository of Machine Learning Databases, `http://www.ics.uci.edu/~mlearn/MLRepository.html`, University of California, Department of Information and Computer Science, Irvine, CA, 1998.
7. Daniel Larose, *Data Mining Methods and Models*, Wiley-Interscience, Hoboken, NJ (to appear 2005).

EXERCISES

1. Describe the possible situations when no further splits can be made at a decision node.

2. Suppose that our target variable is continuous numeric. Can we apply decision trees directly to classify it? How can we work around this?

3. True or false: Decision trees seek to form leaf nodes to maximize heterogeneity in each node.

4. Discuss the benefits and drawbacks of a binary tree versus a bushier tree.

TABLE E6.4 Decision Tree Data

Occupation	Gender	Age	Salary
Service	Female	45	$48,000
	Male	25	$25,000
	Male	33	$35,000
Management	Male	25	$45,000
	Female	35	$65,000
	Male	26	$45,000
	Female	45	$70,000
Sales	Female	40	$50,000
	Male	30	$40,000
Staff	Female	50	$40,000
	Male	25	$25,000

Consider the data in Table E6.4. The target variable is salary. Start by discretizing salary as follows:

- Less than $35,000 Level 1
- $35,000 to less than $45,000 Level 2
- $45,000 to less than $55,000 Level 3
- Above $55,000 Level 4

5. Construct a classification and regression tree to classify *salary* based on the other variables. Do as much as you can by hand, before turning to the software.

6. Construct a C4.5 decision tree to classify *salary* based on the other variables. Do as much as you can by hand, before turning to the software.

7. Compare the two decision trees and discuss the benefits and drawbacks of each.

8. Generate the full set of decision rules for the CART decision tree.

9. Generate the full set of decision rules for the C4.5 decision tree.

10. Compare the two sets of decision rules and discuss the benefits and drawbacks of each.

Hands-on Analysis

For the following exercises, use the *churn* data set available at the book series Web site. Normalize the numerical data and deal with the correlated variables.

11. Generate a CART decision tree.

12. Generate a C4.5-type decision tree.

13. Compare the two decision trees and discuss the benefits and drawbacks of each.

14. Generate the full set of decision rules for the CART decision tree.

15. Generate the full set of decision rules for the C4.5 decision tree.

16. Compare the two sets of decision rules and discuss the benefits and drawbacks of each.

CHAPTER 7

NEURAL NETWORKS

INPUT AND OUTPUT ENCODING

NEURAL NETWORKS FOR ESTIMATION AND PREDICTION

SIMPLE EXAMPLE OF A NEURAL NETWORK

SIGMOID ACTIVATION FUNCTION

BACK-PROPAGATION

GRADIENT DESCENT METHOD

BACK-PROPAGATION RULES

EXAMPLE OF BACK-PROPAGATION

TERMINATION CRITERIA

LEARNING RATE

MOMENTUM TERM

SENSITIVITY ANALYSIS

APPLICATION OF NEURAL NETWORK MODELING

The inspiration for neural networks was the recognition that complex learning systems in animal brains consisted of closely interconnected sets of neurons. Although a particular neuron may be relatively simple in structure, dense networks of interconnected neurons could perform complex learning tasks such as classification and pattern recognition. The human brain, for example, contains approximately 10^{11} neurons, each connected on average to $10,000$ other neurons, making a total of $1{,}000{,}000{,}000{,}000{,}000 = 10^{15}$ synaptic connections. *Artificial neural networks* (hereafter, *neural networks*) represent an attempt at a very basic level to imitate the type of nonlinear learning that occurs in the networks of neurons found in nature.

As shown in Figure 7.1, a real neuron uses dendrites to gather inputs from other neurons and combines the input information, generating a nonlinear response ("firing") when some threshold is reached, which it sends to other neurons using the axon. Figure 7.1 also shows an artificial neuron model used in most neural networks.

Discovering Knowledge in Data: An Introduction to Data Mining, By Daniel T. Larose
ISBN 0-471-66657-2

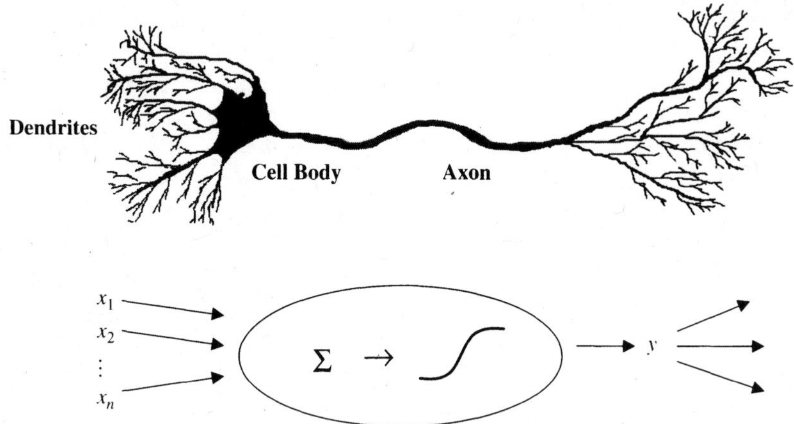

Figure 7.1 Real neuron and artificial neuron model. (Sketch of neuron courtesy of Chantal Larose.)

The inputs (x_i) are collected from upstream neurons (or the data set) and combined through a combination function such as summation (Σ), which is then input into a (usually nonlinear) activation function to produce an output response (y), which is then channeled downstream to other neurons.

What types of problems are appropriate for neural networks? One of the advantages of using neural networks is that they are quite robust with respect to noisy data. Because the network contains many nodes (artificial neurons), with weights assigned to each connection, the network can learn to work around these uninformative (or even erroneous) examples in the data set. However, unlike decision trees, which produce intuitive rules that are understandable to nonspecialists, neural networks are relatively opaque to human interpretation, as we shall see. Also, neural networks usually require longer training times than decision trees, often extending into several hours.

INPUT AND OUTPUT ENCODING

One possible drawback of neural networks is that all attribute values must be encoded in a standardized manner, taking values between zero and 1, even for categorical variables. Later, when we examine the details of the back-propagation algorithm, we shall understand why this is necessary. For now, however, how does one go about standardizing all the attribute values?

For continuous variables, this is not a problem, as we discussed in Chapter 2. We may simply apply the *min–max normalization*:

$$X^* = \frac{X - \min(X)}{\text{range}(X)} = \frac{X - \min(X)}{\max(X) - \min(X)}$$

This works well as long as the minimum and maximum values are known and all potential new data are bounded between them. Neural networks are somewhat robust to minor violations of these boundaries. If more serious violations are expected, certain ad hoc solutions may be adopted, such as rejecting values that are outside the boundaries, or assigning such values to either the minimum or maximum value.

Categorical variables are more problematical, as might be expected. If the number of possible categories is not too large, one may use *indicator (flag) variables*. For example, many data sets contain a *gender attribute*, containing values *female*, *male*, and *unknown*. Since the neural network could not handle these attribute values in their present form, we could, instead, create indicator variables for *female* and *male*. Each record would contain values for each of these two indicator variables. Records for females would have a value of 1 for *female* and 0 for *male*, while records for males would have a value of 0 for *female* and 1 for *male*. Records for persons of unknown gender would have values of 0 for *female* and 0 for *male*. In general, categorical variables with k classes may be translated into $k - 1$ indicator variables, as long as the definition of the indicators is clearly defined.

Be wary of recoding unordered categorical variables into a single variable with a range between zero and 1. For example, suppose that the data set contains information on a *marital status* attribute. Suppose that we code the attribute values *divorced*, *married*, *separated*, *single*, *widowed*, and *unknown*, as 0.0, 0.2, 0.4, 0.6, 0.8, and 1.0, respectively. Then this coding implies, for example, that *divorced* is "closer" to *married* than it is to *separated*, and so on. The neural network would be aware only of the numerical values in the *marital status* field, not of their preencoded meanings, and would thus be naive of their true meaning. Spurious and meaningless findings may result.

With respect to output, we shall see that neural network output nodes always return a continuous value between zero and 1 as output. How can we use such continuous output for classification?

Many classification problems have a dichotomous result, an up-or-down decision, with only two possible outcomes. For example, "Is this customer about to leave our company's service?" For dichotomous classification problems, one option is to use a single output node (such as in Figure 7.2), with a threshold value set a priori which would separate the classes, such as "leave" or "stay." For example, with the threshold of "leave if $output \geq 0.67$," an output of 0.72 from the output node would classify that record as likely to leave the company's service.

Single output nodes may also be used when the classes are clearly ordered. For example, suppose that we would like to classify elementary school reading prowess based on a certain set of student attributes. Then we may be able to define the thresholds as follows:

- If $0 \leq output < 0.25$, classify *first-grade reading level*.
- If $0.25 \leq output < 0.50$, classify *second-grade reading level*.
- If $0.50 \leq output < 0.75$, classify *third-grade reading level*.
- If $output > 0.75$, classify *fourth-grade reading level*.

Fine-tuning of the thresholds may be required, tempered by experience and the judgment of domain experts.

Not all classification problems, however, are soluble using a single output node only. For instance, suppose that we have several unordered categories in our target variable, as, for example, with the *marital status* variable above. In this case we would choose to adopt *1-of-n output encoding*, where one output node is used for each possible category of the target variable. For example, if *marital status* was our target variable, the network would have six output nodes in the output layer, one for each of the six classes *divorced*, *married*, *separated*, *single*, *widowed*, and *unknown*. The output node with the highest value is then chosen as the classification for that particular record.

One benefit of using 1-of-*n* output encoding is that it provides a measure of confidence in the classification, in the form of the difference between the highest-value output node and the second-highest-value output node. Classifications with low confidence (small difference in node output values) can be flagged for further clarification.

NEURAL NETWORKS FOR ESTIMATION AND PREDICTION

Clearly, since neural networks produce continuous output, they may quite naturally be used for estimation and prediction. Suppose, for example, that we are interested in predicting the price of a particular stock three months in the future. Presumably, we would have encoded price information using the min–max normalization above. However, the neural network would output a value between zero and 1, which (one would hope) does not represent the predicted price of the stock.

Rather, the min–max normalization needs to be inverted, so that the neural network output can be understood on the scale of the stock prices. In general, this denormalization is as follows:

$$\text{prediction} = \text{output(data range)} + \text{minimum}$$

where *output* represents the neural network output in the (0,1) range, *data range* represents the range of the original attribute values on the nonnormalized scale, and *minimum* represents the smallest attribute value on the nonnormalized scale. For example, suppose that the stock prices ranged from \$20 to \$30 and that the network output was 0.69. Then the predicted stock price in three months is

$$\text{prediction} = \text{output(data range)} + \text{minimum} = 0.69(\$10) + \$20 = \$26.90$$

SIMPLE EXAMPLE OF A NEURAL NETWORK

Let us examine the simple neural network shown in Figure 7.2. A neural network consists of a *layered, feedforward, completely connected* network of artificial neurons, or *nodes*. The *feedforward* nature of the network restricts the network to a single direction of flow and does not allow looping or cycling. The neural network is composed of two or more layers, although most networks consist of three layers: an *input layer*,

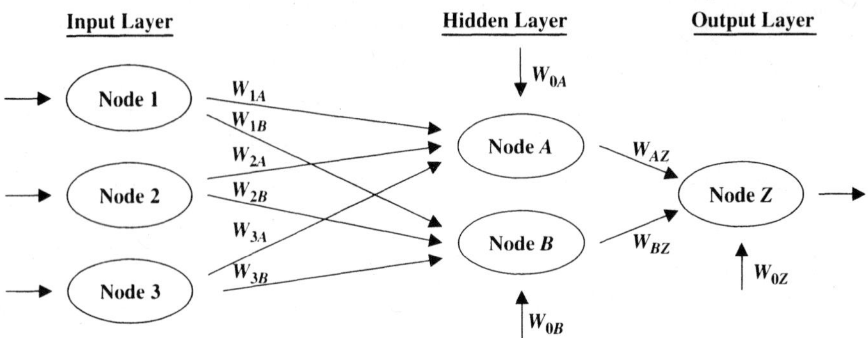

Figure 7.2 Simple neural network.

a *hidden layer*, and an *output layer*. There may be more than one hidden layer, although most networks contain only one, which is sufficient for most purposes. The neural network is *completely connected*, meaning that every node in a given layer is connected to every node in the next layer, although not to other nodes in the same layer. Each connection between nodes has a weight (e.g., W_{1A}) associated with it. At initialization, these weights are randomly assigned to values between zero and 1.

The number of input nodes usually depends on the number and type of attributes in the data set. The number of hidden layers, and the number of nodes in each hidden layer, are both configurable by the user. One may have more than one node in the output layer, depending on the particular classification task at hand.

How many nodes should one have in the hidden layer? Since more nodes in the hidden layer increases the power and flexibility of the network for identifying complex patterns, one might be tempted to have a large number of nodes in the hidden layer. On the other hand, an overly large hidden layer leads to overfitting, memorizing the training set at the expense of generalizability to the validation set. If overfitting is occurring, one may consider reducing the number of nodes in the hidden layer; conversely, if the training accuracy is unacceptably low, one may consider increasing the number of nodes in the hidden layer.

The input layer accepts inputs from the data set, such as attribute values, and simply passes these values along to the hidden layer without further processing. Thus, the nodes in the input layer do not share the detailed node structure that the hidden layer nodes and the output layer nodes share.

We will investigate the structure of hidden layer nodes and output layer nodes using the sample data provided in Table 7.1. First, a *combination function* (usually

TABLE 7.1 Data Inputs and Initial Values for Neural Network Weights

$x_0 = 1.0$	$W_{0A} = 0.5$	$W_{0B} = 0.7$	$W_{0Z} = 0.5$
$x_1 = 0.4$	$W_{1A} = 0.6$	$W_{1B} = 0.9$	$W_{AZ} = 0.9$
$x_2 = 0.2$	$W_{2A} = 0.8$	$W_{2B} = 0.8$	$W_{BZ} = 0.9$
$x_3 = 0.7$	$W_{3A} = 0.6$	$W_{3B} = 0.4$	

summation, Σ) produces a linear combination of the node inputs and the connection weights into a single scalar value, which we will term *net*. Thus, for a given node j,

$$\text{net}_j = \sum_i W_{ij}x_{ij} = W_{0j}x_{0j} + W_{1j}x_{1j} + \cdots + W_{Ij}x_{Ij}$$

where x_{ij} represents the ith input to node j, W_{ij} represents the weight associated with the ith input to node j, and there are $I + 1$ inputs to node j. Note that $x_1, x_2, \ldots, x_I$ represent inputs from upstream nodes, while x_0 represents a *constant* input, analogous to the constant factor in regression models, which by convention uniquely takes the value $x_{0j} = 1$. Thus, each hidden layer or output layer node j contains an "extra" input equal to a particular weight $W_{0j}x_{0j} = W_{0j}$, such as W_{0B} for node B.

For example, for node A in the hidden layer, we have

$$\begin{aligned}\text{net}_A &= \sum_i W_{iA}x_{iA} = W_{0A}(1) + W_{1A}x_{1A} + W_{2A}x_{2A} + W_{3A}x_{3A} \\ &= 0.5 + 0.6(0.4) + 0.8(0.2) + 0.6(0.7) = 1.32\end{aligned}$$

Within node A, this combination function $\text{net}_A = 1.32$ is then used as an input to an activation function. In biological neurons, signals are sent between neurons when the combination of inputs to a particular neuron cross a certain threshold, and the neuron "fires." This is nonlinear behavior, since the firing response is not necessarily linearly related to the increment in input stimulation. Artificial neural networks model this behavior through a nonlinear activation function.

The most common activation function is the sigmoid function:

$$y = \frac{1}{1 + e^{-x}}$$

where e is base of natural logarithms, equal to about 2.718281828. Thus, within node A, the activation would take $\text{net}_A = 1.32$ as input to the sigmoid activation function, and produce an output value of $y = 1/(1 + e^{-1.32}) = 0.7892$. Node A's work is done (for the moment), and this output value would then be passed along the connection to the output node Z, where it would form (via another linear combination) a component of net_Z.

But before we can compute net_Z, we need to find the contribution of node B. From the values in Table 7.1, we have

$$\begin{aligned}\text{net}_B &= \sum_i W_{iB}x_{iB} = W_{0B}(1) + W_{1B}x_{1B} + W_{2B}x_{2B} + W_{3B}x_{3B} \\ &= 0.7 + 0.9(0.4) + 0.8(0.2) + 0.4(0.7) = 1.5\end{aligned}$$

Then

$$f(\text{net}_B) = \frac{1}{1 + e^{-1.5}} = 0.8176$$

Node Z then combines these outputs from nodes A and B, through net_Z, a weighted sum, using the weights associated with the connections between these nodes. Note that the inputs x_i to node Z are not data attribute values but the outputs from the sigmoid functions from upstream nodes:

$$\text{net}_Z = \sum_i W_{iZ}x_{iZ} = W_{0Z}(1) + W_{AZ}x_{AZ} + W_{BZ}x_{BZ}$$
$$= 0.5 + 0.9(0.7892) + 0.9(0.8176) = 1.9461$$

Finally, net_Z is input into the sigmoid activation function in node Z, resulting in

$$f(\text{net}_Z) = \frac{1}{1 + e^{-1.9461}} = 0.8750$$

This value of 0.8750 is the *output* from the neural network for this first pass through the network, and represents the value predicted for the target variable for the first observation.

SIGMOID ACTIVATION FUNCTION

Why use the sigmoid function? Because it combines nearly linear behavior, curvilinear behavior, and nearly constant behavior, depending on the value of the input. Figure 7.3 shows the graph of the sigmoid function $y = f(x) = 1/(1 + e^{-x})$, for $-5 < x < 5$ [although $f(x)$ may theoretically take any real-valued input]. Through much of the center of the domain of the input x (e.g., $-1 < x < 1$), the behavior of $f(x)$ is nearly linear. As the input moves away from the center, $f(x)$ becomes curvilinear. By the time the input reaches extreme values, $f(x)$ becomes nearly constant.

Moderate increments in the value of x produce varying increments in the value of $f(x)$, depending on the location of x. Near the center, moderate increments in the value of x produce moderate increments in the value of $f(x)$; however, near the extremes, moderate increments in the value of x produce tiny increments in the value of $f(x)$. The sigmoid function is sometimes called a *squashing function*, since it takes any real-valued input and returns an output bounded between zero and 1.

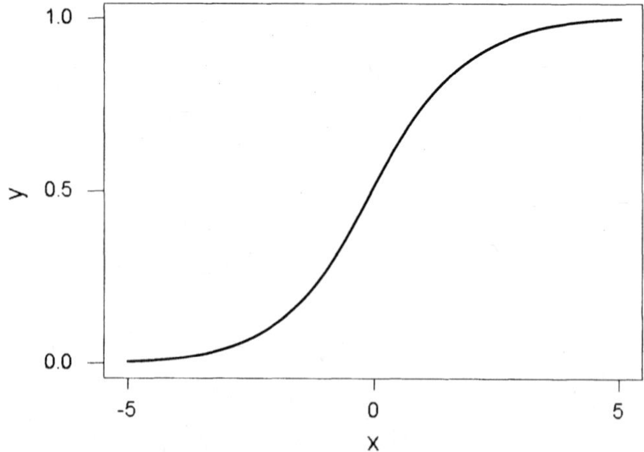

Figure 7.3 Graph of the sigmoid function $y = f(x) = 1/(1 + e^{-x})$.

BACK-PROPAGATION

How does the neural network learn? Neural networks represent a supervised learning method, requiring a large training set of complete records, including the target variable. As each observation from the training set is processed through the network, an output value is produced from the output node (assuming that we have only one output node, as in Figure 7.2). This output value is then compared to the actual value of the target variable for this training set observation, and the error (actual – output) is calculated. This prediction error is analogous to the residuals in regression models. To measure how well the output predictions fit the actual target values, most neural network models use the sum of squared errors:

$$\text{SSE} = \sum_{\text{records}} \sum_{\text{output nodes}} (\text{actual} - \text{output})^2$$

where the squared prediction errors are summed over all the output nodes and over all the records in the training set.

The problem is therefore to construct a set of model weights that will minimize the SSE. In this way, the weights are analogous to the parameters of a regression model. The "true" values for the weights that will minimize SSE are unknown, and our task is to estimate them, given the data. However, due to the nonlinear nature of the sigmoid functions permeating the network, there exists no closed-form solution for minimizing SSE as exists for least-squares regression.

GRADIENT DESCENT METHOD

We must therefore turn to optimization methods, specifically gradient-descent methods, to help us find the set of weights that will minimize SSE. Suppose that we have a set (vector) of m weights $\mathbf{w} = w_0, w_1, w_2, \ldots, w_m$ in our neural network model and we wish to find the values for each of these weights that, together, minimize SSE. We can use the gradient descent method, which *gives us the direction that we should adjust the weights* in order to decrease SSE. The gradient of SSE with respect to the vector of weights $\mathbf{w}$ is the vector derivative:

$$\nabla \text{SSE}(\mathbf{w}) = \left[\frac{\partial \text{SSE}}{\partial w_0}, \frac{\partial \text{SSE}}{\partial w_1}, \ldots, \frac{\partial \text{SSE}}{\partial w_m} \right]$$

that is, the vector of partial derivatives of SSE with respect to each of the weights.

To illustrate how gradient descent works, let us consider the case where there is only a single weight w_1. Consider Figure 7.4, which plots the error SSE against the range of values for w_1. We would prefer values of w_1 that would minimize the SSE. The optimal value for the weight w_1 is indicated as w_1^*. We would like to develop a rule that would help us move our current value of w_1 closer to the optimal value w_1^* as follows: $w_{\text{new}} = w_{\text{current}} + \Delta w_{\text{current}}$, where $\Delta w_{\text{current}}$ is the "change in the current location of w."

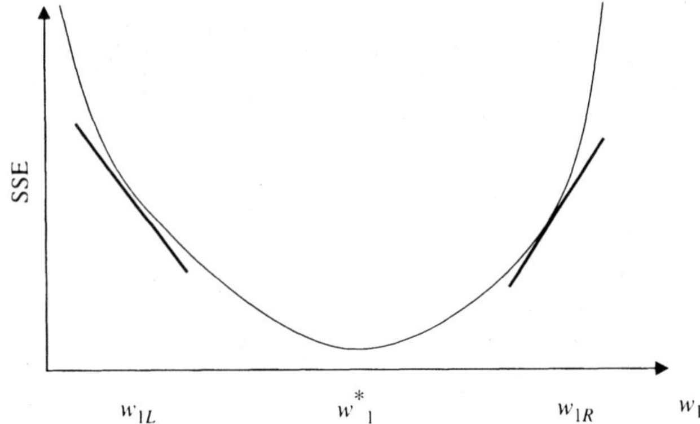

Figure 7.4 Using the slope of SSE with respect to w_1 to find weight adjustment direction.

Now, suppose that our current weight value w_{current} is near w_{1L}. Then we would like to *increase* our current weight value to bring it closer to the optimal value w_1^*. On the other hand, if our current weight value w_{current} were near w_{1R}, we would instead prefer to *decrease* its value, to bring it closer to the optimal value w_1^*. Now the derivative $\partial\text{SSE}/\partial w_1$ is simply the slope of the SSE curve at w_1. For values of w_1 close to w_{1L}, this slope is negative, and for values of w_1 close to w_{1R}, this slope is positive. Hence, the direction for adjusting w_{current} is the negative of the sign of the derivative of SSE at w_{current}, that is, $-\text{sign}(\partial\text{SSE}/\partial w_{\text{current}})$.

Now, how far should w_{current} be adjusted in the direction of $-\text{sign}\,(\partial\text{SSE}/\partial w_{\text{current}})$? Suppose that we use the magnitude of the derivative of SSE at w_{current}. When the curve is steep, the adjustment will be large, since the slope is greater in magnitude at those points. When the curve nearly flat, the adjustment will be smaller, due to less slope. Finally, the derivative is multiplied by a positive constant η (Greek lowercase eta), called the *learning rate*, with values ranging between zero and 1. (We discuss the role of η in more detail below.) The resulting form of $\Delta w_{\text{current}}$ is as follows: $\Delta w_{\text{current}} = -\eta(\partial\text{SSE}/\partial w_{\text{current}})$, meaning that the change in the current weight value equals negative a small constant times the slope of the error function at w_{current}.

BACK-PROPAGATION RULES

The back-propagation algorithm takes the prediction error (actual − output) for a particular record and percolates the error back through the network, assigning partitioned responsibility for the error to the various connections. The weights on these connections are then adjusted to decrease the error, using gradient descent.

Using the sigmoid activation function and gradient descent, Mitchell [1] derives the back-propagation rules as follows:

$$w_{ij,\text{new}} = w_{ij,\text{current}} + \Delta w_{ij} \qquad \text{where} \quad \Delta w_{ij} = \eta\delta_j x_{ij}$$

Now we know that η represents the learning rate and x_{ij} signifies the ith input to node j, but what does δ_j represent? The component δ_j represents the *responsibility* for a particular error belonging to node j. The error responsibility is computed using the partial derivative of the sigmoid function with respect to net_j and takes the following forms, depending on whether the node in question lies in the output layer or the hidden layer:

$$\delta_j = \begin{cases} \text{output}_j(1 - \text{output}_j)(\text{actual}_j - \text{output}_j) & \text{for output layernodes} \\ \text{output}_j(1 - \text{output}_j) \sum\limits_{\text{downstream}} W_{jk}\delta_j & \text{for hidden layer nodes} \end{cases}$$

where $\sum_{\text{downstream}} W_{jk}\delta_j$ refers to the weighted sum of the error responsibilities for the nodes downstream from the particular hidden layer node. (For the full derivation, see Mitchell [1].)

Also, note that the back-propagation rules illustrate why the attribute values need to be normalized to between zero and 1. For example, if income data, with values ranging into six figures, were not normalized, the weight adjustment $\Delta w_{ij} = \eta\delta_j x_{ij}$ would be dominated by the data value x_{ij}. Hence the error propagation (in the form of δ_j) through the network would be overwhelmed, and learning (weight adjustment) would be stifled.

EXAMPLE OF BACK-PROPAGATION

Recall from our introductory example that the output from the first pass through the network was *output* = 0.8750. Assume that the actual value of the target attribute is *actual* = 0.8 and that we will use a learning rate of $\eta = 0.01$. Then the *prediction error* equals $0.8 - 0.8750 = -0.075$, and we may apply the foregoing rules to illustrate how the back-propagation algorithm works to adjust the weights by portioning out responsibility for this error to the various nodes. Although it is possible to update the weights only after all records have been read, neural networks use *stochastic* (or *online*) back-propagation, which updates the weights after each record.

First, the error responsibility δ_Z for node Z is found. Since node Z is an output node, we have

$$\begin{aligned} \delta_Z &= \text{output}_Z(1 - \text{output}_Z)(\text{actual}_Z - \text{output}_Z) \\ &= 0.875(1 - 0.875)(0.8 - 0.875) = -0.0082 \end{aligned}$$

We may now adjust the "constant" weight W_{0Z} (which transmits an "input" of 1) using the back-propagation rules as follows:

$$\begin{aligned} \Delta W_{0Z} &= \eta\delta_Z(1) = 0.1(-0.0082)(1) = -0.00082 \\ w_{0Z,\text{new}} &= w_{0Z,\text{current}} + \Delta w_{0Z} = 0.5 - 0.00082 = 0.49918 \end{aligned}$$

Next, we move upstream to node A. Since node A is a hidden layer node, its error responsibility is

$$\delta_A = \text{output}_A(1 - \text{output}_A) \sum_{\text{downstream}} W_{jk}\delta_j$$

The only node downstream from node A is node Z. The weight associated with this connection is $W_{AZ} = 0.9$, and the error responsibility at node Z is -0.0082, so that $\delta_A = 0.7892(1 - 0.7892)(0.9)(-0.0082) = -0.00123$.

We may now update weight W_{AZ} using the back-propagation rules as follows:

$$\Delta W_{AZ} = \eta\delta_Z \cdot \text{output}_A = 0.1(-0.0082)(0.7892) = -0.000647$$
$$w_{AZ,\text{new}} = w_{AZ,\text{current}} + \Delta w_{AZ} = 0.9 - 0.000647 = 0.899353$$

The weight for the connection between hidden layer node A and output layer node Z has been adjusted from its initial value of 0.9 to its new value of 0.899353.

Next, we turn to node B, a hidden layer node, with error responsibility

$$\delta_B = \text{output}_B(1 - \text{output}_B) \sum_{\text{downstream}} W_{jk}\delta_j$$

Again, the only node downstream from node B is node Z, giving us $\delta_B = 0.8176(1 - 0.8176)(0.9)(-0.0082) = -0.0011$.

Weight W_{BZ} may then be adjusted using the backpropagation rules as follows:

$$\Delta W_{BZ} = \eta\delta_Z \cdot \text{output}_B = 0.1(-0.0082)(0.8176) = -0.00067$$
$$w_{BZ,\text{new}} = w_{BZ,\text{current}} + \Delta w_{BZ} = 0.9 - 0.00067 = 0.89933$$

We move upstream to the connections being used as inputs to node A. For weight W_{1A} we have

$$\Delta W_{1A} = \eta\delta_A x_1 = 0.1(-0.00123)(0.4) = -0.0000492$$
$$w_{1A,\text{new}} = w_{1A,\text{current}} + \Delta w_{1A} = 0.6 - 0.0000492 = 0.5999508.$$

For weight W_{2A} we have

$$\Delta W_{2A} = \eta\delta_A x_2 = 0.1(-0.00123)(0.2) = -0.0000246$$
$$w_{2A,\text{new}} = w_{2A,\text{current}} + \Delta w_{2A} = 0.8 - 0.0000246 = 0.7999754.$$

For weight W_{3A} we have

$$\Delta W_{3A} = \eta\delta_A x_3 = 0.1(-0.00123)(0.7) = -0.0000861$$
$$w_{3A,\text{new}} = w_{3A,\text{current}} + \Delta w_{3A} = 0.6 - 0.0000861 = 0.5999139.$$

Finally, for weight W_{0A} we have

$$\Delta W_{0A} = \eta\delta_A(1) = 0.1(-0.00123) = -0.000123$$
$$w_{0A,\text{new}} = w_{0A,\text{current}} + \Delta w_{0A} = 0.5 - 0.000123 = 0.499877.$$

Adjusting weights W_{0B}, W_{1B}, W_{2B}, and W_{3B} is left as an exercise.

Note that the weight adjustments have been made based on only a single perusal of a single record. The network calculated a predicted value for the target variable, compared this output value to the actual target value, and then percolated the error in prediction throughout the network, adjusting the weights to provide a smaller prediction error. Showing that the adjusted weights result in a smaller prediction error is left as an exercise.

TERMINATION CRITERIA

The neural network algorithm would then proceed to work through the training data set, record by record, adjusting the weights constantly to reduce the prediction error. It may take many passes through the data set before the algorithm's termination criterion is met. What, then, serves as the termination criterion, or stopping criterion? If training time is an issue, one may simply set the number of passes through the data, or the amount of realtime the algorithm may consume, as termination criteria. However, what one gains in short training time is probably bought with degradation in model efficacy.

Alternatively, one may be tempted to use a termination criterion that assesses when the SSE on the training data has been reduced to some low threshold level. Unfortunately, because of their flexibility, neural networks are prone to overfitting, memorizing the idiosyncratic patterns in the training set instead of retaining generalizability to unseen data.

Therefore, most neural network implementations adopt the following cross-validation termination procedure:

1. Retain part of the original data set as a holdout validation set.
2. Proceed to train the neural network as above on the remaining training data.
3. Apply the weights learned from the training data on the validation data.
4. Monitor *two sets of weights*, one "current" set of weights produced by the training data, and one "best" set of weights, as measured by the lowest SSE so far on the validation data.
5. When the current set of weights has significantly greater SSE than the best set of weights, then terminate the algorithm.

Regardless of the stopping criterion used, the neural network is not guaranteed to arrive at the optimal solution, known as the *global minimum* for the SSE. Rather, the algorithm may become stuck in a local minimum, which represents a good, if not optimal solution. In practice, this has not presented an insuperable problem.

- For example, multiple networks may be trained using different initialized weights, with the best-performing model being chosen as the "final" model.
- Second, the *online* or *stochastic* back-propagation method itself acts as a guard against getting stuck in a local minimum, since it introduces a random element to the gradient descent (see Reed and Marks [2]).
- Alternatively, a *momentum* term may be added to the back-propagation algorithm, with effects discussed below.

LEARNING RATE

Recall that the learning rate η, $0 < \eta < 1$, is a constant chosen to help us move the network weights toward a global minimum for SSE. However, what value should η take? How large should the weight adjustments be?

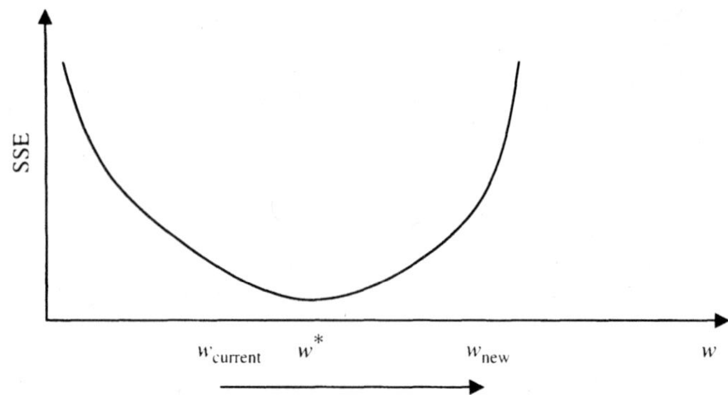

Figure 7.5 Large η may cause algorithm to overshoot global minimum.

When the learning rate is very small, the weight adjustments tend to be very small. Thus, if η is small when the algorithm is initialized, the network will probably take an unacceptably long time to converge. Is the solution therefore to use large values for η? Not necessarily. Suppose that the algorithm is close to the optimal solution and we have a large value for η. This large η will tend to make the algorithm overshoot the optimal solution.

Consider Figure 7.5, where W^* is the optimum value for weight W, which has current value W_{current}. According to the gradient descent rule, $\Delta w_{\text{current}} = -\eta(\partial\text{SSE}/\partial w_{\text{current}})$, W_{current} will be adjusted in the direction of W^*. But if the learning rate η, which acts as a multiplier in the formula for $\Delta w_{\text{current}}$, is too large, the new weight value W_{new} will jump right past the optimal value W^*, and may in fact end up farther away from W^* than W_{current}.

In fact, since the new weight value will then be on the opposite side of W^*, the next adjustment will again overshoot W^*, leading to an unfortunate oscillation between the two "slopes" of the valley and never settling down in the ravine (the minimum). One solution is to allow the learning rate η to change values as the training moves forward. At the start of training, η should be initialized to a relatively large value to allow the network to quickly approach the general neighborhood of the optimal solution. Then, when the network is beginning to approach convergence, the learning rate should gradually be reduced, thereby avoiding overshooting the minimum.

MOMENTUM TERM

The back-propagation algorithm is made more powerful through the addition of a *momentum term* α, as follows:

$$\Delta w_{\text{current}} = -\eta\frac{\partial\text{SSE}}{\partial w_{\text{current}}} + \alpha\Delta w_{\text{previous}}$$

where $\Delta w_{\text{previous}}$ represents the previous weight adjustment, and $0 \le \alpha < 1$. Thus, the new component $\alpha\Delta w_{\text{previous}}$ represents a fraction of the previous weight adjustment for a given weight.

Essentially, the momentum term represents *inertia*. Large values of α will influence the adjustment in the current weight, $\Delta w_{\text{current}}$, to move in the same direction as previous adjustments. It has been shown (e.g., Reed and Marks [2]) that including momentum in the back-propagation algorithm results in the adjustment becoming an exponential average of *all* previous adjustments:

$$\Delta w_{\text{current}} = -\eta \sum_{k=0}^{\infty} \alpha^k \frac{\partial \text{SSE}}{\partial w_{\text{current}-k}}$$

The α^k term indicates that the more recent adjustments exert a larger influence. Large values of α allow the algorithm to "remember" more terms in the adjustment history. Small values of α reduce the inertial effects as well as the influence of previous adjustments, until, with $\alpha = 0$, the component disappears entirely.

Clearly, a momentum component will help to dampen the oscillations around optimality mentioned earlier, by encouraging the adjustments to stay in the same direction. But momentum also helps the algorithm in the early stages of the algorithm, by increasing the rate at which the weights approach the neighborhood of optimality. This is because these early adjustments will probably all be in the same direction, so that the exponential average of the adjustments will also be in that direction. Momentum is also helpful when the gradient of SSE with respect to **w** is flat. If the momentum term α is too large, however, the weight adjustments may again overshoot the minimum, due to the cumulative influences of many previous adjustments.

For an informal appreciation of momentum, consider Figures 7.6 and 7.7. In both figures, the weight is initialized at location I, local minima exist at locations A and C, with the optimal global minimum at B. In Figure 7.6, suppose that we have a small value for the momentum term α, symbolized by the small mass of the "ball" on the curve. If we roll this small ball down the curve, it may never make it over the first hill, and remain stuck in the first valley. That is, the small value for α enables the algorithm to easily find the first trough at location A, representing a local minimum, but does not allow it to find the global minimum at B.

Next, in Figure 7.7, suppose that we have a large value for the momentum term α, symbolized by the large mass of the "ball" on the curve. If we roll this large ball down the curve, it may well make it over the first hill but may then have so much

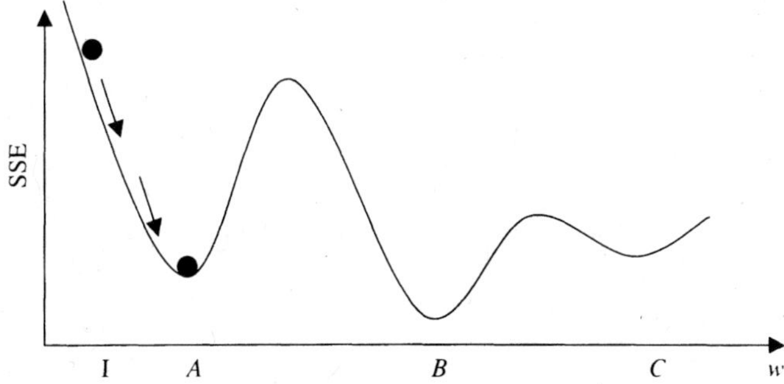

Figure 7.6 Small momentum α may cause algorithm to undershoot global minimum.

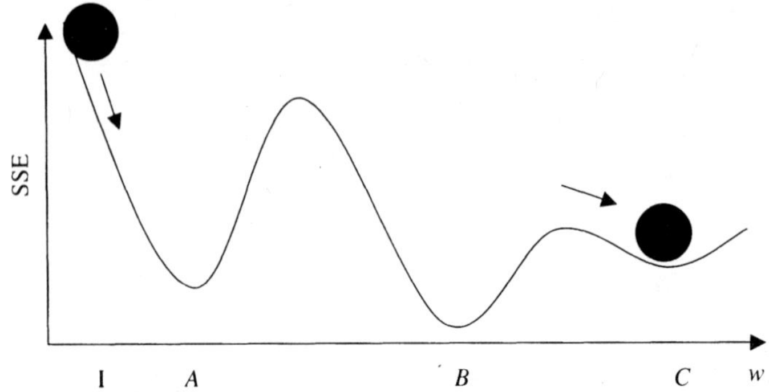

Figure 7.7 Large momentum α may cause algorithm to overshoot global minimum.

momentum that it overshoots the global minimum at location B and settles for the local minimum at location C.

Thus, one needs to consider carefully what values to set for both the learning rate η and the momentum term α. Experimentation with various values of η and α may be necessary before the best results are obtained.

SENSITIVITY ANALYSIS

One of the drawbacks of neural networks is their opacity. The same wonderful flexibility that allows neural networks to model a wide range of nonlinear behavior also limits our ability to interpret the results using easily formulated rules. Unlike decision trees, no straightforward procedure exists for translating the weights of a neural network into a compact set of decision rules.

However, a procedure is available, called *sensitivity analysis*, which does allow us to measure the relative influence each attribute has on the output result. Using the test data set mentioned above, the sensitivity analysis proceeds as follows:

1. Generate a new observation x_{mean}, with each attribute value in x_{mean} equal to the mean of the various attribute values for all records in the test set.
2. Find the network output for input x_{mean}. Call it $\text{output}_{\text{mean}}$.
3. Attribute by attribute, vary x_{mean} to reflect the attribute minimum and maximum. Find the network output for each variation and compare it to $\text{output}_{\text{mean}}$.

The sensitivity analysis will find that varying certain attributes from their minimum to their maximum will have a greater effect on the resulting network output than it has for other attributes. For example, suppose that we are interested in predicting stock price based on *price–earnings ratio*, *dividend yield*, and other attributes. Also, suppose that varying *price–earnings ratio* from its minimum to its maximum results in an increase of 0.20 in the network output, while varying *dividend yield* from its minimum to its maximum results in an increase of 0.30 in the network output when the other attributes are held constant at their mean value. We conclude that the network is more *sensitive* to variations in dividend yield and that therefore dividend yield is a more important factor for predicting stock prices than is price–earnings ratio.

APPLICATION OF NEURAL NETWORK MODELING

Next, we apply a neural network model using Insightful Miner on the same *adult* data set [3] from the UCal Irvine Machine Learning Repository that we analyzed in Chapter 6. The Insightful Miner neural network software was applied to a training set of 24,986 cases, using a single hidden layer with eight hidden nodes. The algorithm iterated 47 epochs (runs through the data set) before termination. The resulting neural network is shown in Figure 7.8. The squares on the left represent the input nodes. For the categorical variables, there is one input node per class. The eight dark circles represent the hidden layer. The light gray circles represent the constant inputs. There is only a single output node, indicating whether or not the record is classified as having income less than $50,000.

In this algorithm, the weights are centered at zero. An excerpt of the computer output showing the weight values is provided in Figure 7.9. The columns in the first

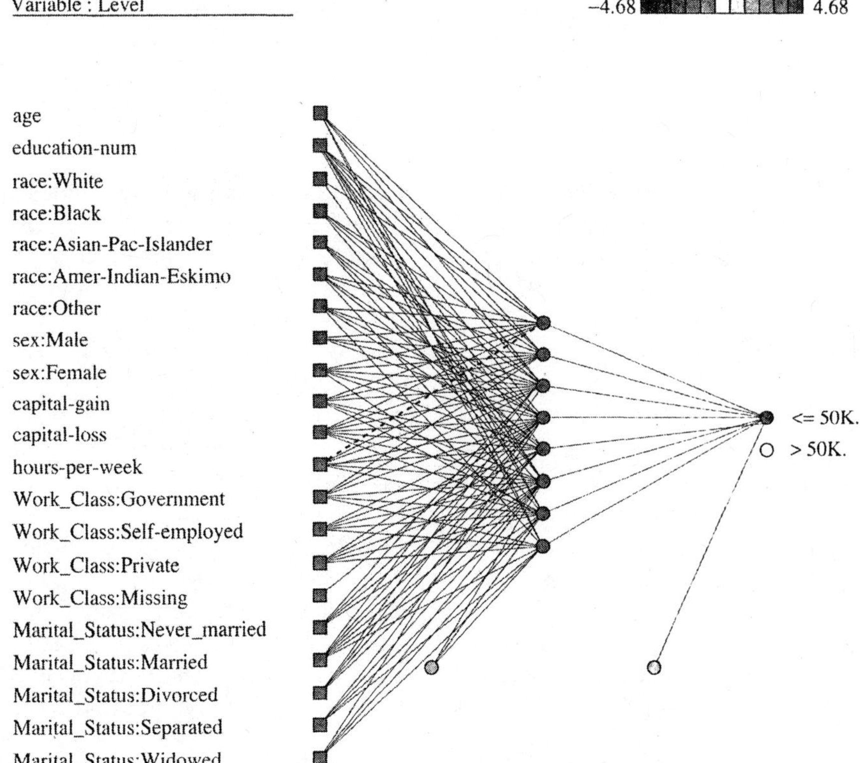

Figure 7.8 Neural network for the adult data set generated by Insightful Miner.

Weights

To/From	1	2	3	4	5	6	7	8	9
22	-0.97	-1.32	-0.18	-0.51	0.69	0.13	-0.25	-0.33	0.30
23	-0.70	-2.97	-0.12	0.34	0.43	0.50	1.03	-0.29	-0.10
24	-0.70	-2.96	-0.24	0.05	0.16	0.46	1.15	-0.16	-0.07
25	0.74	2.86	0.22	0.41	-0.03	-0.59	-1.05	0.18	0.14
26	-0.84	-2.82	-0.23	0.02	-0.16	0.62	1.06	-0.22	-0.20
27	-0.68	-2.89	-0.18	-0.03	-0.03	0.50	1.07	-0.24	-0.12
28	-1.68	-2.54	-0.43	-0.09	0.04	0.54	0.88	-0.18	-0.26
29	-2.11	-1.95	0.01	0.34	0.04	-0.75	-1.16	-0.03	0.38

Weights

To/From	22	23	24	25	26	27	28	29	0
30	0.18	0.59	0.69	-1.40	0.77	0.76	0.74	1.06	-0.08

Figure 7.9 Some of the neural network weights for the income example.

table represent the input nodes: 1 = *age*, 2 = *education-num*, and so on, while the rows represent the hidden layer nodes: 22 = first (top) hidden node, 23 = second hidden node, and so on. For example, the weight on the connection from *age* to the topmost hidden node is −0.97, while the weight on the connection from *Race: American Indian/Eskimo* (the sixth input node) to the last (bottom) hidden node is −0.75. The lower section of Figure7.9 displays the weights from the hidden nodes to the output node.

The estimated prediction accuracy using this very basic model is 82%, which is in the ballpark of the accuracies reported by Kohavi [4]. Since over 75% of the subjects have incomes below $50,000, simply predicted "less than $50,000" for every person would provide a baseline accuracy of about 75%.

However, we would like to know which variables are most important for predicting (classifying) income. We therefore perform a sensitivity analysis using *Clementine*, with results shown in Figure 7.10. Clearly, the amount of capital gains is the best predictor of whether a person has income less than $50,000, followed by the number of years of education. Other important variables include the number of hours worked per week and marital status. A person's gender does not seem to be highly predictive of income.

Of course, there is much more involved with developing a neural network classification model. For example, further data preprocessing may be called for; the

Relative Importance of Inputs

capital-gain	0.719519
education-num	0.486229
hours-per-week	0.289301
Marital_Status	0.27691
age	0.237282
capital-loss	0.228844
race	0.183006
Work_Class	0.119079
sex	0.0641384

Figure 7.10 Most important variables: results from sensitivity analysis.

model would need to be validated using a holdout validation data set, and so on. For a start-to-finish application of neural networks to a real-world data set, from data preparation through model building and sensitivity analysis, see Reference 5.

REFERENCES

1. Tom M. Mitchell, *Machine Learning*, McGraw-Hill, NewYork, 1997.
2. Russell D. Reed and Robert J. Marks II, *Neural Smithing: Supervised Learning in Feedforward Artificial Neural Networks*, MIT Press, Cambridge, MA, 1999.
3. C. L. Blake and C. J. Merz, UCI Repository of Machine Learning Databases, `http://www.ics.uci.edu/~mlearn/MLRepository.html`, University of California, Department of Information and Computer Science, Irvine, CA, 1998.
4. Ronny Kohavi, Scaling up the accuracy of naïve Bayes classifiers: A decision tree hybrid, *Proceedings of the 2nd International Conference on Knowledge Discovery and Data Mining*, Portland, OR, 1996.
5. Daniel Larose, *Data Mining Methods and Models*, Wiley-Interscience, Hoboken, NJ (to appear 2005).

EXERCISES

1. Suppose that you need to prepare the data in Table 6.10 for a neural network algorithm. Define the indicator variables for the *occupation* attribute.

2. Clearly describe each of these characteristics of a neural network:

a. Layered

b. Feedforward

c. Completely connected

3. What is the sole function of the nodes in the input layer?

4. Should we prefer a large hidden layer or a small one? Describe the benefits and drawbacks of each.

5. Describe how neural networks function nonlinearly.

6. Explain why the updating term for the current weight includes the *negative* of the sign of the derivative (slope).

7. Adjust the weights W_{0B}, W_{1B}, W_{2B}, and W_{3B} from the example on back-propagation in the text.

8. Refer to Exercise 7. Show that the adjusted weights result in a smaller prediction error.

9. True or false: Neural networks are valuable because of their capacity for always finding the global minimum of the SSE.

10. Describe the benefits and drawbacks of using large or small values for the learning rate.

11. Describe the benefits and drawbacks of using large or small values for the momentum term.

Hands-on Analysis

For the following exercises, use the data set *churn* located at the book series Web site. Normalize the numerical data, recode the categorical variables, and deal with the correlated variables.

12. Generate a neural network model for classifying *churn* based on the other variables. Describe the topology of the model.

13. Which variables, in order of importance, are identified as most important for classifying *churn*?

14. Compare the neural network model with the CART and C4.5 models for this task in Chapter 6. Describe the benefits and drawbacks of the neural network model compared to the others. Is there convergence or divergence of results among the models?

CHAPTER 8

HIERARCHICAL AND *k*-MEANS CLUSTERING

CLUSTERING TASK

Clustering refers to the grouping of records, observations, or cases into classes of similar objects. A *cluster* is a collection of records that are similar to one another and dissimilar to records in other clusters. Clustering differs from classification in that there is no target variable for clustering. The clustering task does not try to classify, estimate, or predict the value of a target variable. Instead, clustering algorithms seek to segment the entire data set into relatively homogeneous subgroups or clusters, where the similarity of the records within the cluster is maximized, and the similarity to records outside this cluster is minimized.

For example, Claritas, Inc. is a clustering business that provides demographic profiles of each geographic area in the United States, as defined by zip code. One of the clustering mechanisms they use is the PRIZM segmentation system, which describes every U.S. zip code area in terms of distinct lifestyle types. Recall, for example, that the clusters identified for zip code 90210, Beverly Hills, California, were:

- *Cluster 01:* Blue Blood Estates
- *Cluster 10:* Bohemian Mix
- *Cluster 02:* Winner's Circle
- *Cluster 07:* Money and Brains
- *Cluster 08:* Young Literati

Discovering Knowledge in Data: An Introduction to Data Mining, By Daniel T. Larose
ISBN 0-471-66657-2

The description for cluster 01: Blue Blood Estates is "Established executives, professionals, and 'old money' heirs that live in America's wealthiest suburbs. They are accustomed to privilege and live luxuriously—one-tenth of this group's members are multimillionaires. The next affluence level is a sharp drop from this pinnacle."

Examples of clustering tasks in business and research include:

- Target marketing of a niche product for a small-capitalization business that does not have a large marketing budget
- For accounting auditing purposes, to segment financial behavior into benign and suspicious categories
- As a dimension-reduction tool when a data set has hundreds of attributes
- For gene expression clustering, where very large quantities of genes may exhibit similar behavior

Clustering is often performed as a preliminary step in a data mining process, with the resulting clusters being used as further inputs into a different technique downstream, such as neural networks. Due to the enormous size of many present-day databases, it is often helpful to apply clustering analysis first, to reduce the search space for the downstream algorithms. In this chapter, after a brief look at hierarchical clustering methods, we discuss in detail k-means clustering; in Chapter 9 we examine clustering using Kohonen networks, a structure related to neural networks.

Cluster analysis encounters many of the same issues that we dealt with in the chapters on classification. For example, we shall need to determine:

- How to measure similarity
- How to recode categorical variables
- How to standardize or normalize numerical variables
- How many clusters we expect to uncover

For simplicity, in this book we concentrate on Euclidean distance between records:

$$d_{\text{Euclidean}}(\mathbf{x}, \mathbf{y}) = \sqrt{\sum_i (x_i - y_i)^2}$$

where $\mathbf{x} = x_1, x_2, \ldots, x_m$, and $\mathbf{y} = y_1, y_2, \ldots, y_m$ represent the m attribute values of two records. Of course, many other metrics exist, such as *city-block distance*:

$$d_{\text{cityblock}}(\mathbf{x}, \mathbf{y}) = \sum_i |x_i - y_i|$$

or *Minkowski distance*, which represents the general case of the foregoing two metrics for a general exponent q:

$$d_{\text{Minkowski}}(\mathbf{x}, \mathbf{y}) = \sum_i |x_i - y_i|^q$$

For categorical variables, we may again define the "different from" function for

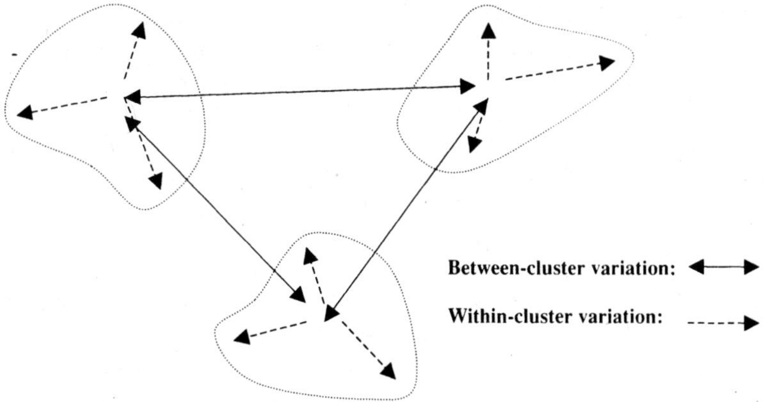

Figure 8.1 Clusters should have small within-cluster variation compared to the between-cluster variation.

comparing the *i*th attribute values of a pair of records:

$$\text{different}(x_i, y_i) = \begin{cases} 0 & \text{if } x_i = y_i \\ 1 & \text{otherwise} \end{cases}$$

where x_i and y_i are categorical values. We may then substitute different(x_i, y_i) for the *i*th term in the Euclidean distance metric above.

For optimal performance, clustering algorithms, just like algorithms for classification, require the data to be normalized so that no particular variable or subset of variables dominates the analysis. Analysts may use either the *min–max normalization* or *Z-score standardization*, discussed in earlier chapters:

$$\textit{Min–max normalization:} \quad X^* = \frac{X - \min(X)}{\text{Range}(X)}$$

$$\textit{Z-score standardization:} \quad X^* = \frac{X - \text{mean}(X)}{\text{SD}(X)}$$

All clustering methods have as their goal the identification of groups of records such that similarity within a group is very high while the similarity to records in other groups is very low. In other words, as shown in Figure 8.1, clustering algorithms seek to construct clusters of records such that the *between-cluster variation* (BCV) is large compared to the *within-cluster variation* (WCV) This is somewhat analogous to the concept behind analysis of variance.

HIERARCHICAL CLUSTERING METHODS

Clustering algorithms are either hierarchical or nonhierarchical. In *hierarchical clustering*, a treelike cluster structure (*dendrogram*) is created through recursive partitioning (divisive methods) or combining (agglomerative) of existing clusters. *Agglomerative clustering methods* initialize each observation to be a tiny cluster of its own. Then, in succeeding steps, the two closest clusters are aggregated into a new combined cluster. In this way, the number of clusters in the data set is reduced by one at each step. Eventually, all records are combined into a single huge cluster. *Divisive clustering methods* begin with all the records in one big cluster, with the most dissimilar records being split off recursively, into a separate cluster, until each record represents its own cluster. Because most computer programs that apply hierarchical clustering use agglomerative methods, we focus on those.

Distance between records is rather straightforward once appropriate recoding and normalization has taken place. But how do we determine *distance between clusters* of records? Should we consider two clusters to be close if their nearest neighbors are close or if their farthest neighbors are close? How about criteria that average out these extremes?

We examine several criteria for determining distance between arbitrary clusters A and B:

- *Single linkage*, sometimes termed the *nearest-neighbor approach*, is based on the minimum distance between any record in cluster A and any record in cluster B. In other words, cluster similarity is based on the similarity of the most similar members from each cluster. Single linkage tends to form long, slender clusters, which may sometimes lead to heterogeneous records being clustered together.
- *Complete linkage*, sometimes termed the *farthest-neighbor approach*, is based on the maximum distance between any record in cluster A and any record in cluster B. In other words, cluster similarity is based on the similarity of the most dissimilar members from each cluster. Complete-linkage tends to form more compact, spherelike clusters, with all records in a cluster within a given diameter of all other records.
- *Average linkage* is designed to reduce the dependence of the cluster-linkage criterion on extreme values, such as the most similar or dissimilar records. In average linkage, the criterion is the average distance of all the records in cluster A from all the records in cluster B. The resulting clusters tend to have approximately equal within-cluster variability.

Let's examine how these linkage methods work, using the following small, one-dimensional data set:

2 5 9 15 16 18 25 33 33 45

Single-Linkage Clustering

Suppose that we are interested in using *single-linkage* agglomerative clustering on this data set. Agglomerative methods start by assigning each record to its own cluster. Then, single linkage seeks the minimum distance between any records in two clusters. Figure 8.2 illustrates how this is accomplished for this data set. The minimum cluster distance is clearly between the single-record clusters which each contain the value 33, for which the distance must be zero for any valid metric. Thus, these two clusters are combined into a new cluster of two records, both of value 33, as shown in Figure 8.2. Note that, after step 1, only nine ($n - 1$) clusters remain. Next, in step 2, the clusters

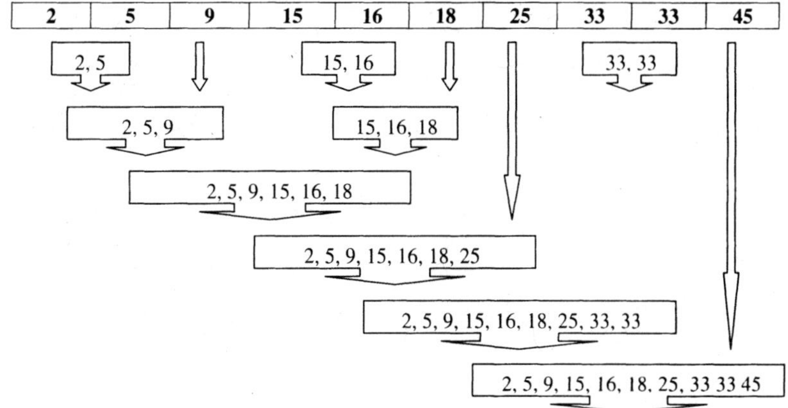

Figure 8.2 Single-linkage agglomerative clustering on the sample data set.

containing values 15 and 16 are combined into a new cluster, since their distance of 1 is the minimum between any two clusters remaining.

Here are the remaining steps:

- *Step 3:* The cluster containing values 15 and 16 (cluster {15,16}) is combined with cluster {18}, since the distance between 16 and 18 (the closest records in each cluster) is two, the minimum among remaining clusters.
- *Step 4:* Clusters {2} and {5} are combined.
- *Step 5:* Cluster {2,5} is combined with cluster {9}, since the distance between 5 and 9 (the closest records in each cluster) is four, the minimum among remaining clusters.
- *Step 6:* Cluster {2,5,9} is combined with cluster {15,16,18}, since the distance between 9 and 15 is six, the minimum among remaining clusters.
- *Step 7:* Cluster {2,5,9,15,16,18} is combined with cluster {25}, since the distance between 18 and 25 is seven, the minimum among remaining clusters.
- *Step 8:* Cluster {2,5,9,15,16,18,25} is combined with cluster {33,33}, since the distance between 25 and 33 is eight, the minimum among remaining clusters.
- *Step 9:* Cluster {2,5,9,15,16,18,25,33,33} is combined with cluster {45}. This last cluster now contains all the records in the data set.

Complete-Linkage Clustering

Next, let's examine whether using the complete-linkage criterion would result in a different clustering of this sample data set. Complete linkage seeks to minimize the distance among the records in two clusters that are farthest from each other. Figure 8.3 illustrates complete-linkage clustering for this data set.

- *Step 1:* Since each cluster contains a single record only, there is no difference between single linkage and complete linkage at step 1. The two clusters each containing 33 are again combined.

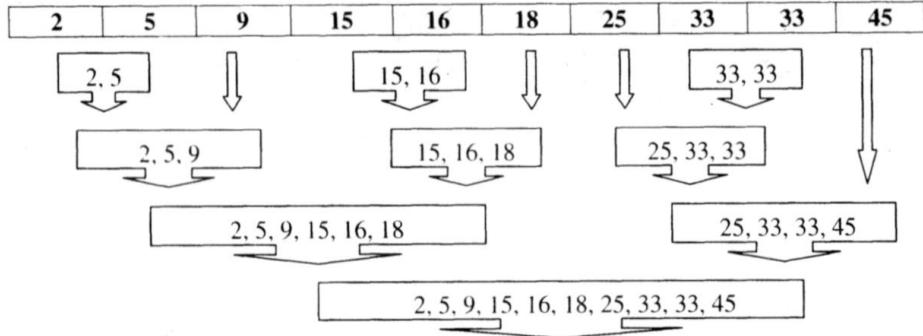

Figure 8.3 Complete-linkage agglomerative clustering on the sample data set.

- *Step 2:* Just as for single linkage, the clusters containing values 15 and 16 are combined into a new cluster. Again, this is because there is no difference in the two criteria for single-record clusters.
- *Step 3:* At this point, complete linkage begins to diverge from its predecessor. In single linkage, cluster {15,16} was at this point combined with cluster {18}. But complete linkage looks at the farthest neighbors, not the nearest neighbors. The farthest neighbors for these two clusters are 15 and 18, for a distance of 3. This is the same distance separating clusters {2} and {5}. The complete-linkage criterion is silent regarding ties, so we arbitrarily select the first such combination found, therefore combining the clusters {2} and {5} into a new cluster.
- *Step 4:* Now cluster {15,16} is combined with cluster {18}.
- *Step 5:* Cluster {2,5} is combined with cluster {9}, since the complete-linkage distance is 7, the smallest among remaining clusters.
- *Step 6:* Cluster {25} is combined with cluster {33,33}, with a complete-linkage distance of 8.
- *Step 7:* Cluster {2,5,9} is combined with cluster {15,16,18}, with a complete-linkage distance of 16.
- *Step 8:* Cluster {25,33,33} is combined with cluster {45}, with a complete-linkage distance of 20.
- *Step 9:* Cluster {2,5,9,15,16,18} is combined with cluster {25,33,33,45}. All records are now contained in this last large cluster.

Finally, with average linkage, the criterion is the average distance of all the records in cluster A from all the records in cluster B. Since the average of a single record is the record's value itself, this method does not differ from the earlier methods in the early stages, where single-record clusters are being combined. At step 3, average linkage would be faced with the choice of combining clusters {2} and {5}, or combining the {15, 16} cluster with the single-record {18} cluster. The average distance between the {15, 16} cluster and the {18} cluster is the average of $|18 - 15|$ and $|18 - 16|$, which is 2.5, while the average distance between clusters {2} and {5} is of course 3. Therefore, average linkage would combine the {15, 16} cluster with cluster {18} at this step, followed by combining cluster {2} with cluster {5}. The reader may verify that the average-linkage criterion leads to the same hierarchical structure for this example as the complete-linkage criterion. In general, average linkage leads to clusters more similar in shape to complete linkage than does single linkage.

k-MEANS CLUSTERING

The k-means clustering algorithm [1] is a straightforward and effective algorithm for finding clusters in data. The algorithm proceeds as follows.

- *Step 1:* Ask the user how many clusters k the data set should be partitioned into.
- *Step 2:* Randomly assign k records to be the initial cluster center locations.
- *Step 3:* For each record, find the nearest cluster center. Thus, in a sense, each cluster center "owns" a subset of the records, thereby representing a partition of the data set. We therefore have k clusters, $C_1, C_2, \ldots, C_k$.
- *Step 4:* For each of the k clusters, find the cluster *centroid*, and update the location of each cluster center to the new value of the centroid.
- *Step 5:* Repeat steps 3 to 5 until convergence or termination.

The "nearest" criterion in step 3 is usually Euclidean distance, although other criteria may be applied as well. The cluster centroid in step 4 is found as follows. Suppose that we have n data points $(a_1, b_1, c_1), (a_2, b_2, c_2), \ldots, (a_n, b_n, c_n)$, the *centroid* of these points is the center of gravity of these points and is located at point $\left(\sum a_i/n, \sum b_i/n, \sum c_i/n\right)$. For example, the points (1,1,1), (1,2,1), (1,3,1), and (2,1,1) would have centroid

$$\left(\frac{1+1+1+2}{4}, \frac{1+2+3+1}{4}, \frac{1+1+1+1}{4}\right) = (1.25, 1.75, 1.00)$$

The algorithm terminates when the centroids no longer change. In other words, the algorithm terminates when for all clusters $C_1, C_2, \ldots, C_k$, all the records "owned" by each cluster center remain in that cluster. Alternatively, the algorithm may terminate when some convergence criterion is met, such as no significant shrinkage in the *sum of squared errors*:

$$\text{SSE} = \sum_{i=1}^{k} \sum_{p \in C_i} d(p, m_i)^2$$

where $p \in C_i$ represents each data point in cluster i and m_i represents the centroid of cluster i.

EXAMPLE OF *k*-MEANS CLUSTERING AT WORK

Let's examine an example of how the k-means algorithm works. Suppose that we have the eight data points in two-dimensional space shown in Table 8.1 and plotted in Figure 8.4 and are interested in uncovering $k = 2$ clusters.

TABLE 8.1 Data Points for k-Means Example

a	b	c	d	e	f	g	h
(1,3)	(3,3)	(4,3)	(5,3)	(1,2)	(4,2)	(1,1)	(2,1)

Let's apply the k-means algorithm step by step.

- *Step 1:* Ask the user how many clusters k the data set should be partitioned into. We have already indicated that we are interested in $k = 2$ clusters.
- *Step 2:* Randomly assign k records to be the initial cluster center locations. For this example, we assign the cluster centers to be $m_1 = (1,1)$ and $m_2 = (2,1)$.
- *Step 3 (first pass):* For each record, find the nearest cluster center. Table 8.2 contains the (rounded) Euclidean distances between each point and each cluster center $m_1 = (1,1)$ and $m_2 = (2,1)$, along with an indication of which cluster center the point is nearest to. Therefore, cluster 1 contains points $\{a,e,g\}$, and cluster 2 contains points $\{b,c,d,f,h\}$. Once cluster membership is assigned, the sum of squared errors may be found:

$$
\begin{aligned}
\text{SSE} &= \sum_{i=1}^{k} \sum_{p \in C_i} d(p,m_i)^2 \\
&= 2^2 + 2.24^2 + 2.83^2 + 3.61^2 + 1^2 + 2.24^2 + 0^2 + 0^2 = 36
\end{aligned}
$$

As remarked earlier, we would like our clustering methodology to maximize the between-cluster variation with respect to the within-cluster variation. Using $d(m_1,m_2)$ as a surrogate for BCV and SSE as a surrogate for WCV, we have:

$$
\frac{\text{BCV}}{\text{WCV}} = \frac{d(m_1,m_2)}{\text{SSE}} = \frac{1}{36} = 0.0278
$$

We expect this ratio to increase with successive passes.

- *Step 4 (first pass):* For each of the k clusters find the cluster *centroid* and update the location of each cluster center to the new value of the centroid. The

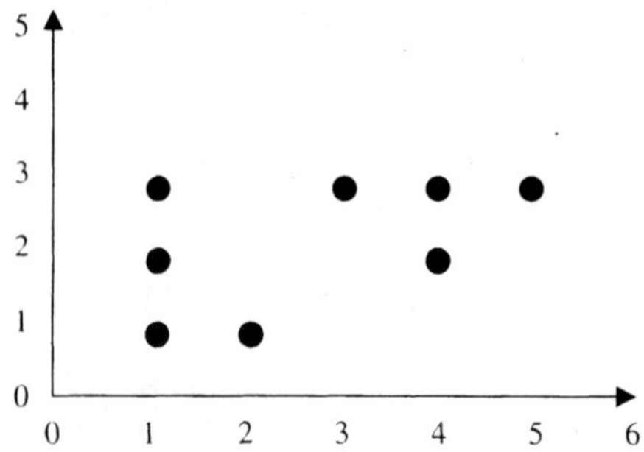

Figure 8.4 How will k-means partition this data into $k = 2$ clusters?

TABLE 8.2 Finding the Nearest Cluster Center for Each Record (First Pass)

Point	Distance from m_1	Distance from m_2	Cluster Membership
a	2.00	2.24	C_1
b	2.83	2.24	C_2
c	3.61	2.83	C_2
d	4.47	3.61	C_2
e	1.00	1.41	C_1
f	3.16	2.24	C_2
g	0.00	1.00	C_1
h	1.00	0.00	C_2

centroid for cluster 1 is $[(1+1+1)/3, (3+2+1)/3] = (1,2)$. The centroid for cluster 2 is $[(3+4+5+4+2)/5, (3+3+3+2+1)/5] = (3.6, 2.4)$. The clusters and centroids (triangles) at the end of the first pass are shown in Figure 8.5. Note that m_1 has moved up to the center of the three points in cluster 1, while m_2 has moved up and to the right a considerable distance, to the center of the five points in cluster 2.

- *Step 5:* Repeat steps 3 and 4 until convergence or termination. The centroids have moved, so we go back to step 3 for our second pass through the algorithm.
- *Step 3 (second pass):* For each record, find the nearest cluster center. Table 8.3 shows the distances between each point and each updated cluster center $m_1 = (1,2)$ and $m_2 = (3.6, 2.4)$, together with the resulting cluster membership. There has been a shift of a single record (h) from cluster 2 to cluster 1. The relatively large change in m_2 has left record h now closer to m_1 than to m_2, so that record h now belongs to cluster 1. All other records remain in the same clusters as previously. Therefore, cluster 1 is {a,e,g,h}, and cluster 2 is {b,c,d,f}. The new sum of squared errors is

$$\text{SSE} = \sum_{i=1}^{k} \sum_{p \in C_i} d(p,m_i)^2 = 1^2 + 0.85^2 + 0.72^2 + 1.52^2 + 0^2 + 0.57^2 + 1^2 + 1.41^2 = 7.88$$

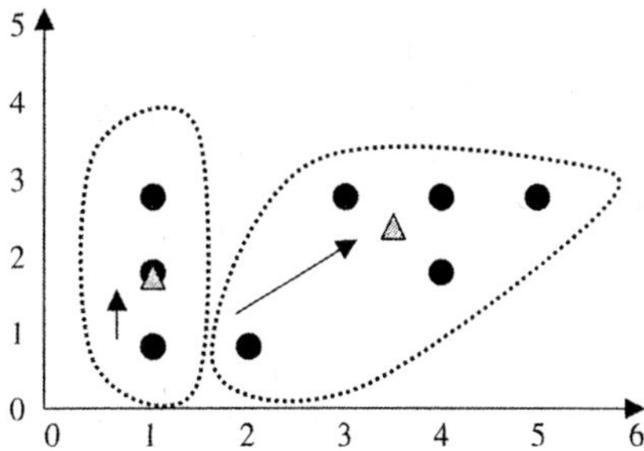

Figure 8.5 Clusters and centroids Δ after first pass through k-means algorithm.

TABLE 8.3 Finding the Nearest Cluster Center for Each Record (Second Pass)

Point	Distance from m_1	Distance from m_2	Cluster Membership
a	1.00	2.67	C_1
b	2.24	0.85	C_2
c	3.16	0.72	C_2
d	4.12	1.52	C_2
e	0.00	2.63	C_1
f	3.00	0.57	C_2
g	1.00	2.95	C_1
h	1.41	2.13	C_2

which is much reduced from the previous SSE of 36, indicating a better clustering solution. We also have:

$$\frac{\text{BCV}}{\text{WCV}} = \frac{d(m_1,m_2)}{\text{SSE}} = \frac{2.63}{7.88} = 0.3338$$

which is larger than the previous 0.0278, indicating that we are increasing the between-cluster variation with respect to the within-cluster variation.

- *Step 4 (second pass):* For each of the k clusters, find the cluster *centroid* and update the location of each cluster center to the new value of the centroid. The new centroid for cluster 1 is $[(1+1+1+2)/4, (3+2+1+1)/4] = (1.25, 1.75)$. The new centroid for cluster 2 is $[(3+4+5+4)/4, (3+3+3+2)/4] = (4, 2.75)$. The clusters and centroids at the end of the second pass are shown in Figure 8.6. Centroids m_1 and m_2 have both moved slightly.
- *Step 5:* Repeat steps 3 and 4 until convergence or termination. Since the centroids have moved, we once again return to step 3 for our third (and as it turns out, final) pass through the algorithm.
- *Step 3 (third pass):* For each record, find the nearest cluster center. Table 8.4 shows the distances between each point and each newly updated cluster center $m_1 = (1.25, 1.75)$ and $m_2 = (4, 2.75)$, together with the resulting cluster membership. Note that no records have shifted cluster membership from the

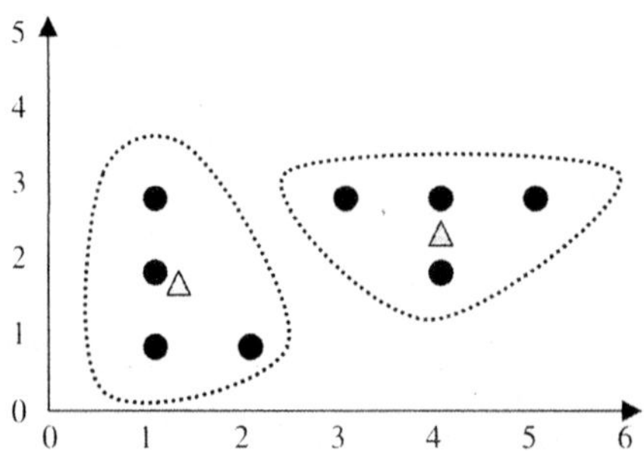

Figure 8.6 Clusters and centroids Δ after second pass through k-means algorithm.

TABLE 8.4 Finding the Nearest Cluster Center for Each Record (Third Pass)

Point	Distance from m_1	Distance from m_2	Cluster Membership
a	1.27	3.01	C_1
b	2.15	1.03	C_2
c	3.02	0.25	C_2
d	3.95	1.03	C_2
e	0.35	3.09	C_1
f	2.76	0.75	C_2
g	0.79	3.47	C_1
h	1.06	2.66	C_2

preceding pass. The new sum of squared errors is

$$\text{SSE} = \sum_{i=1}^{k} \sum_{p \in C_i} d(p,m_i)^2 = 1.27^2 + 1.03^2 + 0.25^2 + 1.03^2 + 0.35^2 + 0.75^2$$
$$+0.79^2 + 1.06^2 = 6.25$$

which is slightly smaller than the previous SSE of 7.88 and indicates that we have our best clustering solution yet. We also have:

$$\frac{\text{BCV}}{\text{WCV}} = \frac{d(m_1,m_2)}{\text{SSE}} = \frac{2.93}{6.25} = 0.4688$$

which is larger than the previous 0.3338, indicating that we have again increased the between-cluster variation with respect to the within-cluster variation. To do so is the goal of every clustering algorithm, in order to produce well-defined clusters such that the similarity within the cluster is high while the similarity to records in other clusters is low.

- *Step 4 (third pass):* For each of the k clusters, find the cluster *centroid* and update the location of each cluster center to the new value of the centroid. Since no records have shifted cluster membership, the cluster centroids therefore also remain unchanged.
- *Step 5:* Repeat steps 3 and 4 until convergence or termination. Since the centroids remain unchanged, the algorithm terminates.

Note that the k-means algorithm cannot guarantee finding the the global minimum SSE, instead often settling at a local minimum. To improve the probability of achieving a global minimum, the analyst should rerun the algorithm using a variety of initial cluster centers. Moore[2] suggests (1) placing the first cluster center on a random data point, and (2) placing the subsequent cluster centers on points as far away from previous centers as possible.

One potential problem for applying the k-means algorithm is: Who decides how many clusters to search for? That is, who decides k? Unless the analyst has a priori knowledge of the number of underlying clusters, therefore, an "outer loop" should be added to the algorithm, which cycles through various promising values of k. Clustering solutions for each value of k can therefore be compared, with the value of k resulting in the smallest SSE being selected.

What if some attributes are more relevant than others to the problem formulation? Since cluster membership is determined by distance, we may apply the same axis-stretching methods for quantifying attribute relevance that we discussed in Chapter 5. In Chapter 9 we examine another common clustering method, Kohonen networks, which are related to artificial neural networks in structure.

APPLICATION OF k-MEANS CLUSTERING USING SAS ENTERPRISE MINER

Next, we turn to the powerful SAS Enterpriser Miner[3] software for an application of the k-means algorithm on the *churn* data set from Chapter 3 (available at the book series Web site; also available from `http://www.sgi.com/tech/mlc/db/`). Recall that the data set contains 20 variables' worth of information about 3333 customers, along with an indication of whether or not that customer churned (left the company).

The following variables were passed to the Enterprise Miner clustering node:

- Flag (0/1) variables
  - International Plan and VoiceMail Plan
- Numerical variables
  - *Account length*, *voice mail messages*, *day minutes*, *evening minutes*, *night minutes*, *international minutes*, and *customer service calls*,
  - After applying min–max normalization to all numerical variables.

The *Enterprise Miner* clustering node uses SAS's FASTCLUS procedure, a version of the k-means algorithm. The number of clusters was set to $k = 3$. The three clusters uncovered by the algorithm varied greatly in size, with tiny cluster 1 containing 92 records, large cluster 2 containing 2411 records, and medium-sized cluster 3 containing 830 records.

Some basic cluster profiling will help us to learn about the types of records falling into each cluster. Figure 8.7 provides a look at the clustering results window of *Enterprise Miner*, containing a pie chart profile of the *International Plan* membership across the three clusters. All members of cluster 1, a fraction of the members of cluster 2, and no members of cluster 3 have adopted the *International Plan*. Note that the left most pie chart represents all records, and is similar to cluster 2.

Next, Figure 8.8 illustrates the proportion of VoiceMail Plan adopters in each cluster. (Note the confusing color reversal for *yes/no* responses.) Remarkably, clusters 1 and 3 contain only VoiceMail Plan adopters, while cluster 2 contains only non-adopters of the plan. In other words, this field was used by the k-means algorithm to create a "perfect" discrimination, dividing the data set perfectly among adopters and nonadopters of the International Plan.

It is clear from these results that the algorithm is relying heavily on the categorical variables to form clusters. The comparison of the means of the numerical variables across the clusters in Table 8.5, shows relatively little variation, indicating that the clusters are similar across these dimensions. Figure 8.9, for example, illustrates that the distribution of *customer service calls* (normalized) is relatively similar in each cluster. If the analyst is not comfortable with this domination of the clustering by the

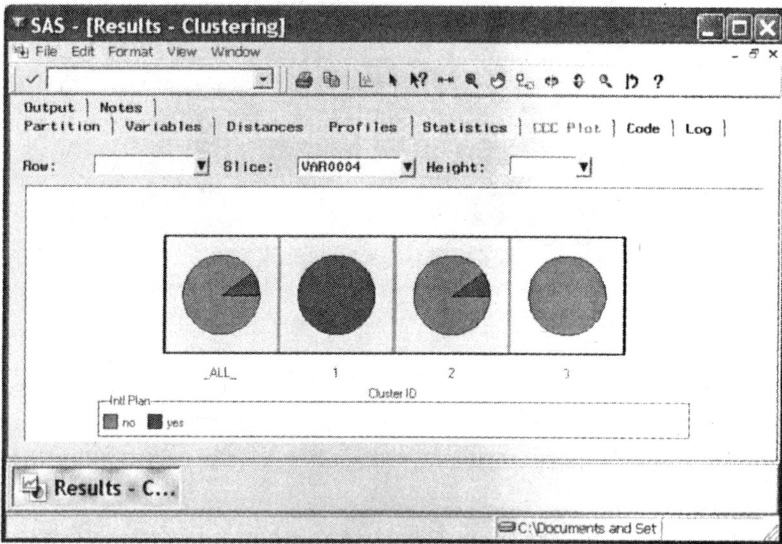

Figure 8.7 Enterprise Miner profile of International Plan adopters across clusters.

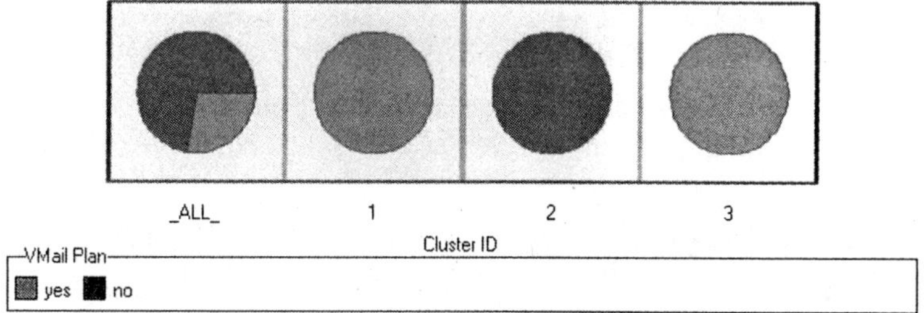

Figure 8.8 VoiceMail Plan adopters and nonadopters are mutually exclusive.

TABLE 8.5 Comparison of Variable Means Across Clusters Shows Little Variation

Cluster	Freq.	AcctLength_m	VMailMessage	DayMins_mm
1	92	0.4340639598	0.5826939471	0.5360015616
2	2411	0.4131940041	0	0.5126334451
3	830	0.4120730857	0.5731159934	0.5093940185

Cluster	EveMins_mm	NightMins_mm	IntMins_mm	CustServCalls_
1	0.5669029659	0.4764366069	0.5467934783	0.1630434783
2	0.5507417372	0.4773586813	0.5119784322	0.1752615328
3	0.5564095259	0.4795138596	0.5076626506	0.1701472557

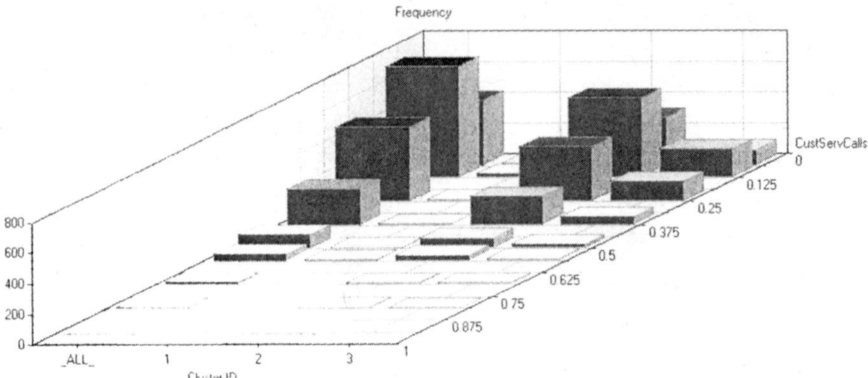

Figure 8.9 Distribution of *customer service calls* is similar across clusters.

categorical variables, he or she can choose to stretch or shrink the appropriate axes, as mentioned earlier, which will help to adjust the clustering algorithm to a more suitable solution.

The clusters may therefore be summarized, using only the categorical variables, as follows:

- *Cluster 1: Sophisticated Users*. A small group of customers who have adopted both the International Plan and the VoiceMail Plan.
- *Cluster 2: The Average Majority*. The largest segment of the customer base, some of whom have adopted the VoiceMail Plan but none of whom have adopted the International Plan.
- *Cluster 3: Voice Mail Users*. A medium-sized group of customers who have all adopted the VoiceMail Plan but not the International Plan.

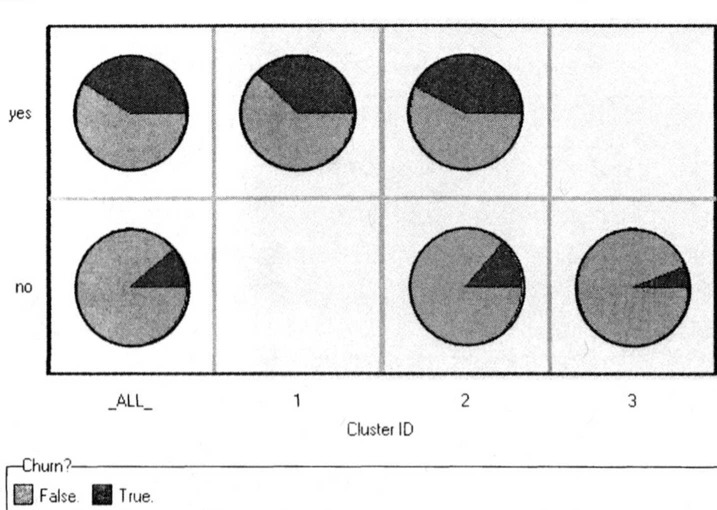

Figure 8.10 Churn behavior across clusters for International Plan adopters and nonadopters.

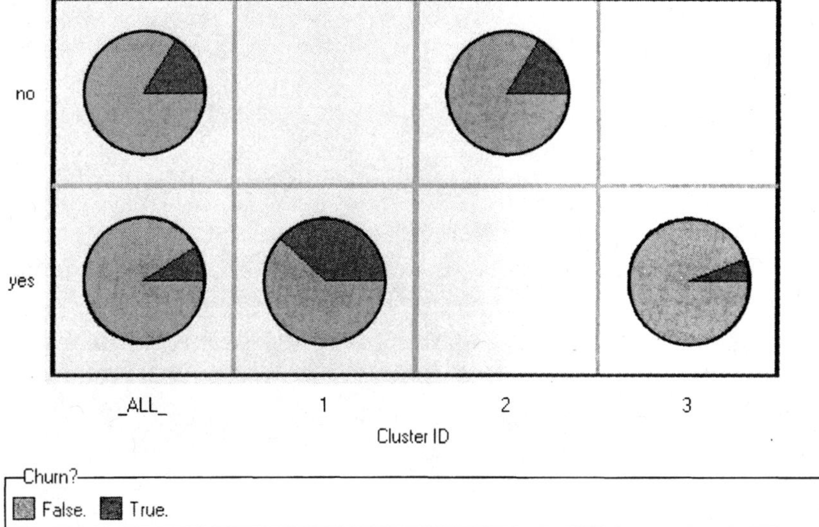

Figure 8.11 Churn behavior across clusters for VoiceMail Plan adopters and nonadopters.

A more detailed clustering profile, including both categorical and numerical variables, is given in Chapter 9.

Using Cluster Membership to Predict Churn

Suppose, however, that we would like to apply these clusters to assist us in the *churn classification* task. We may compare the proportions of churners directly among the various clusters, using graphs such as Figure 8.10. Here we see that overall (the leftmost column of pie charts), the proportion of churners is much higher among those who have adopted the International Plan than among those who have not. This finding was uncovered in Chapter 3. Note that the churn proportion is higher in cluster 1, which contains International Plan adopters, than in cluster 2, which contains a mixture of adopters and nonadopters, and higher still than cluster 3, which contains no such adopters of the International Plan. Clearly, the company should look at the plan to see why the customers who have it are leaving the company at a higher rate.

Now, since we know from Chapter 3 that the proportion of churners is lower among adopters of the VoiceMail Plan, we would expect that the churn rate for cluster 3 would be lower than for the other clusters. This expectation is confirmed in Figure 8.11.

In Chapter 9 we explore using cluster membership as input to downstream data mining models.

REFERENCES

1. J. MacQueen, Some methods for classification and analysis of multivariate observations, *Proceedings of the 5th Berkeley Symposium on Mathematical Statistics and Probability*, Vol. 1, pp. 281–297, University of California Press, Berkeley, CA, 1967.

2. Andrew Moore, *k-Means and Hierarchical Clustering*, Course Notes, `http://www-2.cs.cmu.edu/~awm/tutorials/`, 2001.
3. The SAS Institute, Cary, NC, `www.sas.com`.

EXERCISES

1. To which cluster for the 90210 zip code would you prefer to belong?
2. Describe the goal of all clustering methods.
3. Suppose that we have the following data (one variable). Use single linkage to identify the clusters. Data: 0 0 1 3 3 6 7 9 10 10
4. Suppose that we have the following data (one variable). Use complete linkage to identify the clusters. Data: 0 0 1 3 3 6 7 9 10 10
5. What is an intuitive idea for the meaning of the *centroid* of a cluster?
6. Suppose that we have the following data:

a	b	c	d	e	f	g	h	i	j
(2,0)	(1,2)	(2,2)	(3,2)	(2,3)	(3,3)	(2,4)	(3,4)	(4,4)	(3,5)

   Identify the cluster by applying the k-means algorithm, with $k = 2$. Try using initial cluster centers as far apart as possible.

7. Refer to Exercise 6. Show that the ratio of the between-cluster variation to the within-cluster variation decreases with each pass of the algorithm.
8. Once again identify the clusters in Exercise 6 data, this time by applying the k-means algorithm, with $k = 3$. Try using initial cluster centers as far apart as possible.
9. Refer to Exercise 8. Show that the ratio of the between-cluster variation to the within-cluster variation decreases with each pass of the algorithm.
10. Which clustering solution do you think is preferable? Why?

Hands-on Analysis

Use the *cereals* data set, included at the book series Web site, for the following exercises. Make sure that the data are normalized.

11. Using all of the variables except *name* and *rating*, run the k-means algorithm with k= 5 to identify clusters within the data.
12. Develop clustering profiles that clearly describe the characteristics of the cereals within the cluster.
13. Rerun the k-means algorithm with$k = 3$.
14. Which clustering solution do you prefer, and why?
15. Develop clustering profiles that clearly describe the characteristics of the cereals within the cluster.
16. Use cluster membership to predict *rating*. One way to do this would be to construct a histogram of *rating* based on cluster membership alone. Describe how the relationship you uncovered makes sense, based on your earlier profiles.

CHAPTER 9

KOHONEN NETWORKS

SELF-ORGANIZING MAPS

Kohonen networks were introduced in 1982 by Finnish researcher Tuevo Kohonen [1]. Although applied initially to image and sound analysis, Kohonen networks are nevertheless an effective mechanism for clustering analysis. Kohonen networks represent a type of *self-organizing map* (SOM), which itself represents a special class of neural networks, which we studied in Chapter 7.

The goal of self-organizing maps is to convert a complex high-dimensional input signal into a simpler low-dimensional discrete map [2]. Thus, SOMs are nicely appropriate for cluster analysis, where underlying hidden patterns among records and fields are sought. SOMs structure the output nodes into clusters of nodes, where nodes in closer proximity are more similar to each other than to other nodes that are farther apart. Ritter [3] has shown that SOMs represent a nonlinear generalization of principal components analysis, another dimension-reduction technique.

Self-organizing maps are based on *competitive learning*, where the output nodes compete among themselves to be the winning node (or neuron), the only node to be activated by a particular input observation. As Haykin [2] describes it: "The neurons become *selectively tuned* to various input patterns (stimuli) or classes of input patterns in the course of a competitive learning process." A typical SOM architecture is shown in Figure 9.1. The input layer is shown at the bottom of the figure, with one input node for each field. Just as with neural networks, these input nodes do no processing themselves but simply pass the field input values along downstream.

Discovering Knowledge in Data: An Introduction to Data Mining, By Daniel T. Larose
ISBN 0-471-66657-2

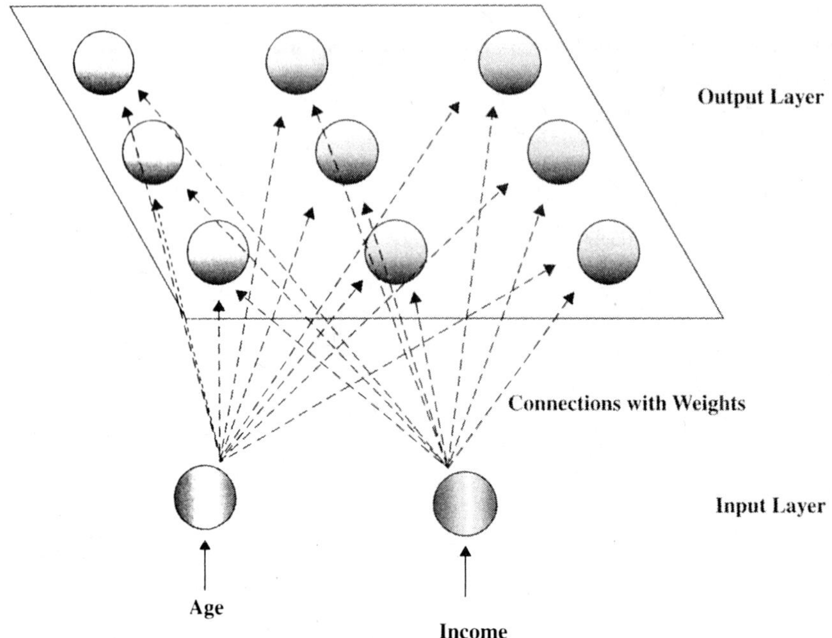

Figure 9.1 Topology of a simple self-organizing map for clustering records by age and income.

Like neural networks, SOMs are *feedforward* and *completely connected. Feedforward* networks do not allow looping or cycling. *Completely connected* means that every node in a given layer is connected to every node in the next layer, although not to other nodes in the same layer. Like neural networks, each connection between nodes has a weight associated with it, which at initialization is assigned randomly to a value between zero and 1. Adjusting these weights represents the key for the learning mechanism in both neural networks and self-organizing maps. Variable values need to be normalized or standardized, just as for neural networks, so that certain variables do not overwhelm others in the learning algorithm.

Unlike most neural networks, however, SOMs have no hidden layer. The data from the input layer is passed along directly to the output layer. The output layer is represented in the form of a lattice, usually in one or two dimensions, and typically in the shape of a rectangle, although other shapes, such as hexagons, may be used. The output layer shown in Figure 9.1 is a 3×3 square.

For a given record (instance), a particular field value is forwarded from a particular input node to every node in the output layer. For example, suppose that the normalized age and income values for the first record in the data set are 0.69 and 0.88, respectively. The 0.69 value would enter the SOM through the input node associated with *age*, and this node would pass this value of 0.69 to every node in the output layer. Similarly, the 0.88 value would be distributed through the *income* input node to every node in the output layer. These values, together with the weights assigned to each of the connections, would determine the values of a *scoring function* (such as

Euclidean distance) for each output node. The output node with the "best" outcome from the scoring function would then be designated as the *winning node*.

Self-organizing maps exhibit three characteristic processes:

1. *Competition*. As mentioned above, the output nodes compete with each other to produce the best value for a particular scoring function, most commonly the Euclidean distance. In this case, the output node that has the smallest Euclidean distance between the field inputs and the connection weights would be declared the winner. Later, we examine in detail an example of how this works.
2. *Cooperation*. The winning node therefore becomes the center of a neighborhood of excited neurons. This emulates the behavior of human neurons, which are sensitive to the output of other neurons in their immediate neighborhood. In self-organizing maps, all the nodes in this neighborhood share in the "excitement" or "reward" earned by the winning nodes, that of *adaptation*. Thus, even though the nodes in the output layer are not connected directly, they tend to share common features, due to this neighborliness parameter.
3. *Adaptation*. The nodes in the neighborhood of the winning node participate in adaptation, that is, learning. The weights of these nodes are adjusted so as to further improve the score function. In other words, these nodes will thereby have an increased chance of winning the competition once again, for a similar set of field values.

KOHONEN NETWORKS

Kohonen networks are self-organizing maps that exhibit *Kohonen learning*. Suppose that we consider the set of m field values for the nth record to be an input vector $\mathbf{x}_n = x_{n1}, x_{n2}, \ldots, x_{nm}$, and the current set of m weights for a particular output node j to be a weight vector $\mathbf{w}_j = w_{1j}, w_{2j}, \ldots, w_{mj}$. In Kohonen learning, the nodes in the neighborhood of the winning node adjust their weights using a linear combination of the input vector and the current weight vector:

$$w_{ij,\text{new}} = w_{ij,\text{current}} + \eta(x_{ni} - w_{ij,\text{current}}) \tag{9.1}$$

where η, $0 < \eta < 1$, represents the *learning rate*, analogous to the neural networks case. Kohonen [4] indicates the learning rate should be a decreasing function of training epochs (runs through the data set) and that a linearly or geometrically decreasing η is satisfactory for most purposes.

The algorithm for Kohonen networks (after Fausett [5]) is shown in the accomponying box. At initialization, the weights are randomly assigned, unless firm a priori knowledge exists regarding the proper value for the weight vectors. Also at initialization, the learning rate η and neighborhood size R are assigned. The value of R may start out moderately large but should decrease as the algorithm progresses. Note that nodes that do not attract a sufficient number of hits may be pruned, thereby improving algorithm efficiency.

KOHONEN NETWORKS ALGORITHM

For each input vector **x**, do:

- *Competition.* For each output node j, calculate the value $D(w_j, x_n)$ of the scoring function. For example, for Euclidean distance, $D(w_j, x_n) = \sqrt{\sum_i (w_{ij} - x_{ni})^2}$. Find the winning node J that minimizes $D(w_j, x_n)$ over all output nodes.
- *Cooperation.* Identify all output nodes j within the neighborhood of J defined by the neighborhood size R. For these nodes, do the following for all input record fields:
  - *Adaptation.* Adjust the weights:

$$w_{ij,\text{new}} = w_{ij,\text{current}} + \eta(x_{ni} - w_{ij,\text{current}})$$

- Adjust the learning rate and neighborhood size, as needed.
- Stop when the termination criteria are met.

EXAMPLE OF A KOHONEN NETWORK STUDY

Consider the following simple example. Suppose that we have a data set with two attributes, *age* and *income*, which have already been normalized, and suppose that we would like to use a 2 × 2 Kohonen network to uncover hidden clusters in the data set. We would thus have the topology shown in Figure 9.2.

A set of four records is ready to be input, with a thumbnail description of each record provided. With such a small network, we set the neighborhood size to be $R = 0$, so that only the winning node will be awarded the opportunity to adjust its weight. Also, we set the learning rate η to be 0.5. Finally, assume that the weights have been randomly initialized as follows:

$$w_{11} = 0.9 \qquad w_{21} = 0.8 \qquad w_{12} = 0.9 \qquad w_{22} = 0.2$$
$$w_{13} = 0.1 \qquad w_{23} = 0.8 \qquad w_{14} = 0.1 \qquad w_{24} = 0.2$$

For the first input vector, $\mathbf{x}_1 = (0.8, 0.8)$, we perform the following competition, cooperation, and adaptation sequence.

- *Competition.* We compute the Euclidean distance between this input vector and the weight vectors for each of the four output nodes:

$$\textit{Node 1: } D(w_1, x_1) = \sqrt{\sum_i (w_{i1} - x_{1i})^2} = \sqrt{(0.9 - 0.8)^2 + (0.8 - 0.8)^2} = 0.1$$

$$\textit{Node 2: } D(w_2, x_1) = \sqrt{(0.9 - 0.8)^2 + (0.2 - 0.8)^2} = 0.61$$

$$\textit{Node 3: } D(w_3, x_1) = \sqrt{(0.1 - 0.8)^2 + (0.8 - 0.8)^2} = 0.70$$

$$\textit{Node 4: } D(w_4, x_1) = \sqrt{(0.1 - 0.8)^2 + (0.2 - 0.8)^2} = 0.92$$

The winning node for this first input record is therefore node 1, since it minimizes the score function D, the Euclidean distance between the input vector for this record, and the vector of weights, over all nodes.

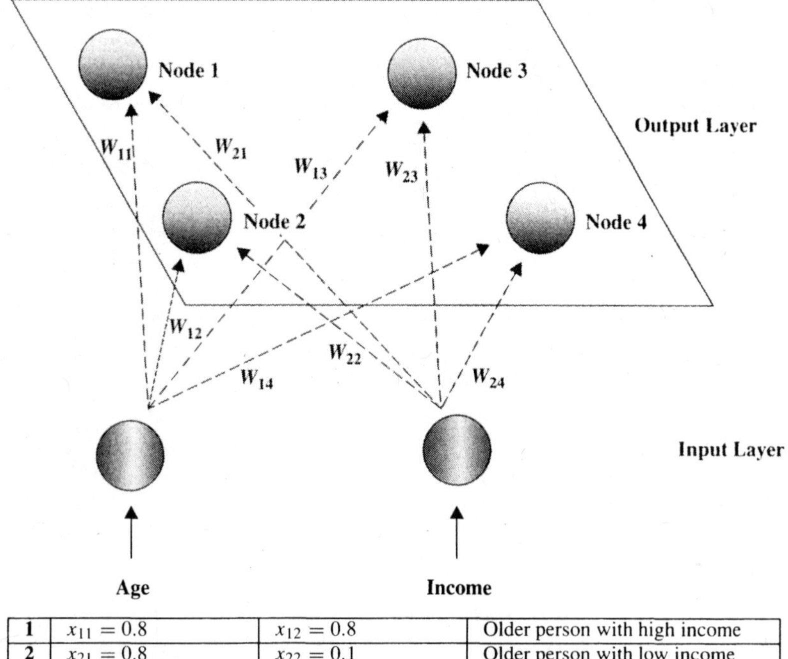

1	$x_{11} = 0.8$	$x_{12} = 0.8$	Older person with high income
2	$x_{21} = 0.8$	$x_{22} = 0.1$	Older person with low income
3	$x_{31} = 0.2$	$x_{32} = 0.9$	Younger person with high income
4	$x_{41} = 0.1$	$x_{42} = 0.1$	Younger person with low income

Figure 9.2 Example: topology of the 2 × 2 Kohonen network.

Note *why* node 1 won the competition for the first record, (0.8, 0.8). Node 1 won because its weights (0.9, 0.8) are more similar to the field values for this record than are the other nodes' weights. For this reason, we may expect node 1 to exhibit an affinity for records of older persons with high-income. In other words, we may expect node 1 to uncover a *cluster* of older, high-income persons.

- *Cooperation*. In this simple example we have set the neighborhood size $R = 0$ so that the level of cooperation among output nodes is nil! Therefore, only the winning node, node 1, will be rewarded with a weight adjustment. (We omit this step in the remainder of the example.)
- *Adaptation*. For the winning node, node 1, the weights are adjusted as follows:

$$w_{ij,\text{new}} = w_{ij,\text{current}} + \eta(x_{ni} - w_{ij,\text{current}})$$

For $j = 1$ (node 1), $n = 1$ (the first record) and learning rate $\eta = 0.5$, this becomes $w_{i1,\text{new}} = w_{i1,\text{current}} + 0.5(x_{1i} - w_{i1,\text{current}})$ for each field:

$$\text{For } age\text{: } w_{11,\text{new}} = w_{11,\text{current}} + 0.5(x_{11} - w_{11,\text{current}})$$
$$= 0.9 + 0.5(0.8 - 0.9) = 0.85$$
$$\text{For } income\text{: } w_{21,\text{new}} = w_{21,\text{current}} + 0.5(x_{12} - w_{21,\text{current}})$$
$$= 0.8 + 0.5(0.8 - 0.8) = 0.8$$

Note the type of adjustment that takes place. The weights are nudged in the direction of the fields' values of the input record. That is, w_{11}, the weight on the *age* connection for the winning node, was originally 0.9, but was adjusted in the direction of the normalized value for *age* in the first record, 0.8. Since the learning rate $\eta = 0.5$, this adjustment is half (0.5) of the distance between the current weight and the field value. This adjustment will help node 1 to become even more proficient at capturing the records of older, high-income persons.

Next, for the second input vector, $\mathbf{x}_2 = (0.8, 0.1)$, we have the following sequence.

- *Competition*

$$\textit{Node 1: } D(w_1, x_2) = \sqrt{\sum_i (w_{i1} - x_{2i})^2} = \sqrt{(0.9 - 0.8)^2 + (0.8 - 0.1)^2}$$
$$= 0.71$$
$$\textit{Node 2: } D(w_2, x_2) = \sqrt{(0.9 - 0.8)^2 + (0.2 - 0.1)^2} = 0.14$$
$$\textit{Node 3: } D(w_3, x_2) = \sqrt{(0.1 - 0.8)^2 + (0.8 - 0.1)^2} = 0.99$$
$$\textit{Node 4: } D(w_4, x_2) = \sqrt{(0.1 - 0.8)^2 + (0.2 - 0.1)^2} = 0.71$$

Winning node: node 2. Note that node 2 won the competition for the second record, (0.8, 0.1), because its weights (0.9, 0.2) are more similar to the field values for this record than are the other nodes' weights. Thus, we may expect node 2 to "collect" records of older persons with low income. That is, node 2 will represent a cluster of older, low-income persons.

- *Adaptation*. For the winning node, node 2, the weights are adjusted as follows: For $j = 2$ (node 2), $n = 2$ (the first record) and learning rate $\eta = 0.5$, we have $w_{i2,\text{new}} = w_{i2,\text{current}} + 0.5(x_{2i} - w_{i2,\text{current}})$ for each field:

$$\text{For } \textit{age}\text{: } w_{12,\text{new}} = w_{12,\text{current}} + 0.5(x_{21} - w_{12,\text{current}})$$
$$= 0.9 + 0.5(0.8 - 0.9) = 0.85$$
$$\text{For } \textit{income}\text{: } w_{22,\text{new}} = w_{22,\text{current}} + 0.5(x_{22} - w_{22,\text{current}})$$
$$= 0.2 + 0.5(0.1 - 0.2) = 0.15$$

Again, the weights are updated in the direction of the field values of the input record. Weight w_{12} undergoes the same adjustment w_{11} above, since the current weights and *age* field values were the same. Weight w_{22} for income is adjusted downward, since the *income* level of the second record was lower than the current *income* weight for the winning node. Because of this adjustment, node 2 will be even better at catching records of older, low-income persons.

Next, for the third input vector, $\mathbf{x}_3 = (0.2, 0.9)$, we have the following sequence.

- *Competition*

$$\textit{Node 1: } D(w_1, x_3) = \sqrt{\sum_i (w_{i1} - x_{3i})^2} = \sqrt{(0.9 - 0.2)^2 + (0.8 - 0.9)^2}$$
$$= 0.71$$
$$\textit{Node 2: } D(w_2, x_3) = \sqrt{(0.9 - 0.2)^2 + (0.2 - 0.9)^2} = 0.99$$

$$\textit{Node 3: } D(w_3, x_3) = \sqrt{(0.1 - 0.2)^2 + (0.8 - 0.9)^2} = 0.14$$

$$\textit{Node 4: } D(w_4, x_3) = \sqrt{(0.1 - 0.2)^2 + (0.2 - 0.9)^2} = 0.71$$

The winning node is node 3 because its weights (0.1, 0.8) are the closest to the third record's field values. Hence, we may expect node 3 to represent a cluster of younger, high-income persons.

- *Adaptation*. For the winning node, node 3, the weights are adjusted as follows: $w_{i3,\text{new}} = w_{i3,\text{current}} + 0.5(x_{3i} - w_{i3,\text{current}})$, for each field:

$$\begin{aligned} \text{For } \textit{age: } w_{13,\text{new}} &= w_{13,\text{current}} + 0.5(x_{31} - w_{13,\text{current}}) \\ &= 0.1 + 0.5(0.2 - 0.1) = 0.15 \\ \text{For } \textit{income: } w_{23,\text{new}} &= w_{23,\text{current}} + 0.5(x_{32} - w_{23,\text{current}}) \\ &= 0.8 + 0.5(0.9 - 0.8) = 0.85 \end{aligned}$$

Finally, for the fourth input vector, $\mathbf{x}_4 = (0.1, 0.1)$, we have the following sequence.

- *Competition*

$$\begin{aligned} \textit{Node 1: } D(w_1, x_4) &= \sqrt{\textstyle\sum_i (w_{i4} - x_{4i})^2} = \sqrt{(0.9 - 0.1)^2 + (0.8 - 0.1)^2} \\ &= 1.06 \end{aligned}$$

$$\textit{Node 2: } D(w_2, x_4) = \sqrt{(0.9 - 0.1)^2 + (0.2 - 0.1)^2} = 0.81$$

$$\textit{Node 3: } D(w_3, x_4) = \sqrt{(0.1 - 0.1)^2 + (0.8 - 0.1)^2} = 0.70$$

$$\textit{Node 4: } D(w_4, x_4) = \sqrt{(0.1 - 0.1)^2 + (0.2 - 0.1)^2} = 0.10$$

The winning node is node 4 because its weights (0.1, 0.2) have the smallest Euclidean distance to the fourth record's field values. We may therefore expect node 4 to represent a cluster of younger, low-income persons.

- *Adaptation*. For the winning node, node 4, the weights are adjusted as follows: $w_{i4,\text{new}} = w_{i4,\text{current}} + 0.5(x_{4i} - w_{i4,\text{current}})$, for each field:

$$\begin{aligned} \text{For } \textit{age}\text{: } w_{14,\text{new}} &= w_{14,\text{current}} + 0.5(x_{41} - w_{14,\text{current}}) \\ &= 0.1 + 0.5(0.1 - 0.1) = 0.10 \\ \text{For } \textit{income}\text{: } w_{24,\text{new}} &= w_{24,\text{current}} + 0.5(x_{42} - w_{24,\text{current}}) \\ &= 0.2 + 0.5(0.1 - 0.2) = 0.15 \end{aligned}$$

Thus, we have seen that the four output nodes will represent four distinct clusters if the network continues to be fed data similar to the four records shown in Figure 9.2. These clusters are summarized in Table 9.1.

Clearly, the clusters uncovered by the Kohonen network in this simple example are fairly obvious. However, this example does serve to illustrate how the network operates at a basic level, using competition and Kohonen learning.

TABLE 9.1 Four Clusters Uncovered by Kohonen Network

Cluster	Associated with:	Description
1	Node 1	Older person with high income
2	Node 2	Older person with low income
3	Node 3	Younger person with high income
4	Node 4	Younger person with low income

CLUSTER VALIDITY

To avoid spurious results, and to assure that the resulting clusters are reflective of the general population, the clustering solution should be validated. One common validation method is to split the original sample randomly into two groups, develop cluster solutions for each group, and then compare their profiles using the methods below or other summarization methods.

Now, suppose that a researcher is interested in performing further inference, prediction, or other analysis downstream on a particular field, and wishes to use the clusters as predictors. Then, it is important that the researcher not include the field of interest as one of the fields used to build the clusters. For example, in the example below, clusters are constructed using the *churn* data set. We would like to use these clusters as predictors for later assistance in classifying customers as churners or not. Therefore, we must be careful not to include the *churn* field among the variables used to build the clusters.

APPLICATION OF CLUSTERING USING KOHONEN NETWORKS

Next, we apply the Kohonen network algorithm to the *churn* data set from Chapter 3 (available at the book series Web site; also available from `http://www.sgi.com/tech/mlc/db/`). Recall that the data set contains 20 variables worth of information about 3333 customers, along with an indication of whether that customer churned (left the company) or not. The following variables were passed to the Kohonen network algorithm, using Clementine:

- Flag (0/1) variables
  - International Plan and VoiceMail Plan
- Numerical variables
  - *Account length*, *voice mail messages*, *day minutes*, *evening minutes*, *night minutes*, *international minutes*, and *customer service calls*
  - After applying min–max normalization to all numerical variables

The topology of the network was as in Figure 9.3, with every node in the input layer being connected with weights (not shown) to every node in the output

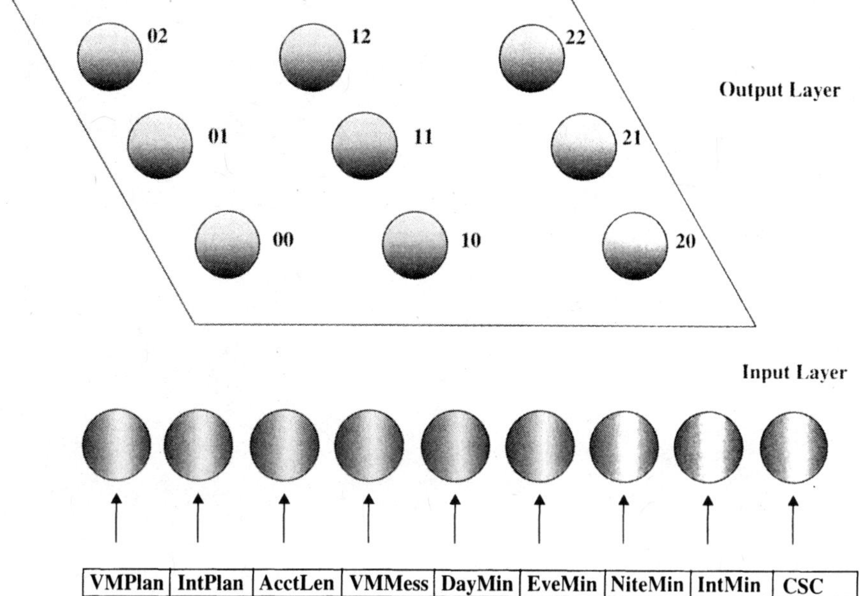

Figure 9.3 Topology of 3 × 3 Kohonen network used for clustering the churn data set.

layer, which are labeled in accordance with their use in the Clementine results. The Kohonen learning parameters were set in Clementine as follows. For the first 20 cycles (passes through the data set), the neighborhood size was set at $R = 2$, and the learning rate was set to decay linearly starting at $\eta = 0.3$. Then, for the next 150 cycles, the neighborhood size was reset to $R = 1$ while the learning rate was allowed to decay linearly from $\eta = 0.3$ to at $\eta = 0$.

As it turned out, the Clementine Kohonen algorithm used only six of the nine available output nodes, as shown in Figure 9.4, with output nodes 01, 11, and 21 being pruned. [Note that each of the six clusters is actually of constant value in this plot, such as (0,0), (1,2), and so on. A random shock (*x, y agitation*, artificial noise) was introduced to illustrate the size of the cluster membership.]

Interpreting the Clusters

How are we to interpret these clusters? How can we develop cluster profiles? Consider Figure 9.5, which is a bar chart of the clusters, with a VoiceMail Plan overlay. Clusters 02 and 12 contain records only if they are adopters of the VoiceMail Plan, while clusters 00, 10, and 20 contain records if and only if they have not adopted the VoiceMail Plan. Cluster 22 contains only a tiny portion of voicemail adopters. Excepting this small proportion of records in cluster 22, the clustering algorithm has found a high-quality discrimination along this dimension, dividing the data set nearly perfectly among adopters and nonadopters of the VoiceMail Plan.

Figure 9.5 also indicates to us the relative sizes of the various clusters. Clusters smaller than a certain threshold size may not be considered significant, with the

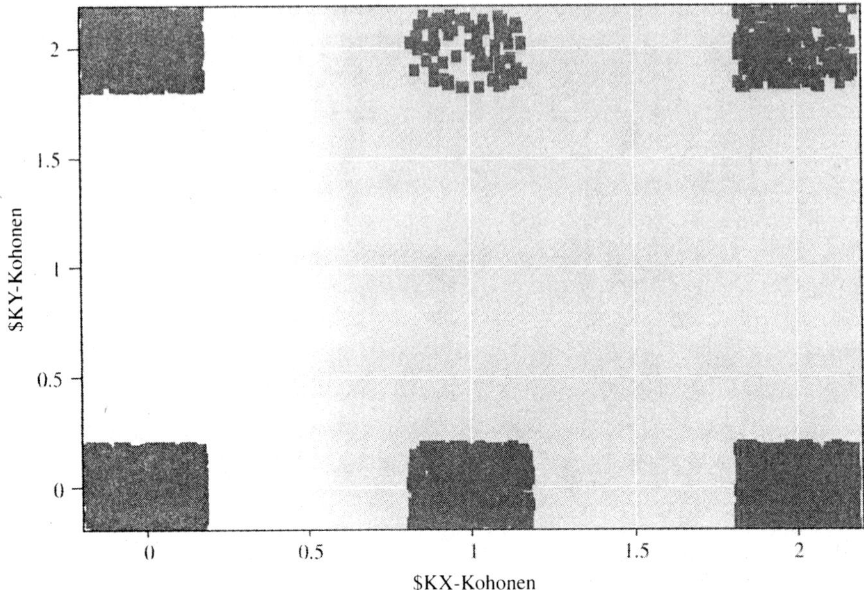

Figure 9.4 Clementine uncovered six clusters.

threshold varying according to the size of the data set, the area of application, and the task at hand. Here, cluster 12 contains only 77 records, representing a rather small 2.31% of the data set. However, as we mentioned, it is nicely discriminating with respect to the VoiceMail Plan. The distribution graph loses the geographic mapping information present in the original cluster plot in Figure 9.4. Recall that because of the neighborliness parameter, clusters that are closer together should be more similar than clusters than are farther apart. Consider the original plot, this time with an overlay of membership in the VoiceMail Plan, as in Figure 9.6. This plot clearly illustrates the contiguity of the two clusters, containing only customers who belong to the VoiceMail Plan, and which therefore makes these clusters more similar. Cluster 22 in the upper right also contains a few of these customers, but none of the clusters along the bottom row contain any customers who adopted the VoiceMail Plan.

Value	Proportion	%	Count
00		24.69	823
02		24.9	830
10		16.11	537
12		2.31	77
20		24.6	820
22		7.38	246

VMail Plan

no yes

Figure 9.5 Clusters 02 and 12 contain only adopters of the VoiceMail Plan.

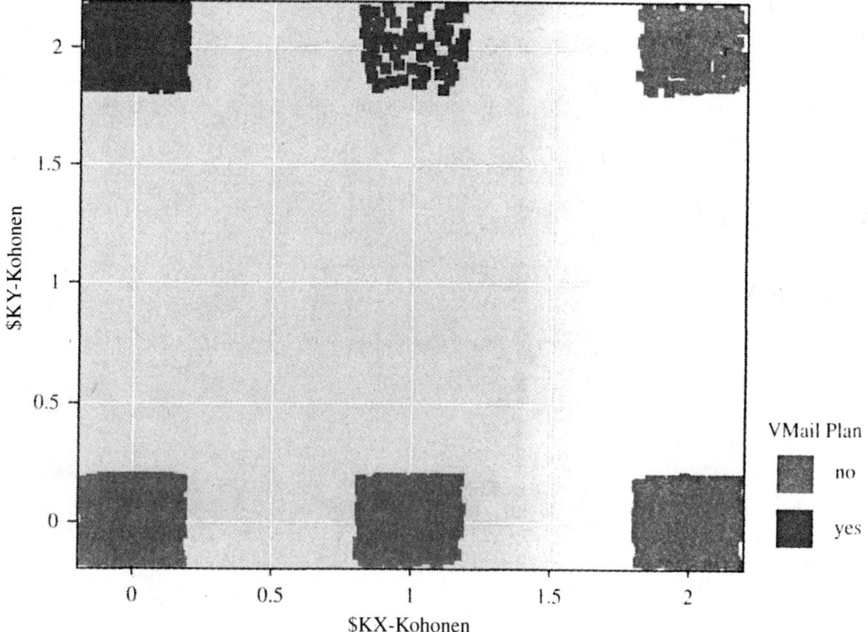

Figure 9.6 Similar clusters are closer to each other.

Next, consider Figure 9.7, which is a distribution plot of the clusters, with an International Plan overlay. Clusters 12 and 22 contain records if and only if they are adopters of the international plan, while the other clusters contain records if and only if they have not adopted the international plan. This time, the clustering algorithm has found another "perfect" discrimination along this dimension, dividing the data set perfectly among adopters and nonadopters of the International Plan.

We see that cluster 12 represents a special subset of customers, those who have adopted both the International Plan and the VoiceMail Plan. This is a well-defined subset of the customer base, which perhaps explains why the Kohonen network uncovered it, even though this subset represents only 2.31% of the customers. Figure 9.8

Value	Proportion	%	Count
00		24.69	823
02		24.9	830
10		16.11	537
12		2.31	77
20		24.6	820
22		7.38	246

Intl Plan
no yes

Figure 9.7 Clusters 12 and 22 contain only adopters of the International Plan.

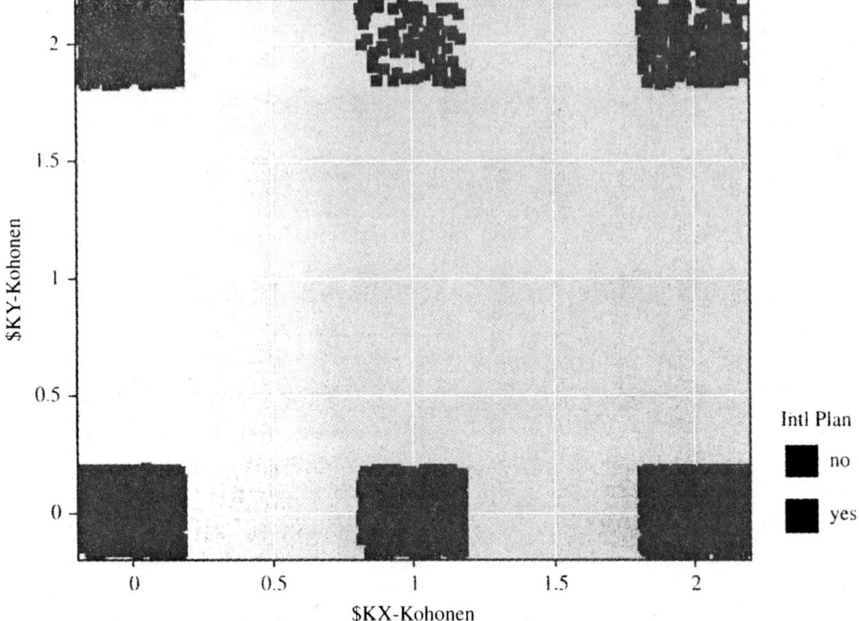

Figure 9.8 Plot of clusters with International Plan overlay.

underscores the contiguity of clusters 12 and 22, due in part to their similarity in the International Plan dimension.

These findings are supported by the web graph in Figure 9.9, which shows the connections among the clusters (at bottom), nonadopters of the plans on the upper left, and adopters of the plans on the upper right. Note that cluster 12 is the only cluster with connections to both *yes* nodes, that cluster 02 shows a connection to the

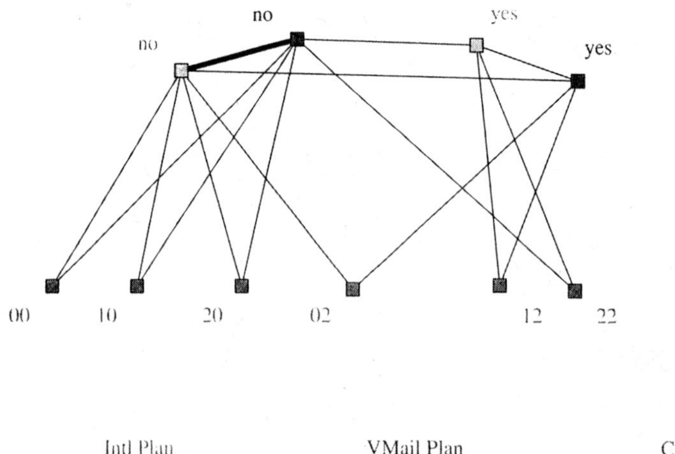

Figure 9.9 Web graph of relationship between clusters and plans.

TABLE 9.2 Cluster Mean Values for Numerical Variables

Cluster	Account Length	VMail Message	Day Mins	Eve Mins	Night Mins	Intl Mins	Cust Serv	Records
00	62.329	0.000	189.256	200.249	209.246	10.203	1.467	852
02	100.722	29.229	178.695	202.366	201.483	10.153	1.531	830
10	101.240	0.000	179.208	202.060	199.434	10.379	1.627	520
12	107.120	31.229	188.781	208.319	203.990	10.919	1.494	83
20	140.948	0.000	167.969	198.451	194.123	10.113	1.694	808
22	103.017	0.529	187.713	202.421	193.789	10.528	1.454	240

yes node for the VoiceMail Plan, and that cluster 22 shows a connection to the *yes* node for the International Plan.

In general, not all clusters are guaranteed to offer obvious interpretability. The data analyst should team up with a domain expert to discuss the relevance and applicability of the clusters uncovered using Kohonen or other methods. Here, however, most of the clusters appear fairly clear-cut and self-explanatory. To complete the profile of our clusters, we consider the cluster mean values for the numerical variables, as shown in Table 9.2.

Cluster Profiles

- *Cluster 00*: *Newbie Heavy Users*. Belonging to neither the VoiceMail Plan nor the International Plan, customers in large cluster 00 represent the company's newest customers, on average, with easily the shortest mean account length. These customers set the pace with the highest mean day minutes and night minutes usage.
- *Cluster 02*: *Voice Mail Users*. This large cluster contains members of the VoiceMail Plan, with therefore a high mean number of VoiceMail messages, and no members of the International Plan. Otherwise, the cluster tends toward the middle of the pack for the other variables.
- *Cluster 10*: *Average Customers*. Customers in this medium-sized cluster belong to neither the VoiceMail Plan nor the International Plan. Except for the second-largest mean number of calls to customer service, this cluster otherwise tends toward the average values for the other variables.
- *Cluster 12*: *Power Customers*. This smallest cluster contains customers who belong to both the VoiceMail Plan and the International Plan. These sophisticated customers also lead the pack in usage minutes across two categories and are in second place in the other two categories. The company should keep a watchful eye on this cluster, as they may represent a highly profitable group.
- *Cluster 20*: *Loyal Low-Usage Customers*. Belonging to neither the VoiceMail Plan nor the International Plan, customers in large cluster 20 have nevertheless

been with the company the longest, with by far the largest mean account length, which may be related to the largest number of calls to customer service. This cluster exhibits the lowest average minutes usage for day, evening, and international minutes, and the second lowest night minutes.

- *Cluster 22*: *International Plan Users*. This small cluster contains members of the International Plan and only a few members of the VoiceMail Plan. The number of calls to customer service is lowest, which may mean that they need a minimum of hand-holding. Besides the lowest mean night minutes usage, this cluster tends toward average values for the other variables.

Cluster profiles may of themselves be of actionable benefit to companies and researchers. They may, for example, suggest marketing segmentation strategies in an era of shrinking budgets. Rather than targeting the entire customer base for a mass mailing, for example, perhaps only the most profitable customers may be targeted. Another strategy is to identify those customers whose potential loss would be of greater harm to the company, such as the customers in cluster 12 above. Finally, customer clusters could be identified that exhibit behavior predictive of churning; intervention with these customers could save them for the company.

Suppose, however, that we would like to apply these clusters to assist us in the *churn classification* task. We may compare the proportions of churners among the various clusters, using graphs such as Figure 9.10.

From the figure we can see that customers in clusters 12 (power customers) and 22 (*International Plan users*) are in greatest danger of leaving the company, as shown by their higher overall churn proportions. Cluster 02 (VoiceMail Plan users) has the lowest churn rate. The company should take a serious look at its International Plan to see why customers do not seem to be happy with it. Also, the company should encourage more customers to adopt its VoiceMail Plan, in order to make switching companies more inconvenient. These results and recommendations reflect our findings from Chapter 3, where we initially examined the relationship between churning and the various fields. Note also that clusters 12 and 22 are neighboring clusters; even

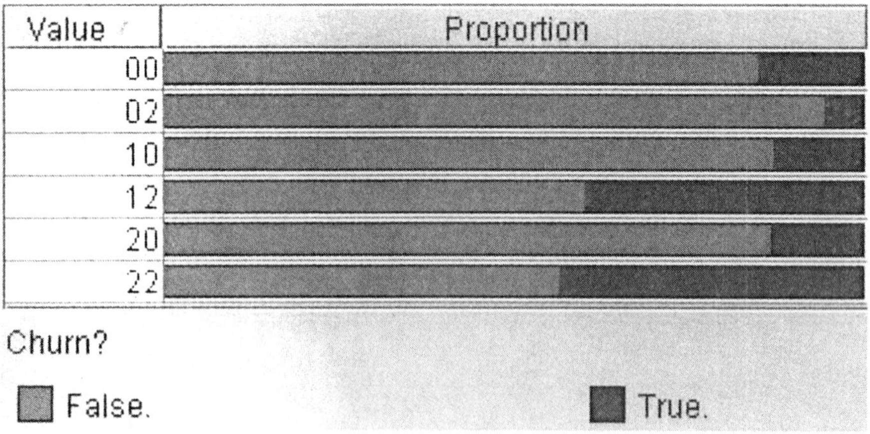

Figure 9.10 Proportions of churners among the clusters.

though *churn* was not an input field for cluster formation, the type of customers who are likely to churn are more similar to each other than to customers not likely to churn.

USING CLUSTER MEMBERSHIP AS INPUT TO DOWNSTREAM DATA MINING MODELS

Cluster membership may be used to enrich the data set and improve model efficacy. Indeed, as data repositories continue to grow and the number of fields continues to increase, clustering has become a common method of dimension reduction.

We will illustrate how cluster membership may be used as input for downstream data mining models, using the *churn* data set and the clusters uncovered above. Each record now has associated with it a cluster membership assigned by the Kohonen networks algorithm. We shall enrich our data set by adding this cluster membership field to the input fields used for classifying churn. A CART decision tree model was run, to classify customers as either churners or nonchurners. The resulting decision tree output is shown in Figure 9.11.

The root node split is on whether *DayMin_mm* (the min–max normalization of *day minutes*) is greater than about 0.75. If so, the second-level split is by cluster, with cluster 02 split off from the remaining clusters. Note that for high day minutes, the mode classification is *True* (churner), but that within this subset, membership in cluster 02 acts to protect from churn, since the 45 customers with high day minutes and membership in cluster 02 have a 97.8% probability of *not* churning. Recall that cluster 02, which is acting as a brake on churn behavior, represents *Voice Mail Users*, who had the lowest churn rate of any cluster.

We turn next to the task of mining association rules in large data sets.

```
DayMins_mm < 0.75384834663626 [Mode: False.] (3,122)
    CustServCalls_mm < 0.388888888888889 [Mode: False.] (2,871)
        Intl Plan in ["no"] [Mode: False.] (2,604)
            DayMins_mm < 0.636402508551881 [Mode: False.] ⇨ False. (2,221, 0.973)
            DayMins_mm >= 0.636402508551881 [Mode: False.] (383)
                EveMins_mm < 0.714324993126203 [Mode: False.] ⇨ False. (332, 0.898)
                EveMins_mm >= 0.714324993126203 [Mode: True.] ⇨ True. (51, 0.667)
        Intl Plan in ["yes"] [Mode: False.] (267)
            IntlMins_mm < 0.655 [Mode: False.] ⇨ False. (219, 0.758)
            IntlMins_mm >= 0.655 [Mode: True.] ⇨ True. (48, 1.0)
    CustServCalls_mm >= 0.388888888888889 [Mode: True.] (251)
        DayMins_mm < 0.456670467502851 [Mode: True.] ⇨ True. (102, 0.873)
        DayMins_mm >= 0.456670467502851 [Mode: False.] ⇨ False. (149, 0.745)
DayMins_mm >= 0.75384834663626 [Mode: True.] (211)
    Cluster in ["02"] [Mode: False.] ⇨ False. (45, 0.978)
    Cluster in ["00" "10" "12" "20" "22"] [Mode: True.] (166)
        EveMins_mm < 0.516222161121804 [Mode: False.] ⇨ False. (57, 0.561)
        EveMins_mm >= 0.516222161121804 [Mode: True.] ⇨ True. (109, 0.927)
```

Figure 9.11 Output of CART decision tree for data set enriched by cluster membership.

REFERENCES

1. Tuevo Kohonen, Self-organized formation of topologically correct feature maps, *Biological Cybernetics*, Vol. 43, pp. 59–69, 1982.
2. Simon Haykin, *Neural Networks: A Comprehensive Foundation*, Prentice Hall, Upper Saddle River, NJ, 1990.
3. Helge Ritter, Self-organizing feature maps: Kohonen maps, in M. A. Arbib, ed., *The Handbook of Brain Theory and Neural Networks*, pp. 846–851, MIT Press, Cambridge, MA, 1995.
4. Tuevo Kohonen, *Self-Organization and Associative Memory*, 3rd ed., Springer-Verlag, Berlin, 1989.
5. Laurene Fausett, *Fundamentals of Neural Networks*, Prentice Hall, Upper Saddle River, NJ, 1994.

EXERCISES

1. Describe some of the similarities between Kohonen networks and the neural networks of Chapter 7. Describe some of the differences.

2. Describe the three characteristic processes exhibited by self-organizing maps such as Kohonen networks. What differentiates Kohonen networks from other self-organizing map models?

3. Using weights and distance, explain clearly why a certain output node will win the competition for the input of a certain record.

4. For larger output layers, what would be the effect of increasing the value of R?

5. Describe what would happen if the learning rate η did not decline?

6. This chapter shows how cluster membership can be used for downstream modeling. Does this apply to the cluster membership obtained by hierarchical and k-means clustering as well?

Hands-on Analysis

Use the *adult* data set at the book series Web site for the following exercises.

7. Apply the Kohonen clustering algorithm to the data set, being careful not to include the *income* field. Use a topology that is not too large, such as 3×3.

8. Construct a scatter plot (with x/y agitation) of the cluster membership, with an overlay of *income*. Discuss your findings.

9. Construct a bar chart of the cluster membership, with an overlay of *income*. Discuss your findings. Compare to the scatter plot.

10. Construct a bar chart of the cluster membership, with an overlay of *marital status*. Discuss your findings.

11. If your software supports this, construct a web graph of *income*, *marital status*, and the other categorical variables. Fine-tune the web graph so that it conveys good information.

12. Generate numerical summaries for the clusters. For example, generate a cluster mean summary.

13. Using the information above and any other information you can bring to bear, construct detailed and informative cluster profiles, complete with titles.

14. Use cluster membership as a further input to a CART decision tree model for classifying income. How important is clustering membership in classifying income?

15. Use cluster membership as a further input to a C4.5 decision tree model for classifying income. How important is clustering membership in classifying income? Compare to the CART model.

CHAPTER **10**

ASSOCIATION RULES

AFFINITY ANALYSIS AND MARKET BASKET ANALYSIS

Affinity analysis is the study of attributes or characteristics that "go together." Methods for affinity analysis, also known as *market basket analysis*, seek to uncover *associations* among these attributes; that is, it seeks to uncover rules for quantifying the relationship between two or more attributes. Association rules take the form "If *antecedent*, then *consequent*," along with a measure of the support and confidence associated with the rule. For example, a particular supermarket may find that of the 1000 customers shopping on a Thursday night, 200 bought diapers, and of the 200 who bought diapers, 50 bought beer. Thus, the association rule would be: "If buy diapers, then buy beer," with a *support* of $50/1000 = 5\%$ and a *confidence* of $50/200 = 25\%$.

Examples of association tasks in business and research include:

- Investigating the proportion of subscribers to your company's cell phone plan that respond positively to an offer of a service upgrade
- Examining the proportion of children whose parents read to them who are themselves good readers

Discovering Knowledge in Data: An Introduction to Data Mining, By Daniel T. Larose
ISBN 0-471-66657-2

- Predicting degradation in telecommunications networks
- Finding out which items in a supermarket are purchased together, and which items are never purchased together
- Determining the proportion of cases in which a new drug will exhibit dangerous side effects

What types of algorithms can we apply to mine association rules from a particular data set? The daunting problem that awaits any such algorithm is the curse of dimensionality: The number of possible association rules grows exponentially in the number of attributes. Specifically, if there are k attributes, we limit ourselves to binary attributes, we account only for the positive cases (e.g., *buy diapers* = *yes*), there are on the order of $k \cdot 2^{k-1}$ possible association rules. Consider that a typical application for association rules is market basket analysis and that there may be *thousands* of binary attributes (*buy beer? buy popcorn? buy milk? buy bread?* etc.), the search

Sketch © 2004 by Chantal Larose

TABLE 10.1 Transactions Made at the Roadside Vegetable Stand

Transaction	Items Purchased
1	Broccoli, green peppers, corn
2	Asparagus, squash, corn
3	Corn, tomatoes, beans, squash
4	Green peppers, corn, tomatoes, beans
5	Beans, asparagus, broccoli
6	Squash, asparagus, beans, tomatoes
7	Tomatoes, corn
8	Broccoli, tomatoes, green peppers
9	Squash, asparagus, beans
10	Beans, corn
11	Green peppers, broccoli, beans, squash
12	Asparagus, beans, squash
13	Squash, corn, asparagus, beans
14	Corn, green peppers, tomatoes, beans, broccoli

problem appears at first glance to be utterly hopeless. For example, suppose that a tiny convenience store has only 100 different items, and a customer could either buy or not buy any combination of those 100 items. Then there are $100 \cdot 2^{99} \simeq 6.4 \times 10^{31}$ possible association rules that await your intrepid search algorithm.

The *a priori algorithm* for mining association rules, however, takes advantage of structure within the rules themselves to reduce the search problem to a more manageable size. Before we examine the a priori algorithm, however, let us consider some basic concepts and notation for association rule mining. We begin with a simple example.

Suppose that a local farmer has set up a roadside vegetable stand and is offering the following items for sale: {asparagus, beans, broccoli, corn, green peppers, squash, tomatoes}. Denote this set of items as I. One by one, customers pull over, pick up a basket, and purchase various combinations of these items, subsets of I. (For our purposes, we don't keep track of how much of each item is purchased, just whether or not that particular item is purchased.) Suppose Table 10.1 lists the transactions made during one fine fall afternoon at this roadside vegetable stand.

Data Representation for Market Basket Analysis

There are two principal methods of representing this type of market basket data: using either the transactional data format or the tabular data format. The *transactional data format* requires only two fields, an *ID* field and a *content* field, with each record representing a single item only. For example, the data in Table 10.1 could be represented using transactional data format as shown in Table 10.2.

In the *tabular data format*, each record represents a separate transaction, with as many 0/1 flag fields as there are items. The data from Table 10.1 could be represented using the tabular data format, as shown in Table 10.3.

TABLE 10.2 Transactional Data Format for the Roadside Vegetable Stand Data

Transaction ID	Items
1	Broccoli
1	Green peppers
1	Corn
2	Asparagus
2	Squash
2	Corn
3	Corn
3	Tomatoes
⋮	⋮

SUPPORT, CONFIDENCE, FREQUENT ITEMSETS, AND THE A PRIORI PROPERTY

Let D be the set of transactions represented in Table 10.1, where each transaction T in D represents a set of items contained in I. Suppose that we have a particular set of items A (e.g., beans and squash), and another set of items B (e.g., asparagus). Then an *association rule* takes the form *if* A, *then* B (i.e., $A \Rightarrow B$), where the *antecedent* A and the *consequent* B are proper subsets of I, and A and B are mutually exclusive. This definition would exclude, for example, trivial rules such as *if beans and squash, then beans*.

TABLE 10.3 Tabular Data Format for the Roadside Vegetable Stand Data

Transaction	Asparagus	Beans	Broccoli	Corn	Green Peppers	Squash	Tomatoes
1	0	0	1	1	1	0	0
2	1	0	0	1	0	1	0
3	0	1	0	1	0	1	1
4	0	1	0	1	1	0	1
5	1	1	1	0	0	0	0
6	1	1	0	0	0	1	1
7	0	0	0	1	0	0	1
8	0	0	1	0	1	0	1
9	1	1	0	0	0	1	0
10	0	1	0	1	0	0	0
11	0	1	1	0	1	1	0
12	1	1	0	0	0	1	0
13	1	1	0	1	0	1	0
14	0	1	1	1	1	0	1

The *support* s for a particular association rule $A \Rightarrow B$ is the proportion of transactions in D that contain both A and B. That is,

$$\text{support} = P(A \cap B) = \frac{\text{number of transactions containing both } A \text{ and } B}{\text{total number of transactions}}.$$

The *confidence* c of the association rule $A \Rightarrow B$ is a measure of the accuracy of the rule, as determined by the percentage of transactions in D containing A that also contain B. In other words,

$$\text{confidence} = P(B|A) = \frac{P(A \cap B)}{P(A)}$$
$$= \frac{\text{number of transactions containing both } A \text{ and } B}{\text{number of transactions containing } A}.$$

Analysts may prefer rules that have either high support or high confidence, and usually both. *Strong rules* are those that meet or surpass certain minimum support and confidence criteria. For example, an analyst interested in finding which supermarket items are purchased together may set a minimum support level of 20% and a minimum confidence level of 70%. On the other hand, a fraud detection analyst or a terrorism detection analyst would need to reduce the minimum support level to 1% or less, since comparatively few transactions are either fraudulent or terror-related.

An *itemset* is a set of items contained in I, and a *k-itemset* is an itemset containing k items. For example, {beans, squash} is a 2-itemset, and {broccoli, green peppers, corn} is a 3-itemset, each from the vegetable stand set I. The *itemset frequency* is simply the number of transactions that contain the particular itemset. A *frequent itemset* is an itemset that occurs at least a certain minimum number of times, having itemset frequency $\geq \phi$. For example, suppose that we set $\phi = 4$. Then itemsets that occur more than four times are said to be *frequent*. We denote the set of frequent k-itemsets as F_k.

MINING ASSOCIATION RULES
The mining of association rules from large databases is a two-steps process: 1. Find all frequent itemsets; that is, find all itemsets with frequency $\geq \phi$. 2. From the frequent itemsets, generate association rules satisfying the minimum support and confidence conditions.

The *a priori algorithm* takes advantage of the a priori property to shrink the search space. The *a priori property* states that if an itemset Z is not frequent, then adding another item A to the itemset Z will not make Z more frequent. That is, if Z is not frequent, $Z \cup A$ will not be frequent. In fact, no *superset* of Z (itemset containing

Z) will be frequent. This helpful property reduces significantly the search space for the a priori algorithm.

A PRIORI PROPERTY
If an itemset Z is not frequent then for any item A, $Z \cup A$ will not be frequent.

HOW DOES THE A PRIORI ALGORITHM WORK (PART 1)? GENERATING FREQUENT ITEMSETS

Consider the set of transactions D represented in Table 10.1. How would the a priori algorithm mine association rules from this data set?

Let $\phi = 4$, so that an itemset is frequent if it occurs four or more times in D. We first find F_1, the frequent 1-itemsets, which represent simply the individual vegetable items themselves. To do so, we may turn to Table 10.3 and take the column sums, which give us the number of transactions containing each particular vegetable. Since each sum meets or exceeds $\phi = 4$, we conclude that each 1-itemset is frequent. Thus, $F_1 = \{$asparagus, beans, broccoli, corn, green peppers, squash, tomatoes$\}$.

Next, we turn to finding the frequent 2-itemsets. In general, to find F_k, the a priori algorithm first constructs a set C_k of candidate k-itemsets by joining F_{k-1} with itself. Then it prunes C_k using the a priori property. The itemsets in C_k that survive the pruning step then form F_k. Here, C_2 consists of all the combinations of vegetables in Table 10.4.

Since $\phi = 4$, we have $F_2 = \{$ {asparagus, beans}, {asparagus, squash}, {beans, corn}, and {beans, squash}, {beans, tomatoes}, {broccoli, green peppers}, {corn, tomatoes} $\}$. Next, we use the frequent itemsets in F_2 to generate C_3, the candidate

TABLE 10.4 Candidate 2-ItemSets

Combination	Count	Combination	Count
Asparagus, beans	5	Broccoli, corn	2
Asparagus, broccoli	1	Broccoli, green peppers	4
Asparagus, corn	2	Broccoli, squash	1
Asparagus, green peppers	0	Broccoli, tomatoes	2
Asparagus, squash	5	Corn, green peppers	3
Asparagus, tomatoes	1	Corn, squash	3
Beans, broccoli	3	Corn, tomatoes	4
Beans, corn	5	Green peppers, squash	1
Beans, green peppers	3	Green peppers, tomatoes	3
Beans, squash	6	Squash, tomatoes	2
Beans, tomatoes	4		

3-itemsets. To do so, we join F_2 with itself, where *itemsets are joined if they have the first $k-1$ items in common* (in alphabetical order). For example, {asparagus, beans} and {asparagus, squash} have the first $k - 1 = 1$ item in common, asparagus. Thus, they are joined into the new candidate itemset {asparagus, beans, squash}. Similarly, {beans, corn} and {beans, squash} have the first item, beans, in common, generating the candidate 3-itemset {beans, corn, squash}. Finally, candidate 3-itemsets {beans, corn, tomatoes} and {beans, squash, tomatoes} are generated in like fashion. Thus, C_3 = { {asparagus, beans, squash}, {beans, corn, squash}, {beans, corn, tomatoes}, {beans, squash, tomatoes} }.

C_3 is then pruned, using the a priori property. For each itemset s in C_3, its size $k - 1$ subsets are generated and examined. If *any* of these subsets are not frequent, s cannot be frequent and is therefore pruned. For example, let s = {asparagus, beans, squash}. The subsets of size $k - 1 = 2$ are generated, as follows: {asparagus, beans}, {asparagus, squash}, and {beans, squash}. From Table 10.4 we see that each of these subsets is frequent and that therefore s = {asparagus, beans, squash} is not pruned. The reader will verify that s = {beans, corn, tomatoes} will also not be pruned.

However, consider s = {beans, corn, squash}. The subset {corn, squash} has frequency $3 < 4 = \phi$, so that {corn, squash} is not frequent. By the a priori property, therefore, {beans, corn, squash} cannot be frequent, is therefore pruned, and does not appear in F_3. Also consider s = {beans, squash, tomatoes}. The subset {squash, tomatoes} has frequency $2 < 4 = \phi$, and hence is not frequent. Again, by the a priori property, its superset {beans, squash, tomatoes} cannot be frequent and is also pruned, not appearing in F_3.

We still need to check the count for these candidate frequent itemsets. The itemset {asparagus, beans, squash} occurs four times in the transaction list, {beans, corn, tomatoes} occurs only three times. Therefore, the latter candidate itemset is also pruned, leaving us with a singleton frequent itemset in F_3: {asparagus, beans, squash}. This completes the task of finding the frequent itemsets for the vegetable stand data D.

HOW DOES THE A PRIORI ALGORITHM WORK (PART 2)? GENERATING ASSOCIATION RULES

Next, we turn to the task of generating association rules using the frequent itemsets. This is accomplished using the following two-step process, for each frequent itemset s:

GENERATING ASSOCIATION RULES

1. First, generate all subsets of s.
2. Then, let ss represent a nonempty subset of s. Consider the association rule $R : ss \Rightarrow (s - ss)$, where $(s - ss)$ indicates the set s without ss. Generate (and output) R if R fulfills the minimum confidence requirement. Do so for every subset ss of s. Note that for simplicity, a single-item consequent is often desired.

TABLE 10.5 Candidate Association Rules for Vegetable Stand Data: Two Antecedents

If *Antecedent*, then *Consequent*	Support	Confidence
If buy asparagus and beans, then buy squash	4/14 = 28.6%	4/5 = 80%
If buy asparagus and squash, then buy beans	4/14 = 28.6%	4/5 = 80%
If buy beans and squash, then buy asparagus	4/14 = 28.6%	4/6 = 66.7%

For example, let s = {asparagus, beans, squash} from F_3. The proper subsets of s are {asparagus}, {beans}, {squash}, {asparagus, beans}, {asparagus, squash}, {beans, squash}. For the first association rule shown in Table 10.5, we let ss = {asparagus, beans}, so that $(s - ss)$ = {squash}. We consider the rule R: {asparagus, beans} $\Rightarrow$ {squash}. The support is the proportion of transactions in which both {asparagus, beans} and {squash} occur, which is 4 (or 28.6%) of the 14 total transactions in D. To find the confidence, we note that {asparagus, beans} occurs in five of the 14 transactions, four of which also contain {squash}, giving us our confidence of 4/5 = 80%. The statistics for the second rule in Table 10.5 arise similarly. For the third rule in Table 10.5, the support is still 4/14 = 28.6%, but the confidence falls to 66.7%. This is because {beans, squash} occurs in six transactions, four of which also contain {asparagus}. Assuming that our minimum confidence criterion is set at 60% and that we desire a single consequent, we therefore have the candidate rules shown in Table 10.5. If our minimum confidence were set at 80%, the third rule would not be reported.

Finally, we turn to single antecedent/single consequent rules. Applying the association rule generation method outlined in the box above, and using the itemsets in F_2, we may generate the candidate association rules shown in Table 10.6.

To provide an overall measure of usefulness for an association rule, analysts sometimes multiply the support times the confidence. This allows the analyst to rank

TABLE 10.6 Candidate Association Rules for Vegetable Stand Data: One Antecedent

If *Antecedent*, then *Consequent*	Support	Confidence
If buy asparagus, then buy beans	5/14 = 35.7%	5/6 = 83.3%
If buy beans, then buy asparagus	5/14 = 35.7%	5/10 = 50%
If buy asparagus, then buy squash	5/14 = 35.7%	5/6 = 83.3%
If buy squash, then buy asparagus	5/14 = 35.7%	5/7 = 71.4%
If buy beans, then buy corn	5/14 = 35.7%	5/10 = 50%
If buy corn, then buy beans	5/14 = 35.7%	5/8 = 62.5%
If buy beans, then buy squash	6/14 = 42.9%	6/10 = 60%
If buy squash, then buy beans	6/14 = 42.9%	6/7 = 85.7%
If buy beans, then buy tomatoes	4/14 = 28.6%	4/10 = 40%
If buy tomatoes, then buy beans	4/14 = 28.6%	4/6 = 66.7%
If buy broccoli, then buy green peppers	4/14 = 28.6%	4/5 = 80%
If buy green peppers, then buy broccoli	4/14 = 28.6%	4/5 = 80%
If buy corn, then buy tomatoes	4/14 = 28.6%	4/8 = 50%
If buy tomatoes, then buy corn	4/14 = 28.6%	4/6 = 66.7%

TABLE 10.7 Final List of Association Rules for Vegetable Stand Data: Ranked by Support × Confidence, Minimum Confidence 80%

If *Antecedent*, then *Consequent*	Support	Confidence	Support × Confidence
If buy squash, then buy beans	6/14 = 42.9%	6/7 = 85.7%	0.3677
If buy asparagus, then buy beans	5/14 = 35.7%	5/6 = 83.3%	0.2974
If buy asparagus, then buy squash	5/14 = 35.7%	5/6 = 83.3%	0.2974
If buy broccoli, then buy green peppers	4/14 = 28.6%	4/5 = 80%	0.2288
If buy green peppers, then buy broccoli	4/14 = 28.6%	4/5 = 80%	0.2288
If buy asparagus and beans, then buy squash	4/14 = 28.6%	4/5 = 80%	0.2288
If buy asparagus and squash, then buy beans	4/14 = 28.6%	4/5 = 80%	0.2288

the rules according to a combination of prevalence and accuracy. Table 10.7 provides such a list for our present data set, after first filtering the rules through a minimum confidence level of 80%.

Compare Table 10.7 with Figure 10.1, the association rules reported by Clementine's version of the a priori algorithm, with minimum 80% confidence, and sorted by support × confidence. The first column indicates the number of instances the antecedent occurs in the transactions. The second column, which Clementine calls "support," is actually not what we defined support to be in this chapter (following Han and Kamber[1], Hand et al.[2], and other texts). Instead, what Clementine calls "support" is the proportion of occurrences of the antecedent alone rather of than the

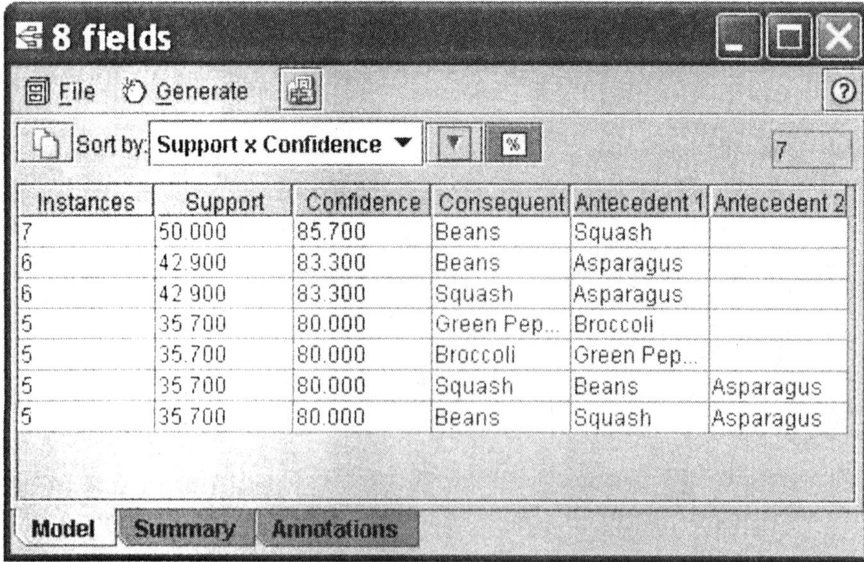

Figure 10.1 Association rules for vegetable stand data, generated by Clementine.

antecedent and the consequent. To find the actual support for the association rule using the Clementine results, multiply the reported "support" times the reported confidence.

Note that after the confidence column, the single consequent appears, followed by the first and second antecedents (if any). Apart from the "support" anomaly, the software's association rules shown in Figure 10.1 represent the same rules as those we found step by step, and by hand, for the vegetable stand data.

Armed with this knowledge, the vegetable stand entrepreneur can deploy marketing strategies that take advantage of the patterns uncovered above. Why do these particular products co-occur in customers' market baskets? Should the product layout be altered to make it easier for customers to purchase these products together? Should personnel be alerted to remind customers not to forget item B when purchasing associated item A?

EXTENSION FROM FLAG DATA TO GENERAL CATEGORICAL DATA

Thus far, we have examined association rules using flag data types only. That is, all of the vegetable stand attributes took the form of Boolean 0/1 flags, resulting in the tabular data format found in Table 10.3, reflecting a straightforward market basket analysis problem. However, association rules are not restricted to flag data types. In particular, the a priori algorithm can be applied to categorical data in general. Let's look at an example.

Recall the normalized *adult* data set analyzed in Chapters 6 and 7. Here in Chapter 10 we apply the a priori algorithm to the categorical variables in that same data set, using Clementine. Minimum support of 10% and minimum confidence of 75% were specified, with the resulting association rules shown in Figure 10.2.

The rules with the highest confidence each have *sex = Male* as the consequent, reflecting the 2:1 male–female ratio in the data set. Recall that there were several values for *Marital_Status* and *Work_Class*, so that these attributes are truly nonflag categorical attributes. The a priori algorithm simply finds the frequent itemsets just as before, this time counting the occurrences of the values of the categorical variables rather than simply the occurrence of the flag.

For example, consider the fifth rule reported in Figure 10.2: "If *Marital_Status = Never_married*, then *Work_Class = Private*," with confidence 76.9%. There were

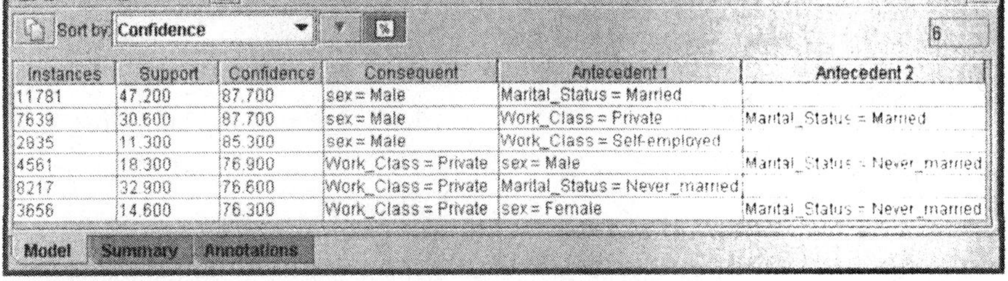

sex & Work_Class & Marital_Status

File Generate

Sort by: Confidence 6

Instances	Support	Confidence	Consequent	Antecedent 1	Antecedent 2
11781	47.200	87.700	sex = Male	Marital_Status = Married	
7639	30.600	87.700	sex = Male	Work_Class = Private	Marital_Status = Married
2835	11.300	85.300	sex = Male	Work_Class = Self-employed	
4561	18.300	76.900	Work_Class = Private	sex = Male	Marital_Status = Never_married
8217	32.900	76.600	Work_Class = Private	Marital_Status = Never_married	
3656	14.600	76.300	Work_Class = Private	sex = Female	Marital_Status = Never_married

Model Summary Annotations

Figure 10.2 Association rules for categorical attributes found by a priori algorithm.

8217 instances in the data set where the attribute *Marital_Status* took the value *Never_married*, which represents 32.9% of the number of records in the data set. (Again, Clementine refers to this as the "support," which is not how most researchers define that term.) The support for this rule is (0.329)(0.766) = 0.252. That is, 25.2% of the records contained the value *Never_married* for *Marital_Status* and the value *Private* for *Work_Class*, thus making this pairing a frequent 2-itemset of categorical attributes.

INFORMATION-THEORETIC APPROACH: GENERALIZED RULE INDUCTION METHOD

The structure of association rules, where the antecedent and consequent are both Boolean statements, makes them particularly well suited for handling categorical data, as we have seen. However, what happens when we try to extend our association rule mining to a broader range of data, specifically, numerical attributes?

Of course, it is always possible to discretize the numerical attributes, for example, by arbitrarily defining income under $30,000 as *low*, income over $70,000 as *high*, and other income as *medium*. Also, we have seen how both C4.5 and CART handle numerical attributes by discretizing the numerical variables at favorable locations. Unfortunately, the a priori algorithm is not well equipped to handle numeric attributes unless they are discretized during preprocessing. Of course, discretization can lead to a loss of information, so if the analyst has numerical inputs and prefers not to discretize them, he or she may choose to apply an alternative method for mining association rules: *generalized rule induction* (GRI). The GRI methodology can handle either categorical or numerical variables as inputs, but still requires categorical variables as outputs.

Generalized rule induction was introduced by Smyth and Goodman in 1992[3]. Rather than using frequent itemsets, GRI applies an information-theoretic approach (as did the C4.5 decision tree algorithm) to determining the "interestingness" of a candidate association rule.

J-Measure

Specifically, GRI applies the *J-measure*:

$$J = p(x)\left[p(y|x)\ln\frac{p(y|x)}{p(y)} + [1 - p(y|x)]\ln\frac{1 - p(y|x)}{1 - p(y)}\right]$$

where

- $p(x)$ represents the probability or confidence of the observed value of x. This is a measure of the coverage of the antecedent. How prevalent is this value of the antecedent attribute? You can calculate $p(x)$ using a frequency distribution for the variable in the antecedent.
- $p(y)$ represents the prior probability or confidence of the value of y. This is a measure of the prevalence of the observed value of y in the consequent.

You can calculate $p(y)$ using a frequency distribution for the variable in the consequent.

- $p(y|x)$ represents the conditional probability, or posterior confidence, of y given that x has occurred. This is a measure of the probability of the observed value of y given that this value of x has occurred. That is, $p(y|x)$ represents an updated probability of observing this value of y after taking into account the additional knowledge of the value of x. In association rule terminology, $p(y|x)$ is measured directly by the confidence of the rule.
- *ln* represents the natural log function (log to the base e).

For rules with more than one antecedent, $p(x)$ is considered to be the probability of the conjunction of the variable values in the antecedent.

As usual, the user specifies desired minimum support and confidence criteria. For GRI, however, the user also specifies how many association rules he or she would like to be reported, thereby defining the size of an association rule table referenced by the algorithm. The GRI algorithm then generates single-antecedent association rules, and calculates J, the value of the J-measure for the rule. If the "interestingness" of the new rule, as quantified by the J-measure, is higher than the current minimum J in the rule table, the new rule is inserted into the rule table, which keeps a constant size by eliminating the rule with minimum J. More specialized rules with more antecedents are then considered.

How can the behavior of the J-statistic be described? Clearly [since $p(x)$ sits outside the brackets], higher values of J will be associated with higher values of $p(x)$. That is, the J-measure will tend to favor those rules whose antecedent value is more prevalent, reflecting higher coverage in the data set. Also, the J-measure tends toward higher values when $p(y)$ and $p(y|x)$ are more extreme (near zero or 1). Hence, the J-measure will also tend to favor those rules whose consequent probability, $p(y)$, is more extreme, or whose rule confidence, $p(y|x)$, is more extreme.

The J-measure favors rules with either very high or very low confidence. Why would we be interested in an association rule with extremely low confidence? For example, suppose that we have a rule R : *If buy beer, then buy fingernail polish*, with confidence $p(y|x) = 0.01\%$, which would presumably be favored by the J-measure, since the confidence is so low. The analyst could then consider the *negative form* of R: *If buy beer, then NOT buy fingernail polish*, with confidence 99.99%. Although such negative rules are often interesting ("I guess we better move that fingernail polish out of the beer section..."), they are often not directly actionable.

Application of Generalized Rule Induction

Let's return to the "adult" data set for an example of how to calculate the J-measure. We applied Clementine's GRI algorithm to the categorical variables in the data set, again specifying minimum support of 10% and minimum confidence of 75%, and setting the rule table maximum size to 30. The results are shown in Figure 10.3.

Let's find the J-measure for the sixth association rule in Figure 10.3: *If Sex = Female and Marital_Status = Never married, then Work_Class = Private*, with

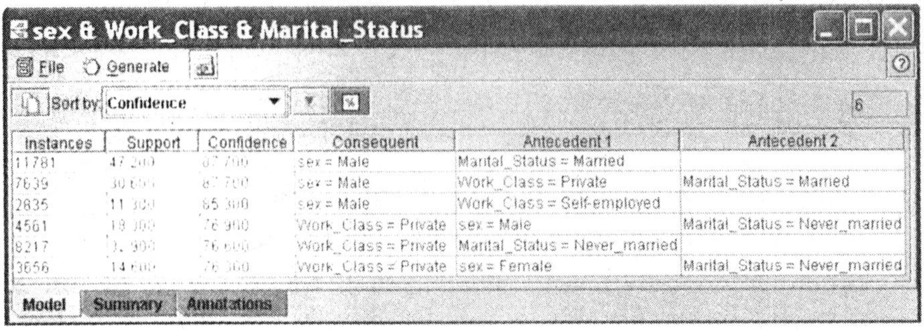

sex & Work_Class & Marital_Status

File Generate

Sort by: Confidence

Instances	Support	Confidence	Consequent	Antecedent 1	Antecedent 2
11781	47.200	87.700	sex = Male	Marital_Status = Married	
7639	30.600	87.700	sex = Male	Work_Class = Private	Marital_Status = Married
2835	11.300	85.300	sex = Male	Work_Class = Self-employed	
4561	18.300	76.900	Work_Class = Private	sex = Male	Marital_Status = Never_married
8217	32.900	76.600	Work_Class = Private	Marital_Status = Never_married	
3656	14.600	76.300	Work_Class = Private	sex = Female	Marital_Status = Never_married

Model | Summary | Annotations

Figure 10.3 Association rules found by the generalized rule induction algorithm.

confidence of 76.3% and support of 11.1% (not 14.6%). We need the following statistics:

- $p(x)$, representing the probability that a randomly chosen record will be that of a never-married female. Clementine provides this directly as $p(x) = 0.1463$.
- $p(y)$, representing the prior probability that a randomly chosen record will have *Private* for the *Work_Class* attribute. Using the frequency distribution in Figure 10.4, we can see that this prior probability is $p(y) = 0.6958$.
- $p(y|x)$,representing the conditional probability that a record has *Private* for the *Work_Class* attribute, given that the record represents a never-married female. This is nothing but the confidence reported for the rule, $p(y|x) = 0.763$.

Plugging these values into the formula for the J-measure, we have

$$
\begin{aligned}
J &= p(x)\left[p(y|x)\ln\frac{p(y|x)}{p(y)} + [1 - p(y|x)]\ln\frac{1 - p(y|x)}{1 - p(y)}\right] \\
&= 0.1463\left[0.763\ln\frac{0.763}{0.6958} + (0.237)\ln\frac{0.237}{0.3042}\right] \\
&= 0.1463\,[0.763\ln(1.0966) + (0.237)\ln(0.7791)] \\
&= 0.001637
\end{aligned}
$$

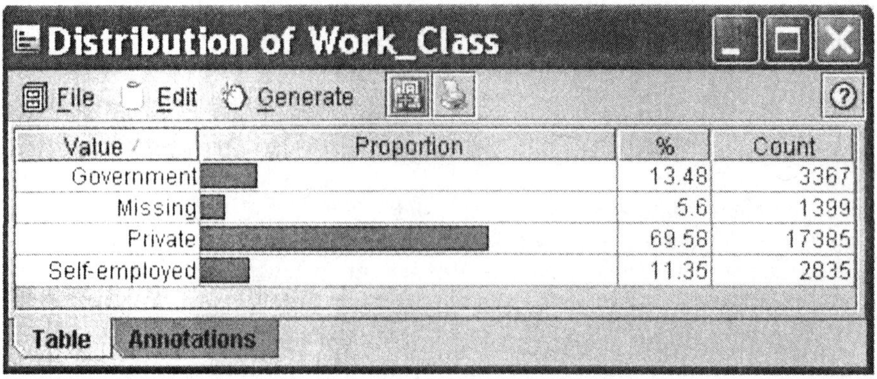

Distribution of Work_Class

File Edit Generate

Value	Proportion	%	Count
Government		13.48	3367
Missing		5.6	1399
Private		69.58	17385
Self-employed		11.35	2835

Table | Annotations

Figure 10.4 Finding $p(y)$: prior probability of *Work_Class* = *Private*.

Instances	Support	Confidence	Consequent	Antecedent 1	Antecedent 2
4310	17.250	95.000	sex = Male	hours-per-week > 0.444	Marital_Status = Married
11781	47.150	88.000	sex = Male	Marital_Status = Married	
7639	30.570	88.000	sex = Male	Work_Class = Private	Marital_Status = Married
6997	28.000	82.000	sex = Male	hours-per-week > 0.444	
6169	24.690	80.000	Marital_Status = Never_married	age < 0.377	
7366	29.480	80.000	Work_Class = Private	age < 0.445	education-num < 0.767
9427	37.730	78.000	Work_Class = Private	age < 0.445	

Figure 10.5 The GRI algorithm generates association rules for numerical antecedents.

As mentioned above, GRI can handle numerical inputs as well as categorical inputs. We illustrate this using Clementine on the *adult* data set, instructing the GRI algorithm to accept both numerical variables and categorical variables as possible antecedents (although, still, only categorical variables are possible consequents). The results, for minimum support and confidence criteria similar to those above, are shown in Figure 10.5.

For example, consider the sixth association rule from Figure 10.5, *If age* <0.445 *and education-num* <0.767, *then Work_Class* = *Private*. Both antecedents are numerical with the variables normalized so that all values are between zero and 1. The antecedent probability is $p(x) = 0.2948$, telling us that 29.48% of all records have *age* <0.445 and *education-num* <0.767. The value for $p(y)$, representing P(*Work_Class*) = *Private*, is still 0.6958 from the previous example. Finally, $p(y|x)$, representing the conditional probability that a record has *Private* for the *Work_Class* attribute given that the record has both *age* <0.445 and *education-num* <0.767, is given by the confidence for the rule, $p(y|x) = 0.80$. Finding the value of the J-measure for this rule is left as an exercise.

WHEN NOT TO USE ASSOCIATION RULES

Association rules need to be applied with care, since their results are sometimes deceptive. Let's look at an example. Turning back to the a priori algorithm, we asked Clementine to mine association rules from the *adult* database using 10% minimum support, 60% minimum confidence, and a maximum of two antecedents. The results are shown in Figure 10.6.

Consider, for example, the third association rule from the bottom, *If Work_Class* = *Government, then sex* = *Male*, with 62.7% confidence. Marketing analysts interested in government workers might be tempted to use this association rule in support of a new marketing strategy aimed at males. However, seen in its proper light, this rule may in fact be quite useless.

One needs to take into account the raw (prior) proportion of males in the data set, which in this case is 66.83%. In other words, applying this association rule actually

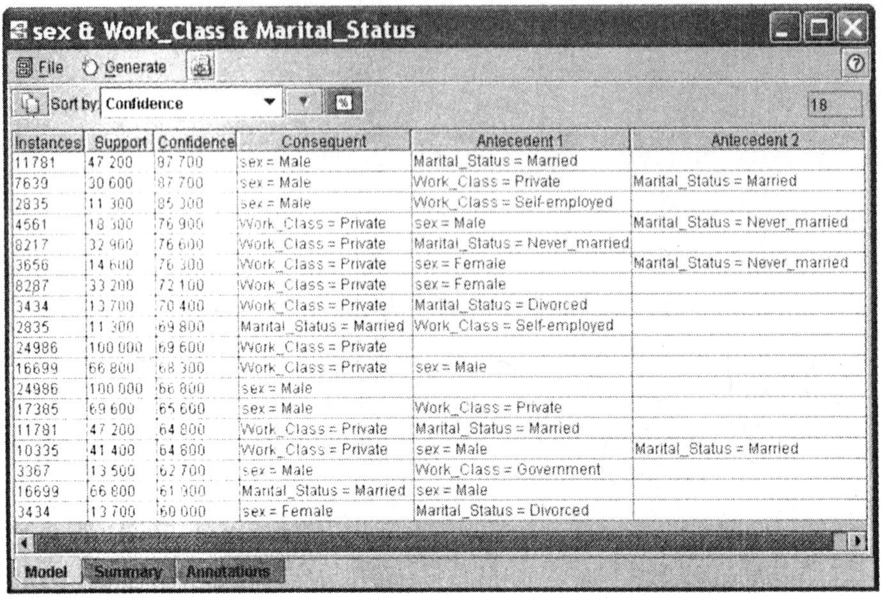

sex & Work_Class & Marital_Status

File Generate

Sort by: Confidence 18

Instances	Support	Confidence	Consequent	Antecedent 1	Antecedent 2
11781	47 200	87 700	sex = Male	Marital_Status = Married	
7639	30 600	87 700	sex = Male	Work_Class = Private	Marital_Status = Married
2835	11 300	85 300	sex = Male	Work_Class = Self-employed	
4561	18 300	76 900	Work_Class = Private	sex = Male	Marital_Status = Never_married
8217	32 900	76 600	Work_Class = Private	Marital_Status = Never_married	
3656	14 600	76 300	Work_Class = Private	sex = Female	Marital_Status = Never_married
8287	33 200	72 100	Work_Class = Private	sex = Female	
3434	13 700	70 400	Work_Class = Private	Marital_Status = Divorced	
2835	11 300	69 800	Marital_Status = Married	Work_Class = Self-employed	
24986	100 000	69 600	Work_Class = Private		
16699	66 800	68 300	Work_Class = Private	sex = Male	
24986	100 000	66 800	sex = Male		
17385	69 600	65 600	sex = Male	Work_Class = Private	
11781	47 200	64 800	Work_Class = Private	Marital_Status = Married	
10335	41 400	64 800	Work_Class = Private	sex = Male	Marital_Status = Married
3367	13 500	62 700	sex = Male	Work_Class = Government	
16699	66 800	61 300	Marital_Status = Married	sex = Male	
3434	13 700	60 000	sex = Female	Marital_Status = Divorced	

Model Summary Annotations

Figure 10.6 Association rules chosen a priori, based on rule confidence.

reduces the probability of randomly selecting a male from 0.6683 to 0.627. You would have been better advised to pull a name out of a hat from the entire data set than apply this rule.

Why, then, if the rule is so useless, did the software report it? The quick answer is that the default ranking mechanism for Clementine's a priori algorithm is confidence. However, it needs to be emphasized here that data miners should never simply believe the computer output without making the effort to understand the models and mechanisms underlying the results. With the onset of sophisticated point-and-click data mining software, poor analysis costing millions of dollars is more prevalent than ever. In a word, *data mining is easy to do badly*. Insightful human expertise and constant human vigilance are required to translate the nuggets hidden in the database into actionable and profitable results.

Other useless rules in the Figure 10.6 results include:

- *If sex = Male and Marital_Status = Married, then Work_Class = Private*
  - Confidence: 64.8%
  - Prior probability of *Work_Class = Private*: 69.58%
- *If Work_Class = Private then sex = Male*
  - Confidence: 65.6%
  - Prior probability of *sex = Male*: 66.83%
- *If sex = Male, then Work_Class = Private*
  - Confidence: 68.3%
  - Prior probability of *Work_Class = Private*: 69.58%

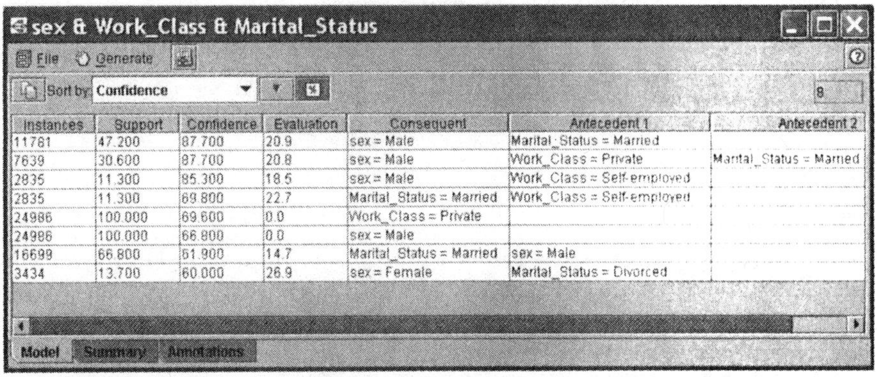

sex & Work_Class & Marital_Status

File Generate

Sort by: Confidence 8

Instances	Support	Confidence	Evaluation	Consequent	Antecedent 1	Antecedent 2
11781	47.200	87.700	20.9	sex = Male	Marital_Status = Married	
7639	30.600	87.700	20.8	sex = Male	Work_Class = Private	Marital_Status = Married
2835	11.300	85.300	18.5	sex = Male	Work_Class = Self-employed	
2835	11.300	69.800	22.7	Marital_Status = Married	Work_Class = Self-employed	
24986	100.000	69.600	0.0	Work_Class = Private		
24986	100.000	66.800	0.0	sex = Male		
16699	66.800	51.900	14.7	Marital_Status = Married	sex = Male	
3434	13.700	60.000	26.9	sex = Female	Marital_Status = Divorced	

Model Summary Annotations

Figure 10.7 Association rules chosen a priori, based on confidence difference.

In each of these cases, a random selection from the database would have provided more efficacious results than applying the association rule. With association rules, one needs to keep in mind the prior probabilities involved. To illustrate, we now ask Clementine to provide us with a priori association rules, but this time using the *confidence difference* as the evaluative measure. Here, rules are favored that provide the greatest increase in confidence from the prior to the posterior. The results are shown in Figure 10.7.

Note that none of the useless rules reported in Figure 10.6 show up in Figure 10.7. Also, note the new column, *Evaluation*, which measures the absolute difference between the prior and posterior confidences. For example, consider the last rule in the list: *If Marital_Status = Divorced, then sex = Female*. This rule (which, recall, applies to the *adult* data set and not necessarily to the U.S. population at large) also happens to have the largest evaluation value for the rules reported. The prior probability in this database of randomly choosing a female is 33.17%, while the confidence for this rule is 60%. This gives us a difference of 0.3317 − 0.60=0.2683 between the prior and posterior confidences. Note that this rule was also reported in Figure 10.6, but was hidden among the useless rules.

Alternatively, analysts may prefer to use the *confidence ratio* to evaluate potential rules. This is defined as

$$\textit{confidence ratio} = 1 - \min\left(\frac{p(y|x)}{p(y)}, \frac{p(y)}{p(y|x)}\right)$$

For example, for the rule: *If Marital_Status = Divorced, then sex = Female*, we have $p(y) = 0.3317$ and $p(y|x) = 0.60$, so that

$$\min\left(\frac{p(y|x)}{p(y)}, \frac{p(y)}{p(y|x)}\right) = \frac{p(y)}{p(y|x)} = \frac{0.3317}{0.60} = 0.5528$$

and the *confidence ratio* equals 1 − 0.5528 = 0.4472. This is confirmed by the evaluation measure for this rule in Figure 10.8.

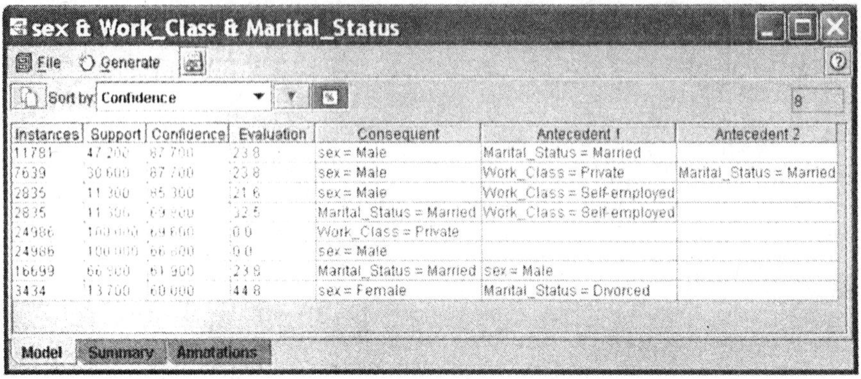

sex & Work_Class & Marital_Status

File Generate

Sort by: Confidence 8

Instances	Support	Confidence	Evaluation	Consequent	Antecedent 1	Antecedent 2
11781	47.200	87.700	23.8	sex = Male	Marital_Status = Married	
7639	30.600	87.700	23.8	sex = Male	Work_Class = Private	Marital_Status = Married
2835	11.300	85.300	21.6	sex = Male	Work_Class = Self-employed	
2835	11.300	69.900	32.5	Marital_Status = Married	Work_Class = Self-employed	
24986	100.000	69.600	0.0	Work_Class = Private		
24986	100.000	66.800	0.0	sex = Male		
16699	66.900	61.900	23.8	Marital_Status = Married	sex = Male	
3434	13.700	60.000	44.8	sex = Female	Marital_Status = Divorced	

Model Summary Annotations

Figure 10.8 Association rules chosen a priori, based on confidence ratio.

Note that in this case, the confidence difference criterion yielded the very same rules as did the confidence ratio criterion. This need not always be the case. In the exercises we explore further the differences among these rule selection criteria.

DO ASSOCIATION RULES REPRESENT SUPERVISED OR UNSUPERVISED LEARNING?

Before we leave the subject of association rules, let us touch on a few topics of interest. First, we may ask whether association rules represent supervised or unsupervised learning. Recall that most data mining methods represent supervised learning, since (1) a target variable is prespecified, and (2) the algorithm is provided with a rich collection of examples where possible association between the target variable and the predictor variables may be uncovered. Conversely, in unsupervised learning, no target variable is identified explicitly. Rather, the data mining algorithm searches for patterns and structure among all the variables. Clustering is perhaps the most common unsupervised data mining method.

Association rule mining, however, can be applied in either a supervised or an unsupervised manner. In market basket analysis, for example, one may simply be interested in "which items are purchased together," in which case no target variable would be identified. On the other hand, some data sets are naturally structured so that a particular variable fulfills the role of consequent, and not antecedent (see the *play* example in the exercises). For example, suppose that political pollsters have collected demographic data in their exit polling, along with the subject's voting preference. In this case, association rules could be mined from this data set, where the demographic information could represent possible antecedents, and the voting preference could represent the single consequent of interest. In this way, association rules could be used to help classify the voting preferences of citizens with certain demographic characteristics, in a supervised learning process.

Thus, the answer to the question is that association rules, while generally used for unsupervised learning, may also be applied for supervised learning for a classification task.

LOCAL PATTERNS VERSUS GLOBAL MODELS

Finally, data analysts need to consider the difference between *models* and *patterns*. A *model* is a global description or explanation of a data set, taking a high-level perspective. Models may be descriptive or inferential. Descriptive models seek to summarize the entire data set in a succinct manner. Inferential models aim to provide a mechanism that enables the analyst to generalize from samples to populations. Either way, the perspective is global, encompassing the entire data set. On the other hand, patterns are essentially local features of the data. Recognizable patterns may in fact hold true for only a few variables or a fraction of the records in the data.

Most of the modeling methods we have covered have dealt with global model building. Association rules, on the other hand, are particularly well suited to uncovering local patterns in the data. As soon as one applies the *if* clause in an association rule, one is partitioning a data so that, usually, most of the records do not apply. Applying the *if* clause "drills down" deeper into a data set, with the aim of uncovering a hidden local pattern which may or may not be relevant to the bulk of the data.

For example, consider the following association rule from Table 10.3: *If Work_Class = Self-employed, then Marital_Status = Married*, with confidence 69.8%. We see that this association rule applies to only 2835 (11.3%) of the records and ignores the remaining 88.7% of the data set. Even among these 2835 records, the association rule ignores most of the variables, concentrating on only two. Therefore, this association rule cannot claim to be global and cannot be considered a model in the strict sense. It represents a pattern that is local to these 2835 records and to these two variables.

Then again, finding interesting local patterns is one of the most important goals of data mining. Sometimes, uncovering a pattern within the data can lead to the deployment of new and profitable initiatives. For example, recall from the *churn* data set (Chapter 3) that those customers who belonged to the VoiceMail Plan were at considerably lower risk of churning than other customers (see Figure 10.9). This

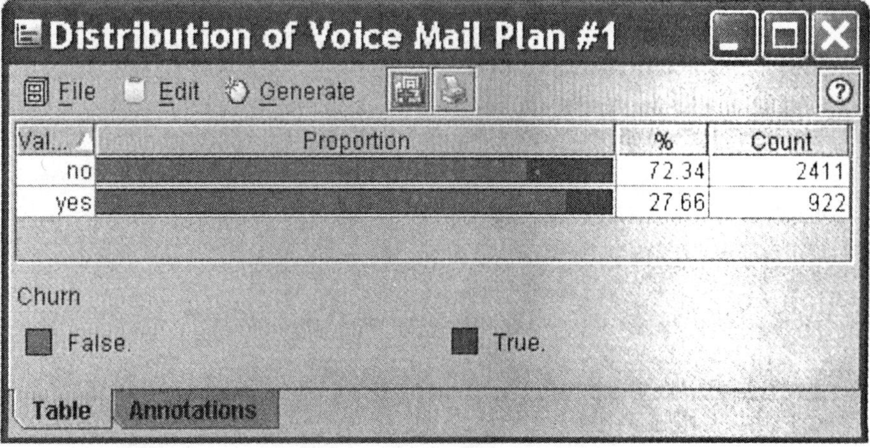

Figure 10.9 Profitable pattern: VoiceMail Plan adopters less likely to churn.

finding affected only 922 (27.7%) of the 3333 records and only two of the variables, and is thus to be considered a local pattern. Nevertheless, the discovery of this nugget could lead to policy changes which, if properly deployed, could lead to increased profits for the cell phone company.

REFERENCES

1. Jiawei Han and Micheline Kamber, *Data Mining Concepts and Techniques*, Morgan Kaufmann, San Francisco, CA, 2001.
2. David Hand, Heikki Mannila, and Padhraic Smith, *Principles of Data Mining*, MIT Press, Cambridge, MA, 2001.
3. Padhraic Smyth and Rodney M. Goodman, An information theoretic approach to rule induction from databases, *IEEE Transactions on Knowledge and Data Engineering*, Vol. 4, No. 4, August 1992.
4. J. Ross Quinlan, *C4.5: Programs for Machine Learning*, Morgan Kaufmann, San Francisco, CA, 1993.

EXERCISES

1. Describe the two main methods of representing market basket data. What are the benefits and drawbacks of each?

2. Describe support and confidence. Express the formula for confidence using support.

3. Restate the a priori property in your own words.

For the following several exercises, consider the following data set from Quinlan [4] shown as Table E10. The goal is to develop association rules using the a priori algorithm for trying to predict when a certain (evidently indoor) game may be played. Therefore, unlike the vegetable stand example, we may restrict our itemset search to items that include the attribute *play*.

4. Let $\phi = 3$. Generate the frequent 1-itemsets.

5. Let $\phi = 3$. Generate the frequent 2-itemsets.

6. Let $\phi = 3$. Generate the frequent 3-itemsets.

7. Using 75% minimum confidence and 20% minimum support, generate one-antecedent association rules for predicting *play*.

8. Using 75% minimum confidence and 20% minimum support, generate two-antecedent association rules for predicting *play*.

9. Multiply the observed support times the confidence for each of the rules in Exercises 7 and 8, and rank them in a table.

10. Verify your manually found results using association rule software.

11. For each of the association rules found above by the a priori algorithm, find the J-measure. Then order the rules by J-measure. Compare the ordering with that from the a priori support $\times$ confidence ordering.

12. Find the value of the J-measure for the sixth rule from Figure 10.5.

TABLE E10 Weather Data Set for Association Rule Mining

No.	*Outlook*	*Temperature*	*Humidity*	*Windy*	*Play*
1	sunny	hot	high	false	no
2	sunny	hot	high	true	no
3	overcast	hot	high	false	yes
4	rain	mild	high	false	yes
5	rain	cool	normal	false	yes
6	rain	cool	normal	true	no
7	overcast	cool	normal	true	yes
8	sunny	mild	high	false	no
9	sunny	cool	normal	false	yes
10	rain	mild	normal	false	yes
11	sunny	mild	normal	true	yes
12	overcast	mild	high	true	yes
13	overcast	hot	normal	false	yes
14	rain	mild	high	true	no

Hands-on Analysis

Use the *churn* data set, given at the book series Web site, for the following exercises. Make sure that the numerical variables are normalized and that correlated variables are accounted for.

13. Apply the a priori algorithm to uncover association rules for predicting either churn or nonchurn behavior. Specify reasonable lower bounds for support and confidence. Which attributes are not applicable?

14. Compare the results from Exercise 13 with the results from the EDA and decision tree analysis in Chapters 3 and 6. Discuss similarities and differences. Which analysis format do you prefer? Do you find a confluence of results?

15. Apply the confidence difference criterion for rule selection, and rerun the a priori algorithm. Order the rules by magnitude of confidence difference. Discuss similarities and differences with the set of rules above.

16. Apply the confidence ratio criterion for rule selection and rerun the a priori algorithm. Order the rules by magnitude of confidence difference. Discuss similarities and differences with the set of rules above.

17. Apply the GRI algorithm to uncover association rules for predicting either churn or nonchurn behavior. Specify reasonable lower bounds for support and confidence.

18. Compare the results from the a priori algorithm with those of the GRI algorithm. Which algorithm yields a richer set of rules, and why? Which algorithm is probably preferable for this particular data set? Why?

CHAPTER **11**

MODEL EVALUATION TECHNIQUES

As you may recall from Chapter 1, the CRISP cross-industry standard process for data mining consists of six phases, to be applied in an iterative cycle:

1. Business understanding phase
2. Data understanding phase
3. Data preparation phase
4. Modeling phase
5. Evaluation phase
6. Deployment phase

Nestled between the modeling and deployment phases comes the crucial evaluation phase, techniques for which are discussed in this chapter. By the time we arrive at the evaluation phase, the modeling phase has already generated one or more candidate models. It is of critical importance that these models be evaluated for quality and effectiveness *before* they are deployed for use in the field. Deployment

Discovering Knowledge in Data: An Introduction to Data Mining, By Daniel T. Larose
ISBN 0-471-66657-2

of data mining models usually represents a capital expenditure and investment on the part of the company. If the models in question are invalid, the company's time and money are wasted. In this chapter we examine model evaluation techniques for each of the six main tasks of data mining: description, estimation, prediction, classification, clustering, and association.

MODEL EVALUATION TECHNIQUES FOR THE DESCRIPTION TASK

In Chapter 3 we learned how to apply exploratory data analysis (EDA) to learn about the salient characteristics of a data set. EDA represents a popular and powerful technique for applying the descriptive task of data mining. On the other hand, because descriptive techniques make no classifications, predictions, or estimates, an objective method for evaluating the efficacy of these techniques can be elusive. The watchword is common sense. Remember that data mining models should be as *transparent* as possible. That is, the results of the data mining model should describe clear patterns that are amenable to intuitive interpretation and explanation. The effectiveness of your EDA is best evaluated by the clarity of understanding elicited in your target audience, whether a group of managers evaluating your new initiative or the evaluation board of the U.S. Food and Drug Administration assessing the efficacy of a new pharmaceutical submission.

If one insists on using a quantifiable measure to assess description, one may apply the *minimum descriptive length principle*. Other things being equal, *Occam's razor* (a principle named after the medieval philosopher William of Occam) states that simple representations are preferable to complex ones. The minimum descriptive length principle quantifies this, saying that the best representation (or description) of a model or body of data is the one that minimizes the information required (in bits) to encode (1) the model and (2) the exceptions to the model.

MODEL EVALUATION TECHNIQUES FOR THE ESTIMATION AND PREDICTION TASKS

For estimation and prediction models, which employ supervised methods, we are provided with both the estimated (or predicted) value $\hat{y}$ of the numeric target variable and the actual value y. Therefore, a natural measure to assess model adequacy is to examine the *estimation error*, or *residual*, $|y - \hat{y}|$. Since the average residual is always equal to zero, we cannot use it for model evaluation; some other measure is needed.

The usual measure used to evaluate estimation or prediction models is the *mean square error* (MSE):

$$\text{MSE} = \frac{\sum_i (y_i - \hat{y}_i)^2}{n - p - 1}$$

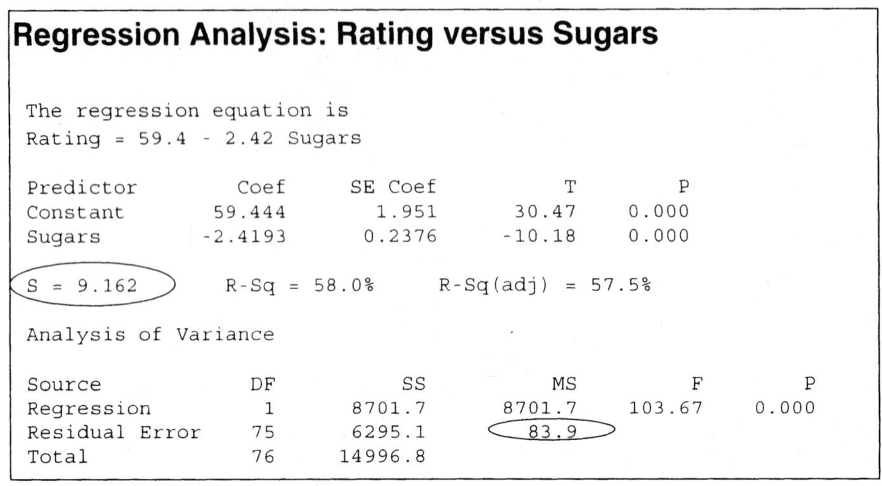

Regression Analysis: Rating versus Sugars

```
The regression equation is
Rating = 59.4 - 2.42 Sugars

Predictor        Coef     SE Coef        T       P
Constant       59.444       1.951    30.47   0.000
Sugars        -2.4193      0.2376   -10.18   0.000

S = 9.162        R-Sq = 58.0%      R-Sq(adj) = 57.5%

Analysis of Variance

Source            DF          SS        MS        F       P
Regression         1      8701.7    8701.7   103.67   0.000
Residual Error    75      6295.1      83.9
Total             76     14996.8
```

Figure 11.1 Minitab regression output, with MSE and s indicated.

where p represents the number of model parameters. Models are preferred that minimize MSE. The square root of MSE can be regarded as an estimate of the typical error in estimation or prediction when using the particular model. In context, this is known as the *standard error of the estimate* and denoted by $s = \sqrt{\text{MSE}}$.

For example, consider Figure 11.1 (excerpted from Chapter 4), which provides the Minitab regression output for the estimated nutritional rating based on sugar content for 77 breakfast cereals. Both MSE $= 83.9$ and $s = 9.162$ are circled on the output. The value of 9.162 for s indicates that the estimated prediction error from using this regression model to predict nutrition rating based on sugar content is 9.162 rating points.

Is this good enough to proceed to model deployment? That depends on the objectives of the business or research problem. Certainly the model is simplicity itself, with only one predictor and one response; however, perhaps the prediction error is too large to consider deployment. Compare this estimated prediction error with the value of s obtained by the multiple regression in Figure 4.10: $s = 1.015$. Here, the estimated error in prediction has been reduced to barely one ratings point. However, there is a cost: The multiple regression model contains eight different predictors, so that the model is more complex than previously. As with so much else in statistical analysis and data mining, there is a trade-off between model complexity and prediction error. The domain experts for the business or research problem in question need to determine where the point of diminishing returns lies.

In Chapter 7 we examined an evaluation measure that was related to MSE:

$$\text{SSE} = \sum_{\text{records}} \sum_{\text{output nodes}} (\text{actual} - \text{output})^2$$

which represents roughly the numerator of MSE above. Again, the goal is to minimize the sum of squared errors over all output nodes.

MODEL EVALUATION TECHNIQUES FOR THE CLASSIFICATION TASK

Perhaps the most widespread usage of supervised data mining involves the classification task. Recall that in classification, there is a target categorical variable. The data mining model examines a large set of records, each record containing information on the target variable as well as a set of input or predictor variables. The analyst would like to be able to generate a classification for the target variable for new records, or persons, not currently in the database, based on other characteristics associated with that person. Using a training set, where information is available about both the predictor variables and the (already classified) target variable, the algorithm learns which combinations of variables are associated with which classes of the target categorical variable. Then the algorithm would look at new records, in the test and validation sets, for which no information about income bracket is available. Based on the classifications in the training set, the algorithm would assign classifications to the new records.

The question is: How well is our classification algorithm functioning? Classification assignments could conceivably be made based on coin flips, tea leaves, goat entrails, or a crystal ball. Which evaluative methods should we use to assure ourselves that the classifications made by our data mining algorithm are efficacious and accurate? Are we outperforming the coin flips?

In this chapter we examine the following evaluative concepts, methods, and tools: *error rate, false positives, false negatives, error cost adjustment, lift, lift charts,* and *gains charts,* in the context of the C5.0 model for classifying income from Chapter 6.

ERROR RATE, FALSE POSITIVES, AND FALSE NEGATIVES

Recall from Chapter 6 that we applied a C5.0 model for classifying whether a person's income was low (≤50,000) or high (>50,000), based on a set of predictor variables which included capital gain, capital loss, marital status, and so on. Let us evaluate the performance of that decision tree classification model, using the notions of error rate, false positives, and false negatives.

Clementine provides us with a matrix of the correct and incorrect classifications made by the algorithm, termed the *confusion matrix,* shown in Figure 11.2. The columns represent the predicted classifications, and the rows represent the actual (true) classifications, for each of the 24,986 records. There are 19,002 records whose actual value for the target variable *income* is ≤50,000, and there are 5984 records whose actual value *income* is >50,000. The C5.0 algorithm classified 20,162 of the records as having *income* ≤50,000, and 4824 records as having *income* >50,000.

Of the 20,162 records whose income is predicted by the algorithm to be ≤50,000, 17,845 of these records actually do have low income. However, the algorithm incorrectly classified 2317 of these 20,162 records as having *income* >50,000.

Now, suppose that this analysis is being carried out for a financial lending firm, which is interested in determining whether or not a loan applicant's income is >50,000. A classification of *income* >50,000 is considered to be *positive,* since

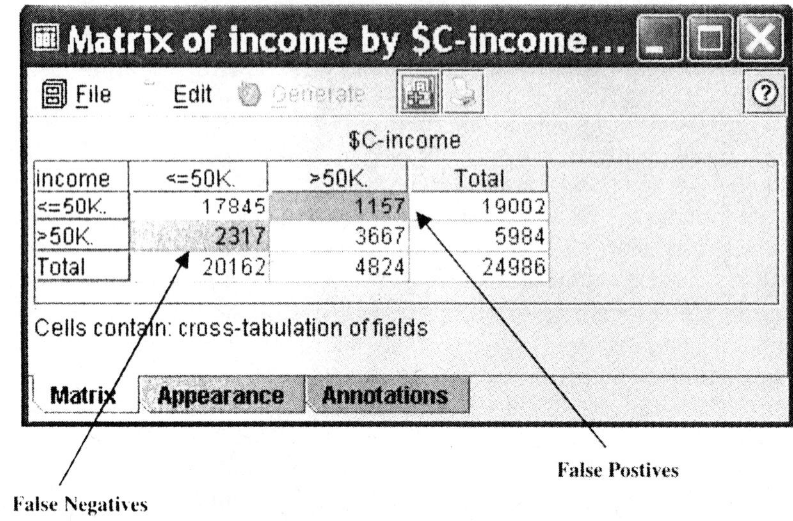

Figure 11.2 Confusion matrix of correct and incorrect classifications.

the lending firm would then proceed to extend the loan to the person in question. A classification of *income* $\leq$ 50,000 is considered to be *negative*, since the firm would proceed to deny the loan application to the person, based on low income (in this simplified scenario). Assume that in the absence of other information, the default decision would be to deny the loan due to low income.

Thus, the 20,162 classifications (predictions) of *income* $\leq$50,000 are said to be *negatives*, and the 4824 classifications of *income* >50,000 are said to be *positives*. The 2317 negative classifications that were made in error are said to be *false negatives*. That is, a false negative represents a record that is classified as negative but is actually positive. Of the 4824 positive classifications, 1157 actually had low incomes, so that there are 1157 false positives. A *false positive* represents a record that is classified as positive but is actually negative.

The *overall error rate*, or simply *error rate*, is the sum of the false negatives and false positives, divided by the total number of records. Here we have

$$\text{overall error rate} = \frac{2317 + 1157}{24{,}986} = 0.1390$$

To find the *false negative rate*, divide the number of false negatives by the total number of negative classifications. Similarly, to find the *false positive rate*, divide the number of false positives by the total number of positive classifications. Here we have

$$\text{false negative rate} = \frac{2317}{20{,}162} = 0.1149$$

$$\text{false positive rate} = \frac{1157}{4824} = 0.2398$$

That is, using the present C5.0 decision tree model, we are more than twice as likely to classify an applicant's income incorrectly as high than to classify an applicant's income incorrectly as low. Using error rate, false positive rate, and false negative rate, analysts may compare the accuracy of various models. For example, a C5.0 decision tree model may be compared against a CART decision tree model or a neural network model. Model choice decisions can then be rendered based on the relative rankings of these evaluation measures.

As an aside, in the parlance of hypothesis testing, since the default decision is to find that the applicant has low income, we would have the following hypotheses:

$$H_0\text{: } income \leq 50{,}000$$
$$H_a\text{: } income > 50{,}000$$

where H_0 represents the default, or null, hypothesis, and H_a represents the alternative hypothesis, which requires evidence to support it. A false positive would be considered a *type I error* in this setting, incorrectly rejecting the null hypothesis, while a false negative would be considered a *type II error*, incorrectly accepting the null hypothesis.

MISCLASSIFICATION COST ADJUSTMENT TO REFLECT REAL-WORLD CONCERNS

Consider this situation from the standpoint of the lending institution. Which error, a false negative or a false positive, would be considered more damaging from the lender's point of view? If the lender commits a false negative, an applicant who had high income gets turned down for a loan: an unfortunate but not very expensive mistake.

On the other hand, if the lender commits a false positive, an applicant who had low income would be awarded the loan. This error greatly increases the chances that the applicant will default on the loan, which is very expensive for the lender. Therefore, the lender would consider the false positive to be the more damaging type of error and would prefer to minimize the false positive rate. The analyst would therefore adjust the C5.0 algorithm's misclassification cost matrix to reflect the lender's concerns. An example of such an adjustment is shown in Figure 11.3, which shows that the false positive cost is increase from 1 to 2, while the false negative cost remains at 1. Thus, a false positive would be considered twice as damaging as a false negative. The analyst may wish to experiment with various cost values for the two types of errors, to find the combination best suited to the task and business problem at hand.

How did the misclassification cost adjustment affect the performance of the algorithm? Which rate would you expect to increase or decrease, the false negative or the false positive? Do you have an intuition of what might happen to the overall error rate?

Well, we would expect that the false positive rate would decrease, since the cost of making such an error has been doubled. Fewer false positives probably means more false negatives, however. Unfortunately, the overall error rate will probably increase, since there are many more negative predictions made than positive, giving the false negative rate a greater weight in the computation of the overall error rate.

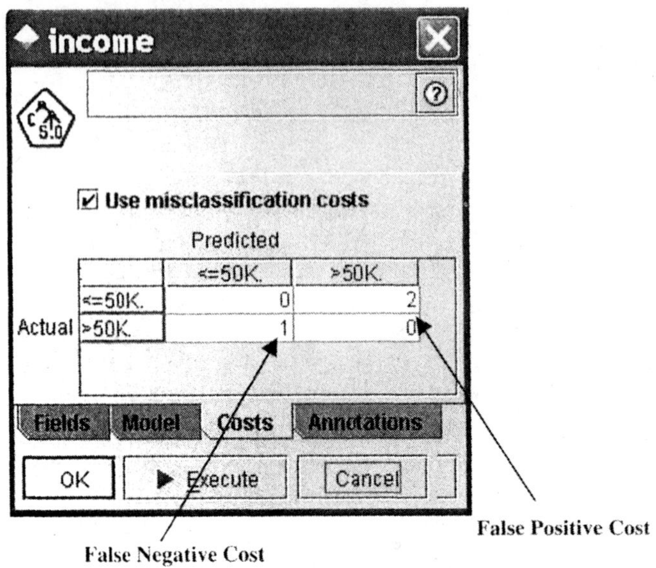

Figure 11.3 Adjusting the cost matrix to reflect higher cost of false positives.

The C5.0 algorithm was rerun, this time including the misclassification cost adjustment. The resulting confusion matrix is shown in Figure 11.4. As expected, the false negative rate has increased, while the false positive rate has decreased. Whereas previously, false positives were twice as likely to occur, this time the false positive rate is lower than the false negative rate. As desired, the false positive rate has decreased. However, this has come at a cost. The algorithm, hesitant to classify records as positive

Matrix of income by $C-income...

File Edit Generate

$C-income

income	<=50K.	>50K.	Total
<=50K.	18753	249	19002
>50K.	3551	2433	5984
Total	22304	2682	24986

Cells contain: cross-tabulation of fields

Matrix Appearance Annotations

Figure 11.4 Confusion matrix after misclassification cost adjustment.

due to the higher cost, instead made many more negative classifications, and therefore more false negatives.

$$\text{false negative rate} = \frac{3551}{22,304} = 0.1592 \qquad \text{up from } 0.1149 \text{ previously}$$

$$\text{false positive rate} = \frac{249}{2682} = 0.0928 \qquad \text{down from } 0.2398 \text{ previously}$$

Unfortunately, the overall error rate has climbed as well:

$$\text{overall error rate} = \frac{3551 + 249}{24,986} = 0.1521 \qquad \text{up from } 0.1390 \text{ previously}$$

Nevertheless, a higher overall error rate and a higher false negative rate are considered a "good trade" by this lender, which is eager to reduce the loan default rate, which is very costly to the firm. The decrease in the false positive rate from 23.98% to 9.28% will surely result in significant savings to the financial lending firm, since fewer applicants who cannot afford to repay the loan will be awarded the loan.

DECISION COST/BENEFIT ANALYSIS

Company managers may require that model comparisons be made in terms of cost/benefit analysis. For example, in comparing the original C5.0 model before the misclassification cost adjustment (call this *model 1*) against the C5.0 model using the misclassification cost adjustment (call this *model 2*), managers may prefer to have the respective error rates, false negatives and false positives, translated into dollars and cents.

Analysts can provide model comparison in terms of anticipated profit or loss by associating a cost or benefit with each of the four possible combinations of correct and incorrect classifications. For example, suppose that the analyst makes the cost/benefit value assignments shown in Table 11.1. The \$25 cost associated with a negative decision reflect the nominal costs associated with processing loan rejections. The "−\$200" cost is actually the anticipated average interest revenue to be collected from applicants whose income is actually >50,000. The \$500 reflects the average cost

TABLE 11.1 Cost/Benefit Table for Each Combination of Correct/Incorrect Decision

Outcome	Classification	Actual Value	Cost	Rationale
True negative	≤50,000	≤50,000	\$25	Nominal cost associated with processing loan rejection
True positive	>50,000	>50,000	−\$200	Anticipated average interest revenue from loans
False negative	≤50,000	>50,000	\$25	Nominal cost associated with processing loan rejection
False positive	>50,000	≤50,000	\$500	Cost of loan default averaged over all loans to ≤50,000 group

of loan defaults, average over all loans to applicants whose income level is low. Of course, the specific numbers assigned here are subject to discussion and are meant for illustration only.

Using the costs from Table 11.1, we can then compare models 1 and 2:

$$\begin{aligned}\text{Cost of model } 1 &= 17{,}845\,(\$25) + 2317\,(\$25) + 1157\,(\$500) + 3667\,(-\$200)\\ &= \$349{,}150\end{aligned}$$

$$\begin{aligned}\text{Cost of model } 2 &= 18{,}753\,(\$25) + 3551\,(\$25) + 249\,(\$500) + 2433\,(-\$200)\\ &= \$195{,}500\end{aligned}$$

The *estimated cost savings* from deploying model 2 rather than model 1 is then

$$\text{estimated cost savings} = \$349{,}150 - \$195{,}500 = \$153{,}650$$

Isn't it amazing what a simple misclassification cost adjustment can mean to the company's bottom line? Thus, even though model 2 suffered from a higher overall error rate and a higher false negative rate, it outperformed model 1 "where it counted," with a lower false positive rate, which for this company's business problem, was crucial.

LIFT CHARTS AND GAINS CHARTS

Lift charts and gains charts are graphical evaluative methods for assessing and comparing the usefulness of classification models. *Lift* is a concept, originally from the marketing field, which seeks to compare the response rates with and without using the classification model. We shall explore these concepts by continuing our examination of the C5.0 models for classifying income.

Suppose that the financial lending firm is interested in identifying high-income persons to put together a targeted marketing campaign for a new platinum credit card. In the past, marketers may have simply canvassed an entire list of contacts without regard to clues about the contact's income. Such blanket initiatives are expensive and tend to have low response rates. It is much better to apply demographic information that the company may have about the list of contacts, build a model to predict which contacts will have high income, and restrict the canvassing to these contacts classified as high income. The cost of the marketing program will then be much reduced and the response rate may be higher.

A good classification model should identify in its positive classifications (the >50,000 column in Figures 11.2 and 11.4), a group that has a higher proportion of positive "hits" than the database as a whole. The concept of *lift* quantifies this. We define *lift* as the proportion of positive hits in the set of the model's positive classifications, divided by the proportion of positive hits in the data set overall:

$$\text{lift} = \frac{\text{proportion of positive hits in set of positive classifications}}{\text{proportion of positive hits in data set as a whole}}$$

For example, in Figure 11.2, model 1 identifies 4824 records as being classified positive (*income* >50,000). This is the set of positive classifications. Of these 4824,

3667 records are positive hits; that is, the actual value of *income* is >50,000. This gives us $3667/4824 = 0.7602$ as the proportion of positive hits in the set of positive classifications. Now, in the data set as a whole, 5984 of the 24,986 records have income >50,000, giving us $5984/24{,}986 = 0.2395$ as the proportion of positive hits in the data set as a whole. The lift, measured at the 4824 records, is therefore $0.7602/0.2395 = 3.17$.

Lift is a function of sample size, which is why we had to specify that the lift of 3.17 for model 1 was measured at $n = 4824$ records. When calculating lift, the software will first sort the records by the probability of being classified positive. The lift is then calculated for every sample size from $n = 1$ to $n =$ the size of the data set. A chart is then produced which graphs lift against the percentile of the data set.

Consider Figure 11.5, which represents the lift chart for model 1. Note that lift is highest at the lowest percentiles, which makes sense since the data are sorted according to the most likely positive hits. The lowest percentiles have the highest proportion of positive hits. As the plot moves from left to right, the positive hits tend to get "used up," so that the proportion steadily decreases until the lift finally equals exactly 1 when the entire data set is considered the sample. Therefore, for any lift chart, the highest lift is always obtained with the smallest sample sizes.

Now, 4824 records represents the 19.3th percentile of the 24,986 total records. Note in Figure 11.5 that the lift just to the left of the 20th percentile would be near

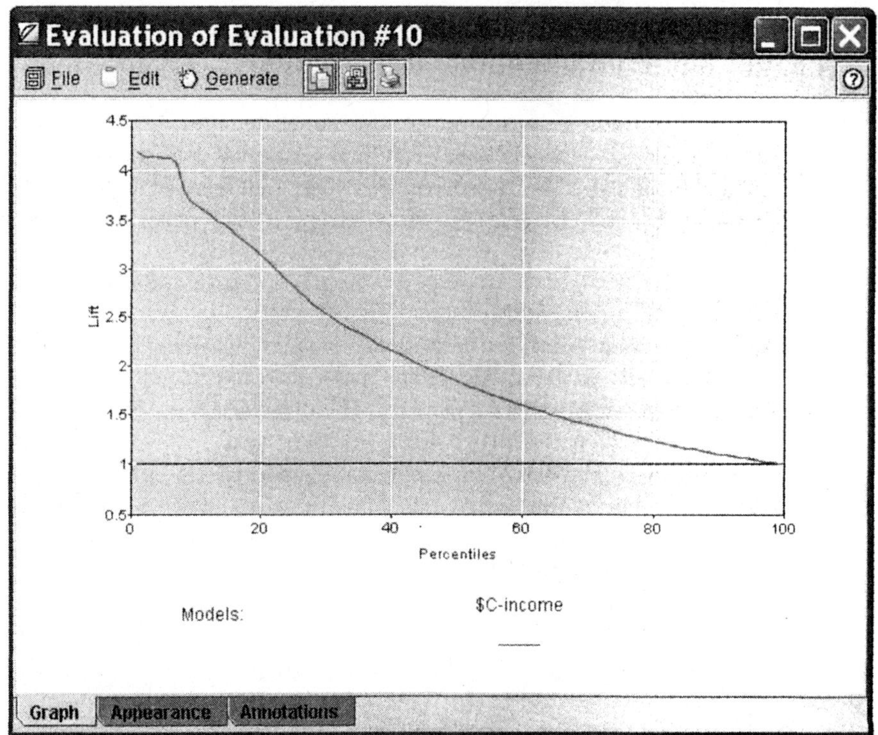

Figure 11.5 Lift chart for model 1: strong lift early, then falls away rapidly.

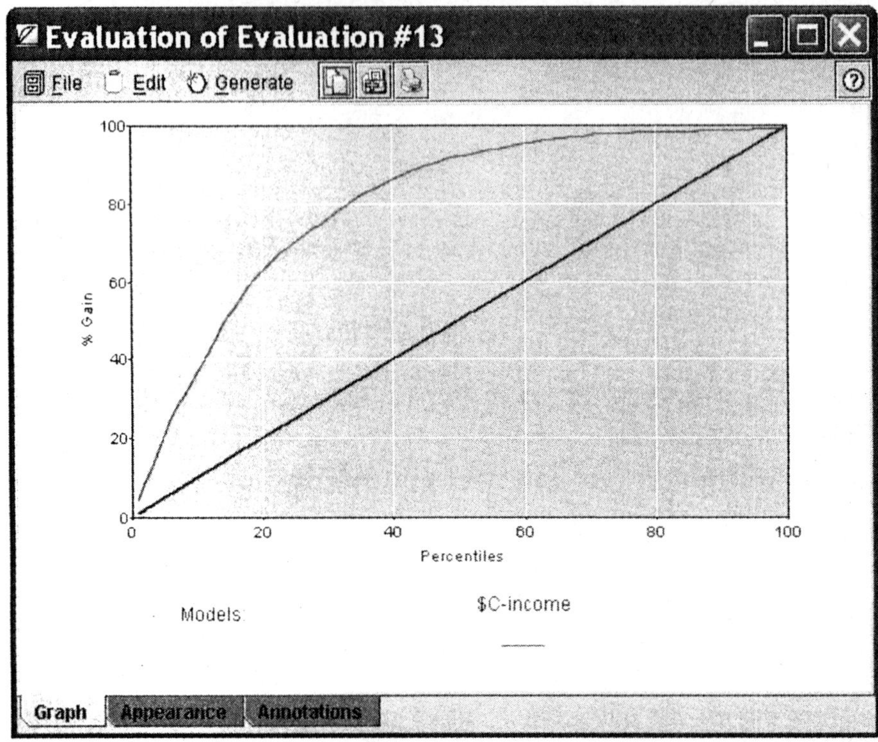

Figure 11.6 Gains chart for model 1.

3.17, as we calculated above. If our market research project required merely the most likely 5% of records, the lift would have been higher, about 4.1, as shown in Figure 11.5. On the other hand, if the project required 60% of all records, the lift would have fallen off to about 1.6. Since the data are sorted by positive propensity, the further we reach into the data set, the lower our overall proportion of positive hits becomes. Another balancing act is required: between reaching lots of contacts and having a high expectation of success per contact.

Lift charts are often presented in their cumulative form, where they are denoted as *cumulative lift charts*, or *gains charts*. The gains chart associated with the lift chart in Figure 11.5 is presented in Figure 11.6. The diagonal on the gains chart is analogous to the horizontal axis at $lift = 1$ on the lift chart. Analysts would like to see gains charts where the upper curve rises steeply as one moves from left to right and then gradually flattens out. In other words, one prefers a deeper "bowl" to a shallower bowl. How do you read a gains chart? Suppose that we canvassed the top 20% of our contact list (percentile = 20). By doing so, we could expect to reach about 62% of the total number of high-income persons on the list. Would doubling our effort also double our results? No. Canvassing the top 40% on the list would enable us to reach approximately 85% of the high-income persons on the list. Past this point, the law of diminishing returns is strongly in effect.

Lift charts and gains charts can also be used to compare model performance. Figure 11.7 shows the combined lift chart for models 1 and 2. The figure shows that

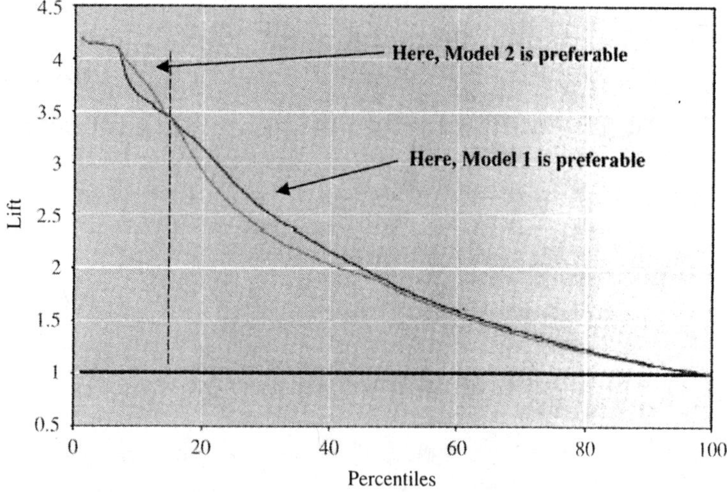

Figure 11.7 Combined lift chart for models 1 and 2.

when it comes to model selection, a particular model may not be uniformly preferable. For example, up to about the 6th percentile, there appears to be no apparent difference in model lift. Then, up to approximately the 17th percentile, model 2 is preferable, provided slightly higher lift. Thereafter, model 1 is preferable.

Hence, if the goal were to canvass up to the top 17% or so of the people on the contact list with high incomes, model 2 would probably be selected. However, if the goal were to extend the reach of the marketing initiative to 20% or more of the likely contacts with high income, model 1 would probably be selected. This question of multiple models and model choice is an important one, which we spend much time discussing in Reference 1.

INTERWEAVING MODEL EVALUATION WITH MODEL BUILDING

In Chapter 1 the graphic representing the CRISP–DM standard process for data mining contained a feedback loop between the model building and evaluation phases. In Chapter 5 (Figure 5.1) we presented a *methodology for supervised modeling*. Where do the methods for model evaluation from Chapter 11 fit into these processes?

We would recommend that model evaluation become a nearly "automatic" process, performed to a certain degree whenever a new model is generated. Therefore, at any point in the process, we may have an accurate measure of the quality of the current or working model. Therefore, it is suggested that model evaluation be interwoven seamlessly into the *methodology for supervised modeling* presented in Chapter 5, being performed on the models generated from each of the training set, test set, and validation set. For example, when we adjust the provisional model to minimize the error rate on the test set, we may have at our fingertips the false positive rate, the false negative rate, the overall error rate, the lift charts, and the gains charts.

These evaluative measures can then point the analyst in the proper direction for best ameliorating any drawbacks of the working model.

CONFLUENCE OF RESULTS: APPLYING A SUITE OF MODELS

In Olympic figure skating, the best-performing skater is not selected by a single judge alone. Instead, a suite of several judges is called upon to select the best skater from among all the candidate skaters. Similarly in model selection, whenever possible, the analyst should not depend solely on a single data mining method. Instead, he or she should seek a *confluence of results* from a suite of different data mining models.

For example, for the *adult* database, Figures 6.5, 6.7, and 7.9, show that the variables listed in Table 11.2 are the most influential (ranked roughly in order of importance) for classifying income, as identified by CART, C5.0, and the neural network algorithm, respectively. Although there is not a perfect match in the ordering of the important variables, there is still much that these three separate classification algorithms have uncovered, including the following:

- All three algorithms identify *Marital_Status*, *education-num*, *capital-gain*, *capital-loss*, and *hours-per-week* as the most important variables, except for the neural network, where *age* snuck in past *capital-loss*.
- None of the algorithms identified either *work-class* or *sex* as important variables, and only the neural network identified *age* as important.
- The algorithms agree on various ordering trends, such as *education-num* is more important than *hours-per-week*.

When we recall the strongly differing mathematical bases on which these three data mining methods are built, it may be considered remarkable that such convincing concurrence prevails among them with respect to classifying income. Remember that CART bases its decisions on the "goodness of split" criterion $\Phi(s|t)$, that C5.0 applies an information-theoretic approach, and that neural network base their learning on back-propagation. Yet these three different algorithms represent streams that broadly speaking, have come together, forming a *confluence* of results. In this way, the models act as validation for each other.

TABLE 11.2 Most Important Variables for Classifying Income, as Identified by CART, C5.0, and the Neural Network Algorithm

CART	C5.0	Neural Network
Marital_Status	*Capital-gain*	*Capital-gain*
Education-num	*Capital-loss*	*Education-num*
Capital-gain	*Marital_Status*	*Hours-per-week*
Capital-loss	*Education-num*	*Marital_Status*
Hours-per-week	*Hours-per-week*	*Age*
		Capital-loss

REFERENCE

1. Daniel Larose, *Data Mining Methods and Models*, Wiley-Interscience, Hoboken, NJ (to appear 2005).

EXERCISES

Hands-on Analysis

Use the *churn* data set at the book series Web site for the following exercises. Make sure that numerical variables are normalized and the correlated variables have been accounted for.

1. Apply a CART model for predicting *churn*. Use default misclassification costs.

- **a.** Determine the false positive rate.
- **b.** Determine the false negative rate.
- **c.** Determine the overall error rate.
- **d.** Determine the overall model accuracy (1 − overall error rate).

2. In a typical churn model, in which interceding with a potential churner is relatively cheap but losing a customer is expensive, which error is more costly, a false negative or a false positive (where positive = customer predicted to churn)? Explain.

3. Based on your answer to Exercise 2, adjust the misclassification costs for your CART model to reduce the prevalence of the more costly type of error. Rerun the CART algorithm. Compare the false positive, false negative, and overall error rates with the previous model. Discuss the trade-off between the various rates in terms of cost for the company.

4. Perform a cost/benefit analysis for the default CART model from exercise 1 as follows. Assign a cost or benefit in dollar terms for each combination of false and true positives and negatives, similar to Table 11.1. Then, using the confusion matrix, find the overall anticipated cost.

5. Perform a cost/benefit analysis for the CART model with the adjusted misclassification costs. Use the same cost/benefits assignments as for the default model. Find the overall anticipated cost. Compare with the default model, and formulate a recommendation as to which model is preferable.

6. Construct a lift chart for the default CART model. What is the estimated lift at 20%? 33%? 40%? 50%?

7. Construct a gains chart for the default CART model. Explain the relationship between this chart and the lift chart.

8. Construct a lift chart for the CART model with the adjusted misclassification costs. What is the estimated lift at 20%? 33%? 40%? 50%?

9. Construct a single lift chart for both of the CART models. Which model is preferable over which regions?

10. Now turn to a C4.5 decision tree model, and redo Exercises 1 to 9. Compare the results. Which model is preferable?

11. Next, apply a neural network model to predict churn.

   a. Determine the false positive rate.

   b. Determine the false negative rate.

   c. Determine the overall error rate.

   d. Determine the overall model accuracy (1 − overall error rate).

12. Construct a lift chart for the neural network model. What is the estimated lift at 20%? 33%? 40%? 50%?

13. Construct a single lift chart which includes the better of the two CART models, the better of the two C4.5 models, and the neural network model. Which model is preferable over which regions?

14. In view of the results obtained above, discuss the overall quality and adequacy of our *churn* classification models.

EPILOGUE

"We've Only Just Begun" An Invitation to *Data Mining Methods and Models*

I hope you have enjoyed *Discovering Knowledge in Data: An Introduction to Data Mining*, and that our experience together has whetted your appetite for learning more about this unique and powerful field of study. In fact, it is true that "we have only just begun" our exploration of data mining. More volumes in this Wiley Interscience data mining series await your examination.

Data Mining Methods and Models, will extend the array of models at our disposal, and will delve deeper into methods and models that we have already encountered. For example, we shall expand our collection of classification models to include *naïve Bayes* methods and *Bayesian networks*.

Further, *Data Mining Methods and Models* will contain chapter case studies, where readers will be shown how to solve actual business and research problems using data mining methods and models on large, real-world data sets. Every step in the process will be demonstrated, from identification of the business problem, through data pre-processing, exploratory data analysis, model development, model assessment, and finally to reporting the results in a form understandable to non-specialists. This is hands-on data mining under real-world conditions.

Beyond this, *Data Mining the Web* will cover the three main facets of web mining, that is, web content mining, web structure mining, and web usage mining. Among the topics that will be examined in this volume are clickstream analysis, preprocessing of web log files, sessionization, path completion, and web log sequence analysis.

Thank you for sharing this experience with me, and I look forward to working with you in the future.

Daniel T. Larose, Ph.D.
Director, Data Mining @CCSU
www.ccsu.edu/datamining

INDEX

Discovering Knowledge in Data: An Introduction to Data Mining, By Daniel T. Larose
ISBN 0-471-66657-2

wruttsoy